SYMPOSIA
READINGS IN PHILOSOPHY

A CUSTOMIZED
READER IN PHILOSOPHY

COMPILED BY

Mr. Craig Derksen
Introduction to Contemporary Moral Issues
PHIL140 Sections 201-209
University of Maryland
Philosophy

PEARSON CUSTOM PUBLISHING

Acquisitions Editor & Director of Database Publishing: Michael Payne
Editor: Colby R. Lawrence
Marketing: Hester Tinti-Kane, Nathan L. Wilbur
Operations Manager: Eric M. Kenney

Copyeditor: Elsa F. Kramer (Apple Press, Inc.)
Proofreader: Amy Krammes (Paperback Writer Communications)
Designer: Julie Gecha
Cover Design: Liza Piper
Composition and Layout: Elizabeth Everett (Enlightened Input)

Cover Art: Courtesy of JOHN GIANNICCHI/ Photo Researchers, Inc.

Printed in the United States of America

10 9 8 7 6 5 4 3 2 1

ISBN: 053679457

PEARSON CUSTOM PUBLISHING
75 Arlington Street, Suite #300/ Boston, MA 02116
Pearson Education Group

Preface

The Philosophy Department of Ohio University and Pearson Custom Publishing are proud to bring you *Symposia: Readings in Philosophy*, an innovative approach to teaching philosophy.

The goal of *Symposia* is to provide a rich archive of high quality philosophical writings for undergraduate courses in philosophy in such a way that both professors and students will have easy and cost-effective access to the minds and ideas that illuminate and help explain the essential questions of life.

This 2001 Edition of *Symposia*—we will be updating and expanding yearly—provides you with access to over **300 readings grouped under 30 topic areas**, from which professors can choose *only* those readings and areas which are germane to their particular course. No longer will professors and students be dependent on the standard large and expensive college reader, which often includes far more material than will be covered in the course, yet often also lacks those *particular* pieces that are viewed as essential by individual instructors. Additionally, we have provided both primary and secondary readings of varying levels of difficulty, as well as a **general introduction to the each of the 30 topical areas,** an opening brief **headnote** and **study questions,** all written by the *Symposia* editors. For each topic area, there is also a **customizable glossary of key terms.**

Overall, it is our hope that you will find *Symposia* to be an essential source of readings in philosophy—a source noted for both its breadth as well as depth—that meets the highest scholarly and pedagogical standards.

✑ Contributors ✑

Contents

Nicomachean Ethics (Book I)
Aristotle 1

The Leviathan
Thomas Hobbes 19

Utilitarianism
John Stuart Mill 39

Foundations of the Metaphysics of Morals
Immanuel Kant 56

Ethical Relativism
H. Gene Blocker 76

Why Abortion is Immoral
Don Marquis 91

A Defense of Abortion
Judith Jarvis Thompson 114

Affirmative Action: An Introduction
Polycarp Ikuenobe 133

Principles of Justice: Rights and Needs
Larry Churchill 140

**Allocating Scarce Medical Resources and the
Availability of Organ Transplantation**
H. T. Engelhardt 153

The Famine Relief Argument
Peter Singer 168

THE NICOMACHEAN ETHICS
Aristotle

Introduction, H. Gene Blocker

JUST AS PLATO WAS the most famous student of Socrates, so Aristotle was the most famous student of Plato. Aristotle (384–322 BCE) came to Athens from Macedonia, where his father practiced medicine, to study with Plato at the Academy. And just as Plato later developed ideas of his own that differed from those of Socrates, so Aristotle later developed ideas that differed significantly from Plato's. As you can clearly see from the first few pages of this reading, Aristotle shared with Plato, as did most of the early Greek thinkers, an understanding of morality in terms of the proper fulfillment of a thing's natural function, or nature. In fact, the first book of Aristotle's *Ethica Nicomachea* is probably the clearest analysis of the teleological-functionalist conception of good ever written. The virtue of each thing must be determined according to how well it performs its unique function; and to discover that proper human function or virtue we must ask what is the final end of all human endeavor (something which is not in turn a means to anything further). And, like Plato, he sees the unique function of man in our capacity for reason and deliberation.

But Aristotle differs from Plato in several important respects. Aristotle rejects Plato's notion that there is an eternal essence (Form) of Good or Justice over and above particular things in the everyday world of our experience, and Aristotle disagrees sharply with Plato that being virtuous is simply a matter of *knowing* what is good. Aristotle believed in Platonic essences, but he insisted they could exist only *in* particular things. By concentrating on justice and goodness as they actually existed in people, Aristotle was led to ask how people actually acquired these virtues. He concluded from his observations of people that they did not become good simply by learning what is good, but by developing good habits through practice and training. Thus, becoming a good person is not, for Aristotle, a theoretical matter like learning Einstein's theory of relativity, but a practical matter like learning how to play tennis, drive a car, speak French, or play the piano. In morality, according to Aristotle, practice makes perfect.

As you read Aristotle ask yourself whether you agree with him that there is a common human nature shared by all people at all times and places. And if so, do you agree that the most distinctive mark of a human being is the ability to think rationally? What is Aristotle's distinction between moral and intellectual virtues? Do you think a moral virtue always exists between two extremes? Finally, do you agree with Aristotle that happiness is the ultimate goal of life, and do you agree with him that being virtuous is a necessary part of human happiness?

E very art and every inquiry, and similarly every action and pursuit, is thought to aim at some good; and for this reason the good has rightly been declared to be that at which all things aim. But a certain difference is found among ends; some are activities, others are products apart from the activities that produce them. Where there are ends apart from the actions, it is the nature of the products to be better than the activities. Now, as there are many actions, arts, and sciences, their ends also are many; the end of the medical art is health, that of shipbuilding a vessel, that of strategy victory, that of economics wealth. But where such arts fall under a single capacity— as bridle-making and the other arts concerned with the equipment of horses fall under the art of riding, and this and every military action under strategy, in the same way other arts fall under yet others—in all of these the ends of the master arts are to be preferred to all the subordinate ends; for it is for the sake of the former that the latter are pursued. It makes no difference whether the activities themselves are the ends of the actions, or something else apart from the activities, as in the case of the sciences just mentioned. . . .

If, then, there is some end of the things we do, which we desire for its own sake (everything else being desired for the sake of this), and if we do not choose everything for the sake of something else (for at that rate the process would go on to infinity, so that our desire would be empty and vain), clearly this must be the good and the chief good. Will not the knowledge of it, then, have a great influence on life? Shall we not, like archers who have a mark to aim at, be more likely to hit upon what is right? If so, we must try, in outline at least to determine what it is. . . .

From Aristotle, *Ethica Nicomachea*, trans. W. D. Ross in *The Oxford Translation of Aristotle* II (Oxford: Oxford University Press, 1925).

Our discussion will be adequate if it has as much clearnes ject-matter admits of, for precision is not to be sought for alike in all discussions, any more than in all the products of the crafts. Now fine and just actions . . . admit of much variety and fluctuation of opinion, so that they may be thought to exist only by convention, and not by nature. And goods also give rise to similar fluctuation because they bring harm to many people; for before now men have been undone by reason of their wealth, and others by reason of their courage. We must be content, then, in speaking of such subjects and with such premises to indicate the truth roughly and in outline, and in speaking about things which are only for the most part true and with premises of the same kind to reach conclusions that are no better. In the same spirit, therefore, should each type of statement be *received;* for it is the mark of an educated man to look for precision in each class of things just so far as the nature of the subject admits; it is evidently equally foolish to accept probable reasoning from a mathematician and to demand from a rhetorician scientific proof.

*   *   *

Let us resume our inquiry and state, in view of the fact that all knowledge and every pursuit aims at some good. . . . what is the highest of all goods achievable by action. Verbally there is very general agreement; for both the general run of men and people of superior refinement say that it is happiness, and identifying living well and doing well with being happy; but with regard to what happiness is they differ, and the many do not give the same account as the wise. For the former think it is some plain and obvious thing, like pleasure, wealth, or honour; they differ, however, from one another—and often even the same man identifies it with different things, with health when he is ill, with wealth when he is poor; but, conscious of their ignorance, they admire those who proclaim some great ideal that is above their comprehension. Now some thought that apart from these many goods there is another which is self-subsistent and causes the goodness of all these as well.

*   *   *

We had perhaps better consider the universal good and discuss thoroughly what is meant by it, although such an inquiry is made an uphill one by the fact that the Forms have been introduced by friends of our own. Yet it would perhaps be thought to be better, indeed to be our duty, for the sake of maintaining the truth even to destroy what touches us closely, especially as we are philosophers or lovers of wisdom; for, while both are dear, piety requires us to honour truth above our friends.

The men who introduced this doctrine did not posit Ideas of classes within which they recognized priority and posteriority (which is the reason why they did not maintain the existence of an Idea embracing all numbers); but the term "good" is used both in the category of substance and in that of quality and in that of relation, and that which is *per se,* i.e. substance, is prior in nature to the relative (for the latter is like an offshoot and accident of being); so that there could not be a common Idea set over all these goods. Further, since "good" has as many senses as "being" (for it is predicated both in the category of substance, as of God and of reason, and in quality, i.e. of the virtues, and in quantity, i.e. of that which is moderate, and in relation, i.e. of the useful, and in time, i.e. of the right opportunity, and in place, i.e. of the right locality and the like), clearly it cannot be something universally present in all cases and single; for then it could not have been predicated in all the categories but in one only. Further, since of the things answering to one Idea there is one science, there would have been one science of all the goods: but as it is there are many sciences even of the things that fall under one cate- gory, e.g. of opportunity, for opportunity in war is studied by strategies and in disease by medicine, and the moderate in food is studied by medicine and in exercise by the science of gymnastics. And one might ask the question, what in the world they *mean* by "a thing itself", if (as is the case) in "man himself" and in a particular man the account of man is one and the same. For in so far as they are man, they will in no respect differ; and if this is so, nei- ther will "good itself" and particular goods, in so far as they are good. But again it will not be good any the more for being eternal, since that which lasts long is no whiter than that which perishes in a day. . . .

An objection to what we have said, however. may be discerned in the fact that the Platonists have not been speaking about *all* goods, and that the goods that are pursued and loved for themselves are called good by reference to a single Form, while those which tend to produce or to preserve these somehow or to prevent their contraries are called so by reference to these, and in a secondary sense. Clearly, then, goods must be spoken of in two ways, and some must be good in themselves, the others by reason of these. Let us separate, then, things good in themselves from things useful, and con- sider whether the former are called good by reference to a single Idea. What sort of goods would one call good in themselves? Is it those that are pursued even when isolated from others, such as intelligence, sight, and certain pleasures and honours? Certainly, if we pursue these also for the sake of something else, yet one would place them among things good in themselves. Or is nothing other than the Idea of good good in itself? In that case the Form will be empty. But if the things we have named are also things good in themselves, the account of the good will have to appear as something identical in them all, as that of whiteness is identical in snow and in white lead. But of honour, wisdom, and pleasure, just in respect of their goodness, the accounts are distinct and diverse. The good, therefore, is not some common element answering to one Idea,

But what then do we mean by the good? It is surely not like the things that only chance to have the same name. Are goods one, then, by being derived from one good or by all contributing to one good, or are they rather one by analogy? Certainly as sight is in the body, so is reason in the soul, and so on in other cases. But perhaps these subjects had better be dismissed for the present; for perfect precision about them would be more appropriate to another branch of philosophy. And similarly with regard to the Idea: even if there is some one good which is universally predicable of goods or is capable of separate and independent existence, clearly it could not be achieved or attained by man, but we are now seeking something attainable. Perhaps, however, some one might think it worth while to recognize this with a view to the goods that *are* attainable and achievable; for having this as a sort of pattern we shall know better the goods that are good for us, and if we know them shall attain them. This argument has some plausibility, but seems to clash with the procedure of the sciences; for all of these, though they aim at some good and seek to supply the deficiency of it, leave on one side the knowledge of *the* good. Yet that all the exponents of the arts should be ignorant of, and should not even seek, so great an aid is not probable. It is hard, too, to see how a weaver or a carpenter will be benefited in regard to his own craft by knowing this "good itself," or how the man who has viewed the Idea itself will be a better doctor or general thereby. For a doctor seems not even to study health in this way, but the health of man, or perhaps rather the health of a particular man; it is individuals that he is healing. . . .

Let us again return to the good we are seeking, and ask what it can be. It seems different in different actions and arts; it is different in medicine, in strategy, and in the other arts likewise. What then is the good of each? Surely that for whose sake everything else is done. In medicine this is health, in strategy victory, in architecture a house, in any other sphere something else, and in every action and pursuit the end; for it is for the sake of this that all men do whatever else they do. Therefore, if there is an end for all that we do, this will be the good achievable by action, and if there are more than one, these will be the goods achievable by action.

So the argument has by a different course reached the same point; but we must try to state this even more clearly. Since there are evidently more than one end, and we choose some of these (e.g., wealth, flutes, and in general instruments) for the sake of something else, clearly not all ends are final ends; but the chief good is evidently something final. Therefore, if there is only one final end, this will be what we are seeking, and if there are more than one, the most final of these will be what we are seeking. Now we call that which is in itself worthy of pursuit more final than that which is worthy of pursuit for the sake of something else, and that which is never desirable for the sake of something else more final than the things that are desirable both in themselves and for the sake of that other thing, and therefore we call final without qualification that which is always desirable in itself and never for the sake of something else.

Now such a thing happiness, above all else, is held to be; for this we choose always for itself and never for the sake of something else, but honour, pleasure, reason, and every virtue we choose indeed for themselves (for if nothing resulted from them we should still choose each of them), but we choose them also for the sake of happiness, judging that by means of them we shall be happy. Happiness, on the other hand, no one chooses for the sake of these, nor, in general, for anything other than itself.

From the point of view of self-sufficiency the same result seems to follow; for the final good is thought to be self-sufficient. Now by self-sufficient we do not mean that which is sufficient for a man by himself, for one who lives a solitary life, but also for parents, children, wife, and in general for his friends and fellow citizens, since man is born for citizenship. But some limit must be set to this; for if we extend our requirements to ancestors and descendants and friends' friends we are in for an infinite series. . . . The self-sufficient we now define as that which when isolated makes life desirable and lacking in nothing; and such we think happiness to be; and further we think it most desirable of all things, without being counted as one good thing among others—if it were so counted it would clearly be made desirable by the addition of even the least of goods; for that which is added becomes an excess of goods, and of goods the greater is always more desirable. Happiness, then, is something final and self-sufficient, and is the end of action.

Presumably, however, to say that happiness is the chief good seems a platitude, and a clearer account of what it is is still desired. This might perhaps be given, if we could first ascertain the function of man. For just as for a flute player, a sculptor, or any artist, and, in general, for all things that have a function or activity, the good and the "well" is thought to reside in the function, so would it seem to be for man, if he has a function. Have the carpenter, then, and the tanner certain functions or activities, and has man none? Is he born without a function? Or as eye, hand, foot, and in general each of the parts evidently has a function, may one lay it down that man similarly has a function apart from all these? What then can this be? Life seems to be common even to plants, but we are seeking what is peculiar to man. Let us exclude, therefore, the life of nutrition and growth. Next there would be a life perception, but *it* also seems to be common even to the horse, the ox, and every animal. There remains, then, an active life of the element that has a rational principle; of this, one part has such a principle in the sense of being obedient to one, the other in the sense of possessing one and exercising thought. And, as "life of the rational element" also has two meanings, we must state that life in the sense of activity is what we mean; for this seems to be the more proper sense of the term. Now if the function of man is an activity of soul which follows or implies a rational principle, and if we say "a so-and-so" and "a good so-and-so" have a function which is the same in kind, e.g., a lyre-player and a good lyre-player, and so without qualification in all cases, eminence in respect of goodness being added to the name of the function (for the function of a lyre-player is to play the lyre, and that of a good lyre-player is to do so well): if this is the case, (and we state the function of man to be a certain kind of life, and this to be an activity or actions of the soul implying a rational principle, and the function of a good man to be the good and noble performance of these, and if any action is well performed when it is performed in accordance with the appropriate excellence: if this is the case,) human good turns out to be activity of soul in accordance with virtue, and if there are more than one virtue, in accordance with the best and most complete.

But we must add "in a complete life." For one swallow does not make a summer, nor does one day; and so too one day, or a short time, does not make a man blessed and happy. . . .

Since happiness is an activity of soul in accordance with perfect virtue, we must consider the nature of virtue. . . .

Some things are said about it, adequately enough, even in the discussion outside our school, and we must use these; e.g., that one element in the soul is irrational and one has a rational principle. Whether these are separated as the parts of the body or of anything divisible are, or are distinct by definition but by nature inseparable, like convex and concave in the circumference of a circle, does not affect the present question.

Of the irrational element one division seems to be widely distributed, and vegetative in its nature, I mean that which causes nutrition and growth; for it is this kind of power of the soul that one must assign to all nurslings and to embryos, and this same power to full-grown creatures; this is more reasonable than to assign some different power to them. Now the excellence of this seems to be common to all species and not specifically human; for this part of faculty seems to function most in sleep, while goodness and badness are least manifest in sleep (whence comes the saying that the happy are no better off than the wretched for half their lives, and this happens naturally enough, since sleep is an inactivity of the soul in that respect in which it is called good or bad). . . .

There seems to be also another irrational element in the soul—one which in a sense, however, shares in a rational principle. For we praise the rational principle of the continent man and of the incontinent, and the part of their soul that has such a principle, since it urges them aright and towards the best objects; but there is found in them also another element naturally opposed to the rational principle, which fights against and resists that principle. For exactly as paralysed limbs when we intend to move them to the right turn on the contrary to the left, so is it with the soul; the impulses of incontinent people move in contrary directions. But while in the body we see that which moves astray, in the soul we do not. No doubt, however, we must nonetheless suppose that in the soul too there is something contrary to the rational principle, resisting and opposing it. In what sense it is distinct from the other elements does not concern us. Now even this seems to have a share in a rational principle, as we said; at any rate in the continent man it obeys the rational principle—and presumably in the temperate and brave man it is still more obedient; for in him it speaks, on all matters, with the same voice as the rational principle.

Therefore the irrational element also appears to be twofold. For the vegetative element in no way shares in a rational principle, but the appetitive, and in general the desiring element in a sense shares in it, in so far as it listens to and obeys it; this is the sense in which we speak of "taking account" of one's father or one's friends, not that in which we speak of "accounting" for a mathematical property. That the irrational element is in some sense persuaded by a rational principle is indicated also by the giving of advice and by all reproof and exhortation. And if this element also must be said to have a rational principle, that which has a rational principle (as well as that which has not) will be twofold, one subdivision having it in the strict sense and in itself, and the other having a tendency to obey as one does one's father.

Virtue too is distinguished into kinds in accordance with this difference; for we say that some of the virtues are intellectual and others moral, philosophic wisdom and understanding and practical wisdom being intellectual, liberality and temperance moral. For in speaking about a man's character we do not say that he is wise or has understanding but that he is good-tempered or temperate; yet we praise the wise man also with respect to his state of mind; and of states of mind we call those which merit praise virtues.

Virtue, then, being of two kinds, intellectual and moral, intellectual virtue in the main owes both its birth and its growth to teaching (for which reason it requires experience and time), while moral virtue comes about as a result of habit, whence also its name *ethike* is one that is formed by a slight variation from the word *ethos* (habit). From this it is also plain that none of the moral virtues arises in us by nature; for nothing that exists by nature can form a habit contrary to its nature. For instance the stone which by nature moves downwards cannot be habituated to move upwards, not even if one tries to train it by throwing it up ten thousand times; nor can fire be habituated to move downwards, nor can anything else that by nature behaves in one way be trained to behave in another. Neither by nature, then, nor contrary to nature do the virtues arise in us; rather we are adapted by nature to receive them, and are made perfect by habit.

Again, of all the things that come to us by nature we first acquire the potentiality and later exhibit the activity (this is plain in the case of the senses; for it was not by often seeing or often hearing that we got these senses, but on the contrary we had them before we used them. and did not come to have them by using them); but the virtues we get by first exercising them, as also happens in the case of the arts as well. For the things we have to learn before we can do them, we learn by doing them, e.g., men become builders by building and lyre-players by playing the lyre; so too we become just by doing just acts, temperate by doing temperate acts, brave by doing brave acts. . . .

Again, it is from the same causes and by the same means that every virtue is both produced and destroyed, and similarly every art; for it is from playing the lyre that both good and bad lyre-players are produced. And the corresponding statement is true of builders and of all the rest; men will be good or bad builders as a result of building well or badly. For if this were not so, there would have been no need of a teacher, but all men would have been born good or bad at their craft. This, then, is the case with the virtues also; by doing the acts that we do in our transactions with other men we become just or unjust, and by doing the acts that we do in the presence of danger, and being habituated to feel fear or confidence, we become brave or cowardly. The same is true of appetites and feelings of anger; some men become temperate and good tempered, others self-indulgent and irascible, by behaving in one way or the other in the appropriate circumstances. Thus, in one word, states of character arise out of like activities. This is why the activities we exhibit must be of a certain kind; it is because the states of character correspond to the differences between these. It makes no small difference, then, whether we form habits of one kind or of another from our very youth; it makes a very great difference, or rather *all* the difference. . . .

Next we must consider what virtue is. Since things that are found in the soul are of three kinds—passions, faculties, states of character—virtue must be one of these. By passions I mean appetite, anger, fear, confidence, envy, joy, friendly feeling, hatred, longing, emulation, pity, and in general the feelings that are accompanied by pleasure or pain; by faculties the things in virtue of which we are said to be capable of feeling these, e.g., of becoming angry or being pained or feeling pity; by states of character the things in virtue of which we stand well or badly with reference to the passions, e.g., with reference to anger we stand badly if we feel it violently or too weakly, and well if we feel it moderately, and similarly with reference to the other passions.

Now neither the virtues nor the vices are *passions,* because we are not called good or bad on the ground of our passions, but are so called on the ground of our virtues and our vices, and because we are neither praised nor blamed for our passions (for the man who feels fear or anger is not praised, nor is the man who simply feels anger blamed, but the man who feels it in a certain way), but for our virtues and our vices we are praised or blamed.

Again, we feel anger and fear without choice, but the virtues are modes of choice or involve choice. Further, in respect of the passions we are said to be moved, but in respect of the virtues and the vices we are said not to be moved but to be disposed in a particular way.

For these reasons also they are not *faculties;* for we are neither called good nor bad, nor praised nor blamed, for the simple capacity of feeling the passions; again, we have the faculties of nature, but we are not made good or bad by nature; we have spoken of this before,

If, then, the virtues are neither passions nor faculties, all that remains is that they should be *states of character.*

Thus we have stated what virtue is in respect of its genus.

We must, however, not only describe virtue as a state of character, but also say what sort of state it is. We may remark, then, that every virtue or excellence both brings into good condition the thing of which it is the excellence and makes the work of that thing be done well; e.g., the excellence of the eye makes both the eye and its work good; for it is by the excellence of the eye that we see well. Similarly the excellence of the horse makes a horse both good in itself and good at running and at carrying its rider and at awaiting the attack of the enemy. Therefore, if this is true in every case, the virtue of man also will be the state of character which makes a man good and which makes him do his own work well.

How this is to happen . . . will be made plain . . . by the following consideration of the specific nature of virtue. In everything that is continuous and divisible it is possible to take more, less, or an equal amount, and that either in terms of the thing itself or relatively to us; and the equal is an intermediate between excess and defect. By the intermediate in the object I mean that which is equidistant from each of the extremes, which is one and the same for all men; by the intermediate relatively to us that which is neither too much nor too little—and this is not one, nor the same for all. For instance, if ten is many and two is few, six is the intermediate, taken in terms of the object; for it exceeds and is exceeded by an equal amount; this is intermediate according to arithimetical proportion. But the intermediate relatively to us is not to be taken so; if ten pounds are too much for a particular person to eat and two too little, it does not follow that the trainer will order six pounds; for this also is perhaps too much for the person who is to take it, or too little. . . . Thus a master of any art avoids excess and defect, but seeks the intermediate and chooses this—the intermediate not in the object but relatively to us.

If it is thus, then, that every art does its work well—by looking to the intermediate and judging its works by this standard (so that we often say of good works of art that it is not possible either to take away or to add any-thing, implying that excess and defect destroy the goodness of works of art, while the mean preserves it; and good artists, as we say, look to this in their work), and if, further, virtue is more exact and better than any art, as nature also is, then virtue must have the quality of aiming at the intermediate. I mean moral virtue; for it is this that is concerned with passions and actions, and in these there is excess, defect, and the intermediate. For instance, both fear and confidence and appetite and anger and pity and in general pleasure and pain may be felt both too much and too little, and in both cases not well; but to feel them at the right times, with reference to the right objects, towards the right people, with the right motive, and in the right way, is what is both intermediate and best, and this is characteristic of virtue. Similarly with regard to actions also there is excess, defect, and the intermediate. Now virtue is concerned with passions and actions, in which excess is a form of failure, and so is defect, while the intermediate is praised and is a form of success; and being praised and being successful are both characteristics of virtue. Therefore virtue is a kind of mean, since, as we have seen, it aims at what is intermediate.

Again, it is possible to fail in many ways (for evil belongs to the class of the unlimited, as the Pythagoreans conjectured, and good to that of the lim-ited), while to succeed is possible only in one way (for which reason also one is easy and the other difficult—to miss the mark easy, to hit it difficult); for these reasons also, then, excess and defect are characteristic of vice, and the mean of virtue;

For men are good in but one way, but bad in many.

Virtue, then, is a state of character concerned with choice, lying in a mean, i.e., the mean relative to us, this being determined by a rational princi-ple, and by that principle by which the man of practical wisdom would deter-mine it. Now it is a mean between two vices, that which depends on excess and that which depends on defect; and again it is a mean because the vices respectively fall short of or exceed what is right in both passions and actions, while virtue both finds and chooses that which is intermediate. Hence in respect of its substance and the definition which states its essence virtue is a mean, with regard to what is best and right and extreme.

But not every action nor every passion admits of a mean; for some have names that already imply badness, e.g., spite, shamelessness, envy, and in the case of actions adultery, theft, murder; for all of these and suchlike things imply by their names that they are themselves bad, and not the excesses or deficiencies of them. It is not possible, then, ever to be right with regard to them; one must always be wrong. Nor does goodness or badness with regard to such things depend on committing adultery with the right woman, at the right time, and in the right way, but simply to do any of them is to go wrong. It would be equally absurd, then, to expect that in unjust, cowardly, and voluptuous action there should be a mean, an excess, and a deficiency; for at that rate there would be a mean of excess and of deficiency, an excess of excess, and a deficiency of deficiency. But as there is no excess and deficiency of temperance and courage because what is intermediate is in a sense an extreme, so too of the actions we have mentioned there is no mean nor any excess and deficiency, but however they are done they are wrong; for in general there is neither a mean of excess and deficiency, nor excess and deficiency of a mean.

We must, however, not only make this general statement, but also apply it to the individual facts. For among statements about conduct those which are general apply more widely, but those which are particular are more genuine, since conduct has to do with individual cases, and our statements must harmonize with the facts in these cases. We may take these cases from our table. With regard to feelings of fear and confidence courage is the mean, of the people who exceed, he who exceeds in fearlessness has no name (many of the states have no name), while the man who exceeds in confidence is rash, and he who exceeds in fear and falls short in confidence is a coward. With regard to pleasures and pains—not all of them, and not so much with regard to the pains—the mean is temperance, the excess self-indulgence. Persons deficient with regard to the pleasures are not often found; hence such persons also have received no name. But let us call them "insensible."

With regard to giving and taking of money the mean is liberality, the excess and the defect prodigality and meanness. In these actions people exceed and fall short in contrary ways; the prodigal exceeds in spending and falls short in taking, while the mean man exceeds in taking and falls short in spending. . . . With regard to money there are also other dispositions—a mean, magnificence (for the magnificent man differs from the liberal man; the former deals with large sums, the latter with small ones), and excess, tastelessness and vulgarity, and a deficiency, niggardliness. . . .

With regard to honour and dishonour the mean is proper pride, the excess is known as a sort of "empty vanity," and the deficiency is undue humility; and as we said liberality was related to magnificence, differing from it by dealing with small sums, so there is a state similarly related to proper pride, being concerned with small honours while that is concerned with great. For it is possible to desire honour as one ought, and more than one ought, and less, and the man who exceeds in his desires is called ambitious, the man who falls short unambitious, while the intermediate person has no name. The dispositions also are nameless, except that that of the ambitious man is called ambition. Hence the people who are at the extremes lay claim to the middle place; and we ourselves sometimes call the intermediate person ambitious and sometimes unambitious, and sometimes praise the ambitious man and sometimes the unambitious. . . .

With regard to anger also there is an excess, a deficiency, and a mean. Although they can scarcely be said to have names, yet since we call the intermediate person good-tempered let us call the mean good temper; of the persons at the extremes let the one who exceeds be called irascible, and his vice irascibility, and the man who falls short an inirascible sort of person, and the deficiency inirascibility.

• • •

What remains is to discuss in outline the nature of happiness, since this is what we state the end of human nature to be. Our discussion will be the more concise if we first sum up what we have said already. We said, then, that it is not a disposition; for if it were it might belong to some one who was asleep throughout his life, living the life of a plant, or, again, to some one who was suffering the greatest misfortunes. If these implications are unacceptable, and we must rather class happiness as an activity, as we have said before, and if some activities are necessary, and desirable for the sake of something else, while others are so in themselves, evidently happiness must be placed among those desirable in themselves, not among those desirable for the sake of something else; for happiness does not lack anything, but is self-sufficient. Now those activities are desirable in themselves from which nothing is sought beyond the activity. And of this nature virtuous actions are thought to be; for to do noble and good deeds is a thing desirable for its own sake.

Pleasant amusements also are thought to be of this nature; we choose them not for the sake of other things; for we are injured rather than benefited by them, since we are led to neglect our bodies and our property. But most of the people who are deemed happy take refuge in such pastimes, which is the reason why those who are ready-witted at them are highly esteemed at the courts of tyrants; they make themselves pleasant companions in the tyrants' favourite pursuits, and that is the sort of man they want. Now these things are thought to be of the nature of happiness because people in despotic positions spend their leisure in them, but perhaps such people prove nothing; for virtue and reason, from which good activities flow, do not depend on despotic position; nor, if these people, who have never tasted pure and generous pleasure, take refuge in the bodily pleasures, should these for that reason be thought more desirable, for boys, too, think the things that are valued among themselves are the best. It is to be expected, then, that, as different things seem valuable to boys and to men, so they should to bad men and to good. Now . . . those things are both valuable and pleasant which are such to the good man; and to each man the activity in accordance with his own disposition is most desirable, and, therefore, to the good man that which is in accordance with virtue. Happiness, therefore, does not lie in amusement; it would, indeed, be strange if the end were amusement, and one were to take trouble and suffer hardship all one's life in order to amuse oneself. For, in a word, everything that we choose we choose for the sake of something else—except happiness, which is an end. Now to exert oneself and work for the sake of amusement seems silly and utterly childish. But to amuse oneself in order that one may exert oneself, as Anacharsis puts it, seems right; for amusement is a sort of relaxation, and we need relaxation because we cannot work continuously. Relaxation, then, is not an end; for it is taken for the sake of activity.

The happy life is thought to be virtuous; now a virtuous life requires exertion, and does not consist in amusement. And we say that serious things are better than laughable things and those connected with amusement, and that the activity of the better of any two things—whether it be two elements of our being or two men—is the more serious; but the activity of the better is *ipso facto* superior and more of the nature of happiness. And any chance person—even a slave—can enjoy the bodily pleasures no less than the best man; but no one assigns to a slave a share in happiness—unless he assigns to him also a share in human life. For happiness does not lie in such occupations, but, as we have said before, in virtuous activities.

If happiness is activity in accordance with virtue, it is reasonable that *it* should be in accordance with the highest virtue; and this will be that of the best thing in us. Whether it be reason or something else that is this element which is thought to be our natural ruler and guide and to take thought of things noble and divine, whether it be itself also divine or only the most divine element in us, the activity of this in accordance with its proper virtue will be perfect happiness. That this activity is contemplative we have already said.

Now this would seem to be in agreement with what we said before and with the truth. For, firstly, this activity is the best (since not only is reason the best thing in us, but the objects of reason are the best of knowable objects); and, secondly, it is the most continuous, since we can contemplate truth more continuously than we can *do* anything. And we think happiness has pleasure mingled with it, but the activity of philosophic wisdom is admittedly the pleasantest of virtuous activities; at all events the pursuit of it is thought to offer pleasures marvellous for their purity and their enduringness, and it is to be expected that those who know will pass their time more pleasantly than those who inquire. And the self-sufficiency that is spoken of must belong most to the contemplative activity. For while a philosopher, as well as a just man or one possessing any other virtue, needs the necessaries of life, when they are sufficiently equipped with things of that sort the just man needs people towards whom and with whom he shall act justly, and the temperate man, the brave man, and each of the others is in the same case, but the philosopher, even when by himself, can contemplate truth, and the better the wiser he is; he can perhaps do so better if he has fellow-workers, but still he is the most self-sufficient. And this activity alone would seem to be loved for its own sake; for nothing arises from it apart from the contemplating, while from practical activities we gain more or less apart from the action. And happiness is thought to depend on leisure, for we are busy that we may have leisure, and make war that we may live in peace. Now the activity of the practical virtues is exhibited in political or military affairs, but the actions concerned with these seem to be unleisurely. War-like actions are completely so (for no one chooses to be at war, or provokes war, for the sake of being at war; any one would seem absolutely murderous if he were to make enemies of his friends in order to bring about battle and slaughter); but the action of the statesman is also unleisurely, and—apart from the political action itself—aims at despotic power and honours, or at all events happiness, for him and his fellow citizens—a happiness different from political action, and evidently sought as being different. So if among virtuous actions, political and military actions are distinguished by nobility and greatness, and these are unleisurely and aim at an end and are not desirable for their own sake, but the activity of reason, which is contemplative, seems both to be superior in serious worth and to aim at no end beyond itself, and to have its pleasure proper to itself (and this augments the activity), and the self-sufficiency, leisureliness, unweariedness (so far as this is possible for man), and all the other attributes ascribed to the supremely happy man are evidently those connected with this activity, it follows that this will be the complete happiness of man, if it be allowed a complete term of life (for none of the attributes of happiness is *in*complete).

But such a life would be too high for man; for it is not in so far as he is man that he will live so, but in so far as something divine is present in him; and by so much as this is superior to our composite nature is its activity superior to that which is the exercise of the other kind of virtue. If reason is divine, then, in comparison with man, the life according to it is divine in comparison with human life. But we must not follow those who advise us, being men, to think of human things, and, being mortal, of mortal things, but must, so far as we can, make ourselves immortal, and strain every nerve to live in accordance with the best thing in us; for even if it be small in bulk, much more does it in power and worth surpass everything. This would seem, too, to be each man himself, since it is the authoritative and better part of him. It would be strange, then, if he were to choose not the life of his self but that of something else. And what we said before will apply now; that which is proper to each thing is by nature best and most pleasant for each thing; for man, therefore, the life according to reason is best and pleasantest, since reason more than anything else *is* man. This life therefore is also the happiest.

But in a secondary degree the life in accordance with the other kind of virtue is happy; for the activities in accordance with this befit our human estate. Just and brave acts, and other virtuous acts, we do in relation to each other, observing our respective duties with regard to contracts and services and all manner of actions and with regard to passions; and all of these seem to be typically human. Some of them seem even to arise from the body, and virtue of character to be in many ways bound up with the passions. Practical wisdom, too, is linked to virtue of character, and this to practical wisdom, since the principles of practical wisdom are in accordance with the moral virtues and rightness in morals is in accordance with practical wisdom. Being connected with the passions also, the moral virtues must belong to our composite nature; and the virtues of our composite nature are human, so, therefore, are the life and the happiness which correspond to these. The excellence of the reason is a thing apart, we must be content to say this much about it, for to describe it precisely is a task greater than our purpose requires. It would seem, however, also to need external equipment but little, or less than moral virtue does. Grant that both need the necessaries, and do so equally, even if the statesman's work is the more concerned with the body and things of that sort; for there will be little difference there; but in what they need for the exercise of their activities there will be much difference. The liberal man will need money for the doing of his liberal deeds, and the just man too will need it for the returning of services (for wishes are hard to discern, and even people who are not just pretend to wish to act justly); and the brave man will need power if he is to accomplish any of the acts that correspond to his virtue, and the temperate man will need opportunity; for how else is either he or any of the others to be recognized? It is debated, too, whether the will or the deed is more essential to virtue, which is assumed to involve both; it is surely clear that its perfection involves both; but for deeds many things are needed, and more, the greater and nobler the deeds are. But the man who is contemplating the truth needs no such thing, at least with a view to the exercise of his activity; indeed they are, one may say, even hindrances, at all events to his contemplation; but in so far as he is a man and lives with a number of people, he chooses to do virtuous acts; he will therefore need such aids to living a human life. . . .

But, being a man, one will also need external prosperity; for our nature is not self-sufficient for the purpose of contemplation, but our body also must be healthy and must have food and other attention. Still, we must not think that the man who is to be happy will need many things or great things, merely because he cannot be supremely happy without external goods; for self-sufficiency and action do not involve excess, and we can do noble acts without ruling earth and sea; for even with moderate advantages one can act virtuously (this is manifest enough; for private persons are thought to do worthy acts no less than despots—indeed even more); and it is enough that we should have so much as that; for the life of the man who is active in accordance with virtue will be happy. . . .

THE LEVIATHAN
Thomas Hobbes

Introduction, H. Gene Blocker

AT THE END OF THE MIDDLE AGES (beginning around 1500) economic and political power began to shift from the nobility to the emerging "middle class." As merchants and trades people rose in prominence, they began to claim privileges for themselves as justifiable "rights"—the right to own and accumulate property, the right to engage in whatever business suited them, the right to move to and live wherever they chose, and the right to self-determination (to rule themselves democratically). But this shift in power relations did not occur quickly or easily. The royal and noble families struggled to maintain their power and engaged in various alliances and schemes to preserve their position and wealth. They were constantly engaged in warfare with one another. England in the sixteenth and seventeenth centuries, for example, was nearly always in chaos. King Charles I was put to death; Cromwell, leader of the British Parliament, was made Protector, and the crown was later restored to King Charles II.

It was in this social context that Thomas Hobbes (1588–1679) began to think about the basis and justification of government. Born prematurely when his mother heard of the approaching Spanish Armada (which signaled the rise of Britain as a major world power), Hobbes said of himself that "Fear and I were born twins." The chaotic political conditions in England were an important part of Hobbes's personal life since he was a tutor to Charles II, and these conditions doubtless influenced his approach to political philosophy. Another influence on his work was his materialist, determinist, and mechanistic approach to the physical world, in keeping with the "new science" of the time.

In order to figure out what would be the best form of government, Hobbes, like other philosophers of his time, devised a "social contract" thought experiment. If there were no government at all, what would life be like? If we think it would be just fine, then we conclude that there is no justification for government at all (i.e., the position known as "anarchism," that there is no justification for the state). But if we think that life would be very bad without a government (that is, without laws, police, judges, legal punishment, etc.), then we conclude that we do need a state and try to figure out what sort of state could fix the problem (that is, what sort state is the best form of government). So Hobbes raised the interesting question of what human beings would be like if there were no civil authority, in what he called the "state of nature." Hobbes viewed human nature (in what he thought was "scientifically") as being egoistic, so that in the state of nature each of us would attempt to better our own condition at the expense of others. In Hobbes's view, in the state of nature each of us has a "natural right" to whatever we can do or obtain. But Hobbes conceives these natural rights more as natural "mights" or "powers," that is, abilities to exercise our autonomy, rather than as "rights" understood as entitlements (justifiable claims upon others). Hobbes imagined the state of nature to be a state of continual warfare of everyone against everyone in which human life would be "nasty, brutish, and short."

However, borrowing an idea from Cicero and other Roman and medieval thinkers, human reason is capable of discovering a "natural law," Hobbes thought, which would tell us to seek peace. In other words, however selfish and aggressive people are, we are not stupid. We realize that by attacking our neighbor we bring trouble on ourselves. While I am out robbing you, you are breaking into my house! We are smart enough, Hobbes thought, to try to work out some sort of negotiated compromise.

He argues that this can be done by forming a social contract with a sovereign by each of us handing to the sovereign virtually all of our natural rights. The sovereign becomes an authority capable of maintaining social order but has no limitations on exercising that authority, short of failing to keep the peace. But why would anyone agree to give up so much freedom—the unlimited freedom in the state of nature to do whatever we thought we had to power to do? Because the state of nature is so bad—it is so completely horrible (nasty, brutish, and short) that anything which can end this misery is worth it. So, for Hobbes the extreme misery of the state of nature justifies an absolute monarchy—and as we mentioned earlier, this was in line with Hobbes's support of soon-to-be King Charles II and of the rights of kings generally. The king does not rule just because he has the right to rule, that is, he has the military power to do so, is justified in ruling absolutely, because of the "social contract" as the only way out of the awful state of nature. Therefore, killing or removing a king is morally wrong, violating the rights of kings according to the negotiated "social contract."

As you read Hobbes ask yourself if you think he is right in his description of the "state of nature." Would it be as bad as he thinks? How do you imagine it? If your picture is different from Hobbes's how can we determine which version is better? In other words, how good is the social contract for deciding such questions if it leads to different results?

————

Nature, the art whereby God hath made and governs the world, is by the *art* of man, as in many other things, so in this also imitated, that it can make an artificial animal. For seeing life is but a motion of limbs, the beginning whereof is in some principal part within; why may we not say, that all *automata* (engines that move themselves by springs and wheels as doth a watch) have an artificial life? For what is the *heart*, but a *spring;* and the *nerves*, but so many *strings;* and the *joints*, but so many *wheels*, giving motion to the whole body, such as was intended by the artificer? Art goes yet further, imitating that rational and most excellent work of nature, *man*. For by art is created that great LEVIATHAN called a COMMONWEALTH, or STATE, . . . which is but an artificial man; though of greater stature and strength than the natural, for whose protection and defence it was intended; and in which the *sovereignty* is an artificial *soul*, as giving life and motion to the whole body; the *magistrates*, and other *officers* of judicature and execution, artificial *joints; reward* and *punishment*, by which fastened to the seat of the sovereignty every joint and member is moved to perform his duty, are the *nerves*, that do the same in the body natural; the *wealth* and *riches* of all the particular members, are the *strength;* . . . the *people's safety*, its *business; counsellors*, by whom all things needful for it to know are suggested unto it, are the *memory; equity*, and *laws*, an artificial *reason* and *will; concord, health; sedition, sickness;* and *civil war, death*. Lastly, the *pacts* and *covenants*, by which the parts of this body politic were at first made, set together, and united, resemble that *fiat*, or the *let us make man*, pronounced by God in the creation. . . .

There be in animals, two sorts of *motions* peculiar to them: one called *vital;* begun in generation, and continued without interruption through their whole life; such as are the *course* of the *blood*, the *pulse*, the *breathing*, the *concoction, nutrition, excretion*, to which motions there needs no help of imagination: the other is *animal motion*, otherwise called *voluntary motion;*

————

From *The Leviathan*, vol. 3, ed. Sir William Molesworth (London: John Bohn, 1839).

as to *go*, to *speak*, to *move* any of our limbs, in such manner as is first fancied in our minds. . . . Sense is motion in the organs and interior parts of man's body, caused by the action of the things we see, hear; and . . . fancy is but the relics of the same motion, remaining after sense, . . . And because *going*, *speaking*, and the like voluntary motions, depend always upon a precedent thought of *whither, which way*, and *what;* it is evident, that the imagination is the first internal beginning of all voluntary motion. . . . These small beginnings of motion, within the body of man, before they appear in walking, speaking, striking, and other visible actions, are commonly called ENDEAVOUR.

This endeavour, when it is toward something which causes it, is called APPETITE, or DESIRE. . . . And when the endeavour is fromward something, it is generally called AVERSION. These words, *appetite* and *aversion*, . . . both of them signify the motions, one of approaching, the other of retiring. . . .

That which men desire, they are also said to LOVE: and to HATE those things for which they have aversion. So that desire and love are the same thing; save that by desire, we always signify the absence of the object; by love, most commonly the presence of the same. So also by aversion, we signify the absence; and by hate, the presence of the object.

Of appetites and aversions, some are born with men; as appetite of food, appetite of excretion, and exoneration. . . . The rest, which are appetites of particular things, proceed from experience, and trial of their effects upon themselves or other men. For of things we know not at all, or believe not to be, we can have no further desire, than to taste and try. But aversion we have for things, not only which we know have hurt us, but also that we do not know whether they will hurt us, or not.

Those things which we neither desire, nor hate, we are said to contemn; CONTEMPT being nothing else but an immobility, . . . in resisting the action of certain things; and proceeding from that the heart is already moved otherwise, by other more potent objects; or from want of experience of them.

And because the constitution of a man's body is in continual mutation, it is impossible that all the same things should always cause in him the same appetites, and aversions: much less can all men consent, in the desire of almost any one and the same object.

But whatsoever is the object of any man's appetite or desire, that is it which he for his part calleth good: and the object of his hate and aversion, evil; and of his contempt, vile and inconsiderable. For these words of good, evil, and contemptible, are ever used with relation to the person that useth them: there being nothing simply and absolutely so; nor any common rule of good and evil, to be taken from the nature of the objects themselves; but from the person of the man, where there is no commonwealth; or, in a commonwealth, from the person that representeth it; or from an arbitrator or judge, whom men disagreeing shall by consent set up, and make his sentence the rule thereof. . . .

When in the mind of man, appetites, and aversions, hopes, and fears, concerning one and the same thing, arise alternately; and divers good and evil consequences of the doing, or omitting the thing propounded, come successively into our thoughts; so that sometimes we have an appetite to it; sometimes an aversion from it; sometimes hope to be able to do it; sometimes despair, or fear to attempt it; the whole sum of desires, aversions, hopes and fears continued till the thing be either done, or thought impossible, is that we call DELIBERATION.

Therefore of things past, there is no *deliberation;* because manifestly impossible to be changed: nor of things known to be impossible, or thought so; because men know, or think such deliberation vain. But of things impossible, which we think possible, we may deliberate; not knowing it is in vain. And it is called *deliberation;* because it is a putting an end to the *liberty* we had of doing, or omitting, according to our own appetite, or aversion.

This alternate succession of appetites, aversions, hopes and fears, is no less in other living creatures than in man: and therefore beasts also deliberate.

Every *deliberation is* then said to *end,* when that whereof they deliberate, is either done, or thought impossible; because till then we retain the liberty of doing, or omitting; according to our appetite, or aversion.

In *deliberation,* the last appetite, or aversion, immediately adhering to the action, or to the omission thereof, is that we call the WILL; the act, not the faculty, of *willing.* And beasts that have *deliberation,* must necessarily also have *will.* . . .

Nature hath made men so equal, in the faculties of the body, and mind; as that though there be found one man sometimes manifestly stronger in body, or of quicker mind than another; yet when all is reckoned together, the difference between man, and man, is not so considerable, as that one man can thereupon claim to himself any benefit, to which another may not pretend, as well as he. For as to the strength of body, the weakest has strength enough to kill the strongest, either by secret machination, or by confederacy with others, that are in the same danger with himself.

And as to the faculties of the mind, setting aside the arts grounded upon words, and especially that skill of proceeding upon general, and infallible rules, called science. . . . I find yet a greater equality amongst men, than that of strength. For prudence, is but experience; which equal time, equally bestows on all men, in those things they equally apply themselves unto. That which may perhaps make such equality incredible, is but a vain conceit of one's own wisdom, which almost all men think they have in a greater degree, than the vulgar; that is, than all men but themselves, and a few others, whom by fame, or for concurring with themselves, they approve. For such is the nature of men, that howsoever they may acknowledge many others to be more witty, or more eloquent, or more learned; yet they will hardly believe there be many so wise as themselves; for they see their own wit at hand, and other men's at a distance. But this proveth rather that men are in that point equal, than unequal. For there is not ordinarily a greater sign of the equal distribution of any thing, than that every man is contented with his share.

From this equality of ability, ariseth equality of hope in the attaining of our ends. And therefore if any two men desire the same thing, which nevertheless they cannot both enjoy, they become enemies; and in the way to their end, which is principally their own conservation, and sometimes their delectation only, endeavour to destroy, or subdue one another. And from hence it comes to pass, that where an invader hath no more to fear, than another man's single power; if one plant, sow, build, or possess a convenient seat, others may probably be expected to come prepared with forces united, to dispossess, and deprive him, not only of the fruit of his labour, but also of his life, or liberty. And the invader again is in the like danger of another.

And from this diffidence of one another, there is no way for any man to secure himself, so reasonable, as anticipation; that is, by force, or wiles, to master the persons of all men he can, so long, till he see no other power great enough to endanger him: and this is no more than his own conservation requireth, and is generally allowed. Also because there be some, that taking pleasure in contemplating their own power in the acts of conquest, which they pursue farther than their security requires; if others, that otherwise would be glad to be at ease within modest bounds, should not by invasion increase their power, they would not be able, long time, by standing only on their defence, to subsist. And by consequence, such augmentation of dominion over men being necessary to a man's conservation, it ought to be allowed him.

Again, men have no pleasure, but on the contrary a great deal of grief, in keeping company, where there is no power able to over-awe them all. For every man looketh that his companion should value him, at the same rate he sets upon himself; and upon all signs of contempt, or undervaluing, naturally endeavours, as far as he dares, (which amongst them that have no common power to keep them in quiet, is far enough to make them destroy each other), to extort a greater value from his contemners, by damage; and from others, by the example.

So that in the nature of man, we find three principal causes of quarrel. First, competition; secondly, diffidence; thirdly, glory.

The first, maketh men invade for gain; the second, for safety; and the third, for reputation. The first use violence, to make themselves masters of other men's persons, wives, children, and cattle; the second, to defend them; the third, for trifles, as a word, a smile, a different opinion, and any other sign of undervalue, either direct in their persons, or by reflection in their kindred, their friends, their nation, their profession, or their name.

Hereby it is manifest, that during the time men live without a common power to keep them all in awe, they are in that condition which is called war; and such a war, as is of every man, against every man. For WAR, consisteth not in battle only, or the act of fighting; but in a tract of time, wherein the will to contend by battle is sufficiently known: and therefore the notion of *time,* is to be considered in the nature of war; as it is in the nature of weather. For as the nature of foul weather, lieth not in a shower or two of rain, but in an inclination thereto of many days together: so the nature of war, consisteth not in actual fighting; but in the known disposition thereto, during all the time there is no assurance to the contrary. All other time is PEACE.

Whatsoever therefore is consequent to a time of war, where every man is enemy to every man; the same is consequent to the time, wherein men live without other security, than what their own strength; and their own invention shall furnish them withal. In such condition, there is no place for industry; because the fruit thereof is uncertain: and consequently no culture of the earth; no navigation, nor use of the commodities that may be imported by sea; no commodious building; no instruments of moving, and removing, such things as require much force; no knowledge of the face of the earth; no account of time; no arts; no letters; no society; and which is worst of all, continual fear, and danger of violent death; and the life of man, solitary, poor, nasty, brutish, and short.

It may seem strange to some man, that has not well weighed these things; that nature should thus dissociate, and render men apt to invade, and destroy one another, and he may therefore, not trusting to this inference, made from the passions, desire perhaps to have the same confirmed by experience. Let him therefore consider with himself, when taking a journey, he arms himself, and seeks to go well accompanied; when going to sleep, he locks his doors; when even in his house he locks his chests; and this when he knows there be laws, and public officers, armed, to revenge all injuries shall be done him; what opinion he has of his fellow-subjects, when he rides armed; of his fellow citizens, when he locks his doors; and of his children, and servants, when he locks his chests. Does he not there as much accuse mankind by his actions, as I do by my words? But neither of us accuse man's nature in it. The desires, and other passions of man, are in themselves no sin. No more are the actions, that proceed from those passions, till they know a law that forbids them: which till laws be made they cannot know: nor can any law be made, till they have agreed upon the person that shall make it.

It may peradventure be thought, there was never such a time, nor condition of war as this; and I believe it was never generally so, over all the world: but there are many places, where they live so now. For the savage people in many places of America, except the government of small families, the concord whereof dependeth on natural lust, have no government at all; and live at this day in that brutish manner, as I said before. Howsoever, it may be perceived what manner of life there would be, where there were no common power to fear, by the manner of life, which men that have formerly lived under a peaceful government, use to degenerate into, in a civil war.

But though there had never been any time, wherein particular men were in a condition of war one against another; yet in all times, kings, and persons of sovereign authority, because of their independency, are in continual jealousies, and in the state and posture of gladiators; having their weapons pointing, and their eyes fixed on one another; that is, their forts, garrisons, and guns upon the frontiers of their kingdoms; and continual spies upon their neighbours; which is a posture of war. But because they uphold thereby, the industry of their subjects; there does not follow from it, that misery, which accompanies the liberty of particular men.

To this war of every man, against every man, this also is consequent, that nothing can be unjust. The notions of right and wrong, justice and injustice have there no place. Where there is no common power, there is no law: where no law, no injustice. Force, and fraud, are in war the two cardinal virtues. Justice, and injustice are none of the faculties neither of the body, nor mind. If they were, they might be in a man that were alone in the world, as well as his senses, and passions. They are qualities, that relate to men in society, not in solitude. It is consequent also to the same condition, that there be no propriety, no dominion, no *mine* and *thine* distinct; but only that to be every man's, that he can get; and for so long, as he can keep it. And thus much for the ill condition, which man by mere nature is actually placed in; though with a possibility to come out of it, consisting partly in the passions, partly in his reason.

The passions that incline men to peace, are fear of death; desire of such things as are necessary to commodious living; and a hope by their industry to obtain them. And reason suggesteth convenient articles of peace, upon which men may be drawn to agreement. These articles, are they, which otherwise are called the Laws of Nature. . . . The right of nature . . . is the liberty each man hath, to use his own power, as he will himself, for the preservation of his own nature; that is to say, of his own life; and consequently, of doing any thing, which in his own judgment, and reason, he shall conceive to be the aptest means thereunto.

By LIBERTY, is understood, according to the proper signification of the word, the absence of external impediments: which impediments, may oft take away part of a man's power to do what he would; but cannot hinder him from using the power left him, according as his judgment, and reason shall dictate to him.

A LAW OF NATURE . . . is a precept or general rule, found out by reason, by which a man is forbidden to do that, which is destructive of his life, or taketh away the means of preserving the same; and to omit that, by which he thinketh it may be best preserved. For though they that speak of this subject, use to confound *right* and *law:* yet they ought to be distinguished; because RIGHT, consisteth in liberty to do, or to forbear: whereas LAW, determineth, and bindeth to one of them: so that law, and right, differ as much, as obligation, and liberty; which in one and the same matter are inconsistent.

And because the condition of man . . . is a condition of war of every one against every one: in which case every one is governed by his own reason; and there is nothing he can make use of, that may not be a help unto him, in preserving his life against his enemies; it followeth, that in such a condition, every man has a right to every thing; even to one another's body. And therefore, as long as this natural right of every man to every thing endureth, there can be no security to any man, how strong or wise soever he be, of living out the time, which nature ordinarily alloweth men to live. And consequently it is a precept, or general rule of reason, *that every man, ought to endeavour peace, as far as he has hope of obtaining it; and when he cannot obtain it, that he may seek, and use, all helps, and advantages of war.* The first branch of which rule, containeth the first, and fundamental law of nature; which is, *to seek peace, and follow it.* The second, the sum of the right of nature; which is, *by all means we can, to defend ourselves.*

From this fundamental law of nature, by which men are commanded to endeavour peace, is derived this second law; *that a man be willing, when others are so too, as far-forth, as for peace, and defence of himself he shall think it necessary, to lay down this right to all things; and be contented with so much liberty against other men, as he would allow other men against himself.* For as long as every man holdeth this right, of doing any thing he liketh; so long are all men in the condition of war. But if other men will not lay down their right, as well as he; then there is no reason for any one, to divest himself of his: for that were to expose himself to prey, which no man is bound to, rather than to dispose himself to peace. . . .

To *lay down* a man's *right* to any thing, is to *divest* himself of the *liberty,* of hindering another of the benefit of his own right to the same. For he that renounceth, or passeth away his right, giveth not to any other man a right which he had not before; because there is nothing to which every man had not right by nature: but only standeth out of his way, that he may enjoy his own original right, without hindrance from him; not without hindrance from another. So that the effect which redoundeth to one man, by another man's defect of right, is but so much diminution of impediments to the use of his own right original.

Right is laid aside, either by simply renouncing it; or by transferring it to another. By *simply* RENOUNCING; when he cares not to whom the benefit thereof redoundeth. By TRANSFERRING; when he intendeth the benefit thereof to some certain person, or persons. And when a man hath in either manner abandoned, or granted away his right; then is he said to be OBLIGED, or BOUND, not to hinder those, to whom such right is granted, or abandoned, from the benefit of it: and that he *ought,* and it is his DUTY, not to make void that voluntary act of his own: and that such hindrance is INJUSTICE, and INJURY.

So that *injury,* or *injustice,* in the controversies of the world, is somewhat like to that, which in the disputations of scholars is called *absurdity.* For as it is there called an absurdity, to contradict what one maintained in the beginning: so in the world, it is called injustice, and injury, voluntarily to undo that, which from the beginning he had voluntarily done. The way by which a man either simply renounceth, or transferreth his right, is a declaration, or signification, by some voluntary and sufficient sign, or signs, that he doth so renounce, or transfer; or hath so renounced, or transferred the same, to him that accepteth it. And these signs are either words only, or actions only; or, as it happeneth most often, both words, and actions. And the same are the BONDS, by which men are bound, and obliged: bonds, that have their strength, not from their own nature, for nothing is more easily broken than a man's word, but from fear of some evil consequence upon the rupture.

Whensoever a man transferreth his right, or renounceth it; it is either in consideration of some right reciprocally transferred to himself; or for some other good he hopeth for thereby. For it is a voluntary act: and of the voluntary acts of every man, the object is some *good to himself*. And therefore there be some rights, which no man can be understood by any words, or other signs, to have abandoned, or transferred. As first a man cannot lay down the right of resisting them, that assault him by force, to take away his life; because he cannot be understood to aim thereby, at any good to himself. The same may be said of wounds, and chains, and imprisonment, both because there is no benefit consequent to such patience; as there is to the patience of suffering another to be wounded, or imprisoned: as also because a man cannot tell, when he seeth men proceed against him by violence, whether they intend his death or not. And lastly the motive, and end for which this renouncing, and transferring of right is introduced, is nothing else but the security of a man's person, in his life, and in the means of so preserving life, as not to be weary of it. And therefore if a man by words, or other signs, seem to despoil himself of the end, for which those signs were intended; he is not to be understood as if he meant it, or that it was his will; but that he was ignorant of how such words and actions were to be interpreted.

The mutual transferring of right, is that which men call CONTRACT. . . .

If a covenant be made, wherein neither of the parties perform presently, but trust one another; in the condition of mere nature, which is a condition of war of every man against every man, upon any reasonable suspicion, it is void: but if there be a common power set over them both, with right and force sufficient to compel performance, it is not void. For he that performeth first, has no assurance the other will perform after; because the bonds of words are too weak to bridle men's ambition, avarice, anger, and other passions, without the fear of some coercive power; which in the condition of mere nature, where all men are equal, and judges of the justness of their own fears, cannot possibly be supposed. And therefore he which performeth first, does but betray himself to his enemy; contrary to the right, he can never abandon, of defending his life, and means of living.

But in a civil estate, where there is a power set up to constrain those that would otherwise violate their faith, that fear is no more reasonable; and for that cause, he which by the covenant is to perform first, is obliged so to do. . . .

He that transferreth any right, transferreth the means of enjoying it, as far as lieth in his power. As he that selleth land, is understood to transfer the herbage, and whatsoever grows upon it: nor can he that sells a mill turn away the stream that drives it. And they that give to a man the right of government in sovereignty, are understood to give him the right of levying money to maintain soldiers; and of appointing magistrates for the administration of justice. . . .

The final cause, end, or design of men, who naturally love liberty, and dominion over others, in the introduction of that restraint upon themselves, in which we see them live in commonwealths, is the foresight of their own preservation, and of a more contented life thereby; that is to say, of getting themselves out from that miserable condition of war, which is necessarily consequent . . . to the natural passions of men, when there is no visible power to keep them in awe, and tie them by fear of punishment to the performance of their covenants, and observation of the laws of nature. . . .

For the laws of nature, as *justice, equity, modesty, mercy,* and, in sum, *doing to others, as we would be done to,* of themselves, without the terror of some power, to cause them to be observed, are contrary to our natural passions, that carry us to partiality, pride, revenge, and the like. And covenants, without the sword, are but words, and of no strength to secure a man at all. Therefore notwithstanding, the laws of nature, which every one hath then kept, when he has the will to keep them, when he can do it safely, if there be no power erected, or not great enough for our security; every man will, and may lawfully rely on his own strength and art, for caution against all other men. And in all places, where men have lived by small families, to rob and spoil one another, has been a trade, and so far from being reputed against the law of nature, that the greater spoils they gained, the greater was their honour; and men observed no other laws therein, but the laws of honour; that is, to abstain from cruelty, leaving to men their lives, and instruments of husbandry. And as small families did then; so now do cities and kingdoms which are but greater families, for their own security, enlarge their dominions, upon all pretences of danger, and fear of invasion, or assistance that may be given to invaders, and endeavour as much as they can, to subdue, or weaken their neighbours, by open force, and secret arts, for want of other caution, justly; and are remembered for it in after ages with honour. . . .

Nor is it enough for the security, which men desire should last all the time of their life, that they be governed, and directed by one judgment, for a limited time; as in one battle, or one war. For though they obtain a victory by their unanimous endeavour against a foreign enemy; yet afterwards, when either they have no common enemy, or he that by one part is held for an enemy, is by another part held for a friend, they must needs by the difference of their interests dissolve, and fall again into a war amongst themselves.

It is true, that certain living creatures, as bees, and ants, live sociably one with another, which are therefore by Aristotle numbered amongst political creatures; and yet have no other direction, than their particular judgments and appetites; nor speech, whereby one of them can signify to another, what he thinks expedient for the common benefit: and therefore some man may perhaps desire to know, why mankind cannot do the same. To which I answer,

> First, that men are continually in competition for honour and dignity, which these creatures are not; and consequently amongst men there ariseth on that ground, envy and hatred, and finally war; but amongst these not so.

> Secondly, that amongst these creatures, the common good differeth not from the private; and being by nature inclined to their private, they procure thereby the common benefit. But man, whose joy consisteth in comparing himself with other men, can relish nothing but what is eminent.

> Thirdly, that these creatures, having not, as man, the use of reason, do not see, nor think they see any fault, in the administration of their common business; whereas amongst men, there are very many, that think themselves wiser, and abler to govern the public, better than the rest; and these strive to reform and innovate, one this way, another that way; and thereby bring it into distraction and civil war.

> Fourthly, that these creatures, though they have some use of voice, in making known to one another their desires, and other affections; yet they want that art of words, by which some men can represent to others, that which is good, in the likeness of evil; and evil, in the likeness of good; and augment, or diminish the apparent greatness of good and evil; discontenting men, and troubling their peace at their pleasure.

Fifthly, irrational creatures cannot distinguish between *injury,* and *damage;* and therefore as long as they be at ease, they are not offended with their fellows: whereas man is then most troublesome, when he is most at ease: for then it is that he loves to shew his wisdom, and control the actions of them that govern the commonwealth.

Lastly, the agreement of these creatures is natural; that of men, is by covenant only, which is artificial: and therefore it is no wonder if there be somewhat else required, besides covenant, to make their agreement constant and lasting; which is a common power, to keep them in awe, and to direct their actions to the common benefit.

The only way to erect such a common power, as may be able to defend them from the invasion of foreigners, and the injuries of one another, and thereby to secure them in such sort, as that by their own industry, and by the fruits of the earth, they may nourish themselves and live contentedly; is, to confer all their power and strength upon one man, or upon one assembly of men, that may reduce all their wills, by plurality of voices, unto one will: which is as much as to say, to appoint one man, or assembly of men, to bear their person; and every one to own, and acknowledge himself to be author of whatsoever he that so beareth their person, shall act, or cause to be acted, in those things which concern the common peace and safety; and therein to submit their wills, every one to his will, and their judgments, to his judgment. This is more than consent, or concord; it is a real unity of them all, in one and the same person, made by covenant of every man with every man, in such manner, as if every man should say to every man, *I authorise and give up my right of governing myself, to this man, or to this assembly of men, on this condition, that thou give up thy right to him, and authorize all his actions in like manner.* This done, the multitude so united in one person, is called a COMMONWEALTH. . . . This is the generation of that great LEVIATHAN, or rather, to speak more reverently, of that *mortal god,* to which we owe under the *immortal God,* our peace and defence. For by this authority, given him by every particular man in the commonwealth, he hath the use of so much power and strength conferred on him, that by terror thereof, he is enabled to perform the wills of them all, to peace at home, and mutual aid against their enemies abroad. And in him consisteth the essence of the commonwealth; which, to define it, is *one person, of whose acts a great multitude, by mutual covenants one with another, have made themselves every one the author, to the end he may use the strength and means of them all, as he shall think expedient, for their peace and common defence.*

And he that carrieth this person, is called SOVEREIGN, and said to have *sovereign power,* and every one besides, his SUBJECT.

The attaining to this sovereign power, is by two ways. One, by natural force; as when a man maketh his children, to submit themselves, and their children to his government, as being able to destroy them if they refuse; or by war subdueth his enemies to his will, giving them their lives on that condition. The other, is when men agree amongst themselves, to submit to some man, or assembly of men, voluntarily, on confidence to be protected by him against all others. This latter, may be called a political commonwealth, or commonwealth by *institution;* and the former, a commonwealth by *acquisition.* And first, I shall speak of a commonwealth by institution.

A *commonwealth* is said to be *instituted,* when a *multitude* of men do agree, and *covenant, every one, with every one,* that to whatsoever *man,* or *assembly of men,* shall be given by the major part, the *right* to *present* the person of them all, that is to say, to be their *representative;* every one, as well he that *voted for it,* as he that *voted against it,* shall *authorize* the actions and judgments, of that man, or assembly of men, in the same manner, as if they were his own, to the end, to live peaceably amongst themselves, and be protected against other men.

From this institution of a commonwealth are derived all the *rights,* and *faculties* of him, or them, on whom sovereign power is conferred by the consent of the people assembled.

First, because they covenant, it is to be understood, they are not obliged by former covenant to anything repugnant hereunto. And consequently they that have already instituted a commonwealth, being thereby bound by covenant, to own the actions, and judgments of one, cannot lawfully make a new covenant, amongst themselves, to be obedient to any other, in any thing whatsoever, without his permission. And therefore, they that are subjects to a monarch, cannot without his leave cast off monarchy, and return to the confusion of a disunited multitude; nor transfer their person from him that beareth it, to another man, or other assembly of men: for they are bound, every man to every man, to own, and be reputed author of all, that he that already is their sovereign, shall do, and judge fit to be done: so that any one man dissenting, all the rest should break their covenant made to that man, which is injustice: and they have also every man given the sovereignty to him that beareth their person; and therefore if they depose him, they take from him that which is his own, and so again it is injustice. Besides, if he that attempteth to depose his sovereign, be killed, or punished by him for such attempt, he is author of his own punishment, as being by the institution, author of all his sovereign shall do: and because it is injustice for a man to do anything, for which he may be punished by his own authority, he is also upon that title, unjust. And whereas some men have pretended for their disobedience to their sovereign, a new covenant, made, not with men, but with God; this also is unjust: for there is no covenant with God, but by mediation of somebody that representeth God's person, which none doth but God's lieutenant, who hath the sovereignty under God. But this pretence of covenant with God, is so evident a lie, even in the pretenders' own consciences, that it is not only an act of an unjust, but also of a vile, and unmanly disposition.

Secondly, because the right of bearing the person of them all, is given to him they make sovereign, by covenant only of one to another, and not of him to any of them; there can happen no breach of covenant on the part of the sovereign; and consequently none of his subjects, by any pretence of forfeiture, can be freed from his subjection. That he which is made sovereign maketh no covenant with his subjects beforehand, is manifest; because either he must make it with the whole multitude, as one party to the covenant; or he must make a several covenant with every man. With the whole, as one party, it is impossible; because as yet they are not one person: and if he make so many several covenants as there be men, those covenants after he hath the sovereignty are void; because what act soever can be pretended by any one of them for breach thereof, is the act both of himself, and of all the rest, because done in the person, and by the right of every one of them in particular. Besides, if any one, or more of them, pretend a breach of the covenant made by the sovereign at his institution; and others, or one other of his subjects, or himself alone, pretend there was no such breach, there is in this case, no judge to decide the controversy; it returns therefore to the sword again; and every man recovereth the right of protecting himself by his own strength, contrary to the design they had in the institution. . . .

Thirdly, because the major part hath by consenting voices declared a sovereign; he that dissented must now consent with the rest; that is, be contented to avow all the actions he shall do, or else justly be destroyed by the rest. For if he voluntarily entered into the congregation of them that were assembled, he sufficiently declared thereby his will, and therefore tacitly covenanted, to stand to what the major part should ordain: and therefore if he refuse to stand thereto, or make protestation against any of their decrees, he does contrary to his covenant, and therefore unjustly. And whether he be of the congregation, or not; and whether his consent be asked, or not, he must either submit to their decrees, or be left in the condition of war he was in before; wherein he might without injustice be destroyed by any man whatsoever.

Fourthly, because every subject is by this institution author of all the actions, and judgments of the sovereign instituted; it follows, that whatsoever he doth, it can be no injury to any of his subjects; nor ought he to be by any of them accused of injustice. For he that doth anything by authority from another, doth therein no injury to him by whose authority he acteth: but by this institution of a commonwealth, every particular man is author of all the sovereign doth: and consequently he that complained of injury from his sovereign, complaineth of that whereof he himself is author; and therefore ought not to accuse any man but himself; no nor himself of injury; because to do injury to one's self, is impossible. It is true that they that have sovereign power may commit iniquity; but not injustice, or injury in the proper signification.

Fifthly, and consequently to that which was said last, no man that hath sovereign power can justly be put to death, or otherwise in any manner by his subjects punished. For seeing every subject is author of the actions of his sovereign; he punisheth another for the actions committed by himself.

And because the end of this institution, is the peace and defence of them all; and whosoever has right to the end, has right to the means; it belongeth of right, to whatsoever man, or assembly that hath the sovereignty, to be judge both of the means of peace and defence, and also of the hindrances, and disturbances of the same; and to do whatsoever he shall think necessary to be done, both beforehand, for the preserving of peace and security, by prevention of discord at home, and hostility from abroad; and, when peace and security are lost, for the recovery of the same. And therefore,

Sixthly, it is annexed to the sovereignty, to be judge of what opinions and doctrines are averse, and what conducing to peace; and consequently, on what occasions, how far, and what men are to be trusted withal, in speaking to multitudes of people; and who shall examine the doctrines of all books before they be published. For the actions of men proceed from their opinions; and in the well-governing of opinions, consisteth the well-governing of men's actions, in order to their peace, and concord. And though in matter of doctrine, nothing ought to be regarded but the truth; yet this is not repugnant to regulating the same by peace. For doctrine repugnant to peace, can no more be true, than peace and concord can be against the law of nature. It is true, that in a commonwealth, where by the negligence, or unskillfulness of governors, and teachers, false doctrines are by time generally received; the contrary truths may be generally offensive. Yet the most sudden, and rough bursting in of a new truth, that can be, does never break the peace, but only sometimes awake the war. For those men that are so remissly governed, that they dare take up arms to defend, or introduce an opinion, are still in war; and their condition not peace, but only a cessation of arms for fear of one another, and they live, as it were, in the precincts of battle continually. It belongeth therefore to him that hath the sovereign power, to be judge, or constitute all judges of opinions and doctrines, as a thing necessary to peace; thereby to prevent discord and civil war.

Seventhly, is annexed to the sovereignty, the whole power of prescribing the rules, whereby every man may know, what goods he may enjoy, and what actions he may do, without being molested by any of his fellow-subjects; and this is it men call *propriety*. . . .

Eighthly, is annexed to the sovereignty, the right of judicature; that is to say, of hearing and deciding all controversies, which may arise concerning law, either civil, or natural; or concerning fact. For without the decision of controversies, there is no protection of one subject, against the injuries of another. . . .

Ninthly, is annexed to the sovereignty, the right of making war and peace with other nations, and commonwealths; that is to say, of judging when it is for the public good, and how great forces are to be assembled, armed, and paid for that end; and to levy money upon the subjects, to defray the expenses thereof. For the power by which the people are to be defended, consisteth in their armies; and the strength of an army, in the union of their strength under one command; which command the sovereign instituted, therefore hath; because the command of the *militia*, without other institution, maketh him that hath it sovereign. And therefore whosoever, is made general of an army, he that hath the sovereign power is always generalissimo.

Tenthly, is annexed to the sovereignty, the choosing of all counsellors, ministers, magistrates, and officers, both in peace, and war. For seeing the sovereign is charged with the end, which is the common peace and defence, he is understood to have power to use such means, as he shall think most fit for his discharge.

Eleventhly, to the sovereign is committed the power of rewarding with riches, or honour, and of punishing with corporal or pecuniary punishment, or with ignominy, every subject according to the law he hath formerly made; or if there be no law made, according as he shall judge most to conduce to the encouraging of men to serve the commonwealth, or deterring of them from doing disservice to the same. . . .

LIBERTY, or FREEDOM, signifieth, properly, the absence of opposition. . . . And according to this proper, and generally received meaning of the word, a FREEMAN, *is he, that in those things, which by his strength and wit he is able to do, is not hindered to do what he has a will to.* . . .

But as men, for the attaining of peace, and conservation of themselves thereby, have made an artificial man, which we call a commonwealth; so also have they made artificial chains, called *civil laws,* which they themselves, by mutual covenants, have fastened at one end, to the lips of that man, or assembly, to whom they have given the sovereign power; and at the other end to their own ears. These bonds, in their own nature but weak, may nevertheless be made to hold, by the danger; though not by the difficulty of breaking them.

In relation to these bonds only it is, that I am to speak now, of the *liberty* of *subjects.* For seeing there is no commonwealth in the world, wherein there be rules enough set down, for the regulating of all the actions, and words of men; as being a thing impossible: it followeth necessarily, that in all kinds of actions by the laws permitted, men have the liberty, of doing what their own reasons shall suggest, for the most profitable to themselves. For if we take liberty in the proper sense, for corporal liberty; that is to say, freedom from chains and prison; it were very absurd for men to clamour as they do, for the liberty they so manifestly enjoy. Again, if we take liberty, for an exemption from laws, it is it no less absurd, for men to demand as they do, that liberty, by which all other men may be masters of their lives. And yet, as absurd as it is, this is it they demand; not knowing that the laws are of no power to protect them, without a sword in the hands of a man, or men, to cause those laws to be put in execution. The liberty of a subject, lieth therefore only in those things, which in regulating their actions, the sovereign hath permitted: such as is the liberty to buy, and sell, and otherwise contract with one another; to choose their own abode, their own diet, their own trade of life, and institute their children as they themselves think fit; and the like.

Nevertheless we are not to understand, that by such liberty, the sovereign power of life and death, is either abolished, or limited. For it has been already shown, that nothing the sovereign representative can do to a subject, on what pretence soever, can properly be called injustice, or injury; because every subject is author of every act the sovereign doth; so that he never wanteth right to anything, otherwise, than as he himself is the subject of God, and bound thereby to observe the laws of nature. And therefore it may, and doth often happen in commonwealths, that a subject may be put to death, by the command of the sovereign power; and yet neither do the other wrong. . . .

UTILITARIANISM
John Stuart Mill (1806–1873)

Introduction, H. Gene Blocker

JOHN STUART MILL WAS ONE of the most important of the early Utilitarians. He is best known for his defense and modification of Utilitarianism. His father, James Mill, raised him from early childhood to promote the cause of Utilitarianism, which James Mill and Jeremy Bentham had founded in 1820.

By the time the younger Mill had reached early adulthood, Utilitarianism had come under attack from all sides. Because of its emphasis on pleasure seeking (hedonism) as the mainspring of human action, many people complained that Utilitarianism demeaned human beings by appealing to their baser instincts. There was also the "problem of justice"—the fact that Utilitarianism seemed to sanction the exploitation of minority groups because it would increase the overall happiness in the larger society.

In the selection below, John Stuart Mill tried to answer these critics. First he distinguished between the "quality" and "quantity" of pleasure. In his view, "higher-quality" pleasures, such as reading poetry or listening to classical music, would be more moral than "quantities" of pleasure gained through drinking beer or eating pizza. Mill also tried to show that Utilitarianism did not in fact advocate injustice. As he explained, a society that was run on just, or fair, principles would be happier than one run unfairly. Also, educators and social planners could teach young people to support socially beneficial principles such as justice.

This last point has led some recent philosophers to identify Mill as a "rule Utilitarian"—someone who believes that we should follow those moral rules that most benefit our entire society. In other words, Mill did not suggest that we should seek simply the "greatest happiness for the greatest number" (a principle of "act Utilitarianism") but that we should follow those moral rules—such as don't tell lies, be honest —that most make for a happy and productive society.

As you read the selection, ask yourself whether Mill's distinction between "quality" and "quantity" of pleasure helped Utilitarianism. From a Utilitarian's perspective, how might one kind of pleasure (such as reading poetry) be "higher" than another (such as watching *The Simpsons*)? If your answer is that higher pleasures have something to do with helping us to develop our full human potential, is that a value that a true Utilitarian would hold? Also, in your opinion, how successful is Mill's argument about the social utility of moral rules such as justice? Most of us would probably agree that fairness and justice are good things in any society. However, can you think of times when it would be more moral, from a Utilitarian point of view, to be unjust? In other words, are there cases in which an unfair act would be worth doing because it would gain important benefits for society overall? Finally, see whether you can state Mill's basic argument for Utilitarianism— then analyze that argument step by step. Which points do you think have merit? Which would you challenge? Why?

CHAPTER II. WHAT UTILITARIANISM IS

The creed which accepts as the foundation of morals, Utility, or the Greatest Happiness Principle, holds that actions are right in proportion as they tend to promote happiness, wrong as they tend to produce the reverse of happiness. By happiness is intended pleasure, and the absence of pain; by unhappiness, pain, and the privation of pleasure. To give a clear view of the moral standard set up by the theory, much more requires to be said; in particular, what things it includes in the ideas of pain and pleasure; and to what extent this is left an open question. But these supplementary explanations do not affect the theory of life on which this theory of morality is grounded— namely, that pleasure, and freedom from pain, are the only things desirable as ends; and that all desirable things (which are as numerous in the utilitarian as in any other scheme) are desirable either for the pleasure inherent in themselves, or as a means to the promotion of pleasure and the prevention of pain.

Now, such a theory of life excites in many minds, and among them in some of the most estimable in feeling and purpose, inveterate dislike. To suppose that life has (as they express it) no higher end than pleasure—no better and nobler object of desire and pursuit—they designate as utterly mean and grovelling; as a doctrine worthy only of swine, to whom the followers of Epicurus were, at a very early period, contemptuously likened; and modern holders of the doctrine are occasionally made the subject of equally polite comparisons by its German, French, and English assailants.

When thus attacked, the Epicureans have always answered, that it is not they, but their accusers, who represent human nature in a degrading light;

since the accusation supposes human beings to be capable of no pleasures except those of which swine are capable. If this supposition were true, the charge could not be gainsaid, but would then be no longer an imputation; for if the sources of pleasure were precisely the same to human beings and to swine, the rule of life which is good enough for the one would be good enough for the other. The comparison of the Epicurean life to that of beasts is felt as degrading, precisely because a beast's pleasures do not satisfy a human being's conceptions of happiness. Human beings have faculties more elevated than the animal appetites, and when once made conscious of them, do not regard anything as happiness which does not include their gratification. I do not, indeed, consider the Epicureans to have been by any means faultless in drawing out their scheme of consequences from the utilitarian principle. To do this in any sufficient manner, many Stoic, as well as Christian elements require to be included. But there is no known Epicurean theory of life which does not assign to the pleasures of the intellect, of the feelings and imagination, and of the moral sentiments, a much higher value as pleasures than to those of mere sensation. It must be admitted, however, that utilitarian writers in general have placed the superiority of mental over bodily pleasures chiefly in the greater permanency, safety, uncostliness. &c., of the former—that is, in their circumstantial advantages rather than in their intrinsic nature. And on all these points, utilitarians have fully proved their case; but they might have taken the other, and, as it may be called, higher ground, with entire consistency. It is quite compatible with the principle of utility to recognise the fact, that some *kinds* of pleasure are more desirable and more valuable than others. It would be absurd that while, in estimating all other things, quality is considered as well as quantity, the estimation of pleasures should be supposed to depend on quantity alone.

If I am asked, what I mean by difference of quality in pleasures, or what makes one pleasure more valuable than another, merely as a pleasure, except its being greater in amount, there is but one possible answer. Of two pleasures, if there be one to which all or almost all who have experience of both give a decided preference, irrespective of any feeling of moral obligation to prefer it, that is the more desirable pleasure. If one of the two is, by those who are competently acquainted with both, placed so far above the other that they prefer it, even though knowing it to be attended with a greater amount of discontent, and would not resign it for any quantity of the other pleasure which their nature is capable of, we are justified in ascribing to the preferred enjoyment a superiority in quality so far outweighing quantity as to render it, in comparison, of small account.

Now it is an unquestionable fact that those who are equally acquainted with, and equally capable of appreciating and enjoying, both, do give a most marked preference to the manner of existence which employs their higher faculties. Few human creatures would consent to be changed into any of the lower animals, for a promise of the fullest allowance of a beast's pleasures, no intelligent human being would consent to be a fool, no instructed person would be an ignoramus, no person of feeling and conscience would be self-ish and base, even though they should be persuaded that the fool, the dunce, or the rascal is better satisfied with his lot than they are with theirs. They would not resign what they possess more than he, for the most complete sat-isfaction of all the desires which they have in common with him. If they ever fancy they would, it is only in cases of unhappiness so extreme, that to escape from it they would exchange their lot for almost any other, however undesirable in their own eyes. A being of higher faculties requires more to make him happy, is capable probably of more acute suffering, and is cer-tainly accessible to it at more points than one of an inferior type, but in spite of these liabilities, he can never really wish to sink into what he feels to be a lower grade of existence. We may give what explanation we please of this unwillingness; we may attribute it to pride, a name which is given indiscrim-inately to some of the most and to some of the least estimable feelings of which mankind are capable: we may refer it to the love of liberty and per-sonal independence, an appeal to which was with the Stoics one of the most effective means for the inculcation of it: to the love of power, or to the love of excitement, both of which do really enter into and contribute to it: but its most appropriate appellation is a sense of dignity, which all human beings possess in one form or other and in some, though by no means in exact, pro-portion to their higher faculties, and which is so essential a part of the happi-ness of those in whom it is strong, that nothing which conflicts with it could be, otherwise than momentarily, an object of desire to them. Whoever sup-poses that this preference takes place at a sacrifice of happiness—that the superior being in anything like the equal circumstances, is not happier than the inferior—confounds the two very different ideas, of happiness, and con-tent. It is indisputable that the being whose capacities of enjoyment are low, has the greatest chance of having them fully satisfied; and a highly-endowed being will always feel that any happiness which he can look for, as the world is constituted, is imperfect. But he can learn to bear its imperfections, if they are at all bearable; and they will not make him envy the being who is indeed unconscious of the imperfections, but only because he feels not at all the good which those imperfections qualify. It is better to be a human being dissatisfied than a pig satisfied; better to be Socrates dissatisfied than a fool satisfied. And if the fool, or the pig, is of a different opinion, it is because they only know their own side of the question. The other party to the comparison knows both sides.

It may be objected that many who are capable of the higher pleasures, occasionally, under the influence of temptation, postpone them to the lower. But this is quite compatible with a full appreciation of the intrinsic superiority of the higher. Men often, from infirmity of character, make their election for the nearer good, though they know it to be the less valuable; and this no less when the choice is between two bodily pleasures, than when it is between bodily and mental. They pursue sensual indulgence to the injury of health, though perfectly aware that health is the greater good. It may be further objected, that many who begin with youthful enthusiasm for everything noble, as they advance in years sink into indolence and selfishness. But I do not believe that those who undergo this very common change, voluntarily choose the lower description of pleasures in preference to the higher. I believe that before they devote themselves exclusively to the one, they have already become incapable of the other. Capacity for the nobler feelings is in most natures a very tender plant, easily killed, not only by hostile influences, but by mere want of sustenance, and in the majority of young persons it speedily dies away if the occupations to which their position in life has devoted them, and the society into which it has thrown them, are not favourable to keeping that higher capacity in exercise. Men lose their high aspirations as they lose their intellectual tastes, because they have not time or opportunity for indulging them; and they addict themselves to inferior pleasures, not because they deliberately prefer them, but because they are either the only ones to which they have access, or the only ones which they are any longer capable of enjoying. It may be questioned whether any one who has remained equally susceptible to both classes of pleasures, ever knowingly and calmly preferred the lower, though many, in all ages, have broken down in an ineffectual attempt to combine both.

From this verdict of the only competent judges, I apprehend there can be no appeal. On a question which is the best worth having of two pleasures, or which of two modes of existence is the most grateful to the feelings, apart from its moral attributes and from its consequences, the judgment of those who are qualified by knowledge of both, or, if they differ, that of the majority among them, must be admitted as final. And there needs be the less hesitation to accept this judgment respecting the quality of pleasures, since there is no other tribunal to be referred to even on the question of quantity. What means are there of determining which is the acutest of two pains, or the intensest of two pleasurable sensations, except the general suffrage of those who are familiar with both? Neither pains nor pleasures are homogeneous, and pain is always heterogeneous with pleasure. What is there to decide whether a particular pleasure is worth purchasing at the cost of a particular pain, except the feelings and judgment of the experienced? When, therefore, those feelings and judgment declare the pleasures derived from the higher faculties to be preferable in *kind*, apart from the question of intensity, to those of which the animal nature, disjoined from the higher faculties, is susceptible, they are entitled on this subject to the same regard.

I have dwelt on this point, as being a necessary part of a perfectly just conception of Utility or Happiness, considered as the directive rule of human conduct. But it is by no means an indispensable condition to the acceptance of the utilitarian standard; for that standard is not the agent's own greatest happiness, but the greatest amount of happiness altogether. And if it may possibly be doubted whether a noble character is always the happier for its nobleness, there can be no doubt that it makes other people happier, and that the world in general is immensely a gainer by it. Utilitarianism, therefore, could only attain its end by the general cultivation of nobleness of character, even if each individual were only benefitted by the nobleness of others, and his own, so far as happiness is concerned, were a sheer deduction from the benefit. But the bare enunciation of such an absurdity as this last, renders refutation superfluous.

According to the Greatest Happiness Principle, as above explained, the ultimate end, with reference to and for the sake of which all other things are desirable (whether we are considering our own good or that of other people), is an existence exempt as far as possible from pain, and as rich as possible in enjoyments, both in point of quantity and quality; the test of quality, and the rule for measuring it against quantity, being the preference felt by those who, in their opportunities of experience, to which must be added their habits of self-consciousness and self-observation, are best furnished with the means of comparison. This, being, according to the utilitarian opinion, the end of human action, is necessarily also the standard of morality; which may accordingly be defined, the rules and precepts for human conduct, by the observance of which an existence such as has been described might be, to the greatest extent possible, secured to all mankind; and not to them only, but, so far as the nature of things admits, to the whole sentient creation.

Against this doctrine, however, arises another class of objectors, who say that happiness, in any form, cannot be the rational purpose of human life and action; because, in the first place, it is unattainable: and they contemptuously ask, What right hast thou to be happy? a question which Mr. Carlyle clenches by the addition, What right, a short time ago, hadst thou even *to be*? Next, they say, that men can do *without* happiness; that all noble human beings have felt this, and could not have become noble but by learning the lesson of Entsagen, or renunciation; which lesson, thoroughly learnt and submitted to, they affirm to be the beginning and necessary condition of all virtue.

The first of these objections would go to the root of the matter were it well-founded; for if no happiness is to be had at all by human beings, the attainment of it cannot be the end of morality, or of any rational conduct. Though, even in that case, something might still be said for the utilitarian theory; since utility includes not solely the pursuit of happiness, but the prevention or mitigation of unhappiness; and if the former aim be chimerical, there will be all the greater scope and more imperative need for the latter, so long at least as mankind think fit to live, and do not take refuge in the simultaneous act of suicide recommended under certain conditions by Novalis. When, however, it is thus positively asserted to be impossible that human life should be happy, the assertion, if not something like a verbal quibble, is at least an exaggeration. If by happiness be meant a continuity of highly pleasurable excitement, it is evident enough that this is impossible. A state of exalted pleasure lasts only moments, or in some cases, and with some intermissions, hours or days, and is the occasional brilliant flash of enjoyment, not Its permanent and steady flame. Of this the philosophers who have taught that happiness is the end of life were as fully aware as those who taunt them. The happiness which they meant was not a life of rapture; but moments of such, in an existence made up of few and transitory pains, many and various pleasures, with a decided predominance of the active over the passive, and having as the foundation of the whole, not to expect more from life than it is capable of bestowing. A life thus composed, to those who have been fortunate enough to obtain it, has always appeared worthy of the name of happiness. And such an existence is even now the lot of many, during some considerable portion of their lives. The present wretched education, and wretched social arrangements, are the only real hindrance to its being attainable by almost all. . . .

I must again repeat, what the assailants of utilitarianism seldom have the justice to acknowledge, that the happiness which forms the utilitarian standard of what is right in conduct, is not the agent's own happiness, but that of all concerned. As between his own happiness and that of others, utilitarianism requires him to be as strictly impartial as a disinterested and benevolent spectator. In the golden rule of Jesus of Nazareth, we read the complete spirit of the ethics of utility. To do as one would be done by, and to love one's neighbour as oneself, constitute the ideal perfection of utilitarian morality. As the means of making the nearest approach to this ideal, utility would enjoin, first, that laws and social arrangements should place the happiness, or (as speaking practically it may be called) the interest, of every individual, as nearly as possible in harmony with the interest of the whole; and secondly, that education and opinion, which have so vast a power over human character, should so use that power as to establish in the mind of every individual an indissoluble association between his own happiness and the good of the whole; especially between his own happiness and the practice of such modes of conduct, negative and positive, as regard for the universal happiness prescribes: so that not only he may be unable to conceive the possibility of happiness to himself, consistently with conduct opposed to the general good, but also that a direct impulse to promote the general good may be in every individual one of the habitual motives of action, and the sentiments connected therewith may fill a large and prominent place in every human being's sentient existence. If the impugners of the utilitarian morality represented it to their own minds in this its true character, I know not what recommendation possessed by any other morality they could possibly affirm to be wanting to it: what more beautiful or more exalted developments of human nature any other ethical system can be supposed to foster, or what springs of action, not accessible to the utilitarian, such systems rely on for giving effect to their mandates.

The objectors to utilitarianism cannot always be charged with representing it in a discreditable light. On the contrary, those among them who entertain anything like a just idea of its disinterested character, sometimes find fault with its standard as being too high for humanity. They say it is exacting too much to require that people shall always act from the inducement of promoting the general interests of society. But this is to mistake the very meaning of a standard of morals, and to confound the rule of action with the motive of it. It is the business of ethics to tell us what are our duties, or by what test we may know them; but no system of ethics requires that the sole motive of all we do shall be a feeling of duty; on the contrary, ninety-nine hundredths of all our actions are done from other motives, and rightly so done, if the rule of duty does not condemn them. It is the more unjust to utilitarianism that this particular misapprehension should be made a ground of objection to it, inasmuch as utilitarian moralists have gone beyond almost all others in affirming that the motive has nothing to do with the morality of the action, though much with the worth of the agent. He who saves a fellow creature from drowning does what is morally right, whether his motive be duty, or the hope of being paid for his trouble: he who betrays the friend that trusts him, is guilty of a crime, even if his object be to serve another friend to whom he is under greater obligations. But to speak only of actions done from the motive of duty, and in direct obedience to principle: it is a misapprehension of the utilitarian mode of thought, to conceive it as implying that people should fix their minds upon so wide a generality as the world, or society at large. The great majority of good actions are intended, not for the benefit of the world, but for that of individuals, of which the good of the world is made up; and the thoughts of the most virtuous man need not on these occasions travel beyond the particular persons concerned, except so far as is necessary to assure himself that in benefiting them he is not violating the rights—that is, the legitimate and authorized expectations—of any one else. The multiplication of happiness is, according to the utilitarian ethics, the object of virtue: the occasions on which any person (except one in a thousand) has it in his power to do this on an extended scale, in other words, to be a public benefactor, are but exceptional; and on these occasions alone is he called on to consider public utility; in every other case, private utility, the interest or happiness of some few persons, is all he has to attend to. Those alone the influence of whose actions extends to society in general, need concern themselves habitually about so large an object. In the case of abstinences indeed—of things which people forbear to do, from moral considerations, though the consequences in the particular case might be beneficial—it would be unworthy of an intelligent agent not to be consciously aware that the action is of a class which, if practised generally, would be generally injurious, and that this is the ground of the obligation to abstain from it. The amount of regard for the public interest implied in this recognition, is no greater than is demanded by every system of morals, for they all enjoin to abstain from whatever is manifestly pernicious to society . . .

Chapter III. Of the Ultimate Sanction of the Principle of Utility

The question is often asked, and properly so, in regard to any supposed moral standard—What is its sanction? what are the motives to obey it? or more specifically, what is the source of its obligation? whence does it derive its binding force? It is a necessary part of moral philosophy to provide the answer to this question; which, though frequently assuming the shape of an objection to the utilitarian morality, as if it had some special applicability to that above others, really arises in regard to all standards. It arises, in fact, whenever a person is called on to *adopt* a standard or refer morality to any basis on which he has not been accustomed to test it. For the customary morality, that which education and opinion have consecrated, is the only one which presents itself to the mind with the feeling of being *in itself* obligatory; and when a person is asked to believe that this morality *derives* its obligation from some general principle round which custom has not thrown the same halo, the assertion is to him a paradox; the supposed corollaries seem to have a more binding force than the original theorem; the superstructure seems to stand better without, than with, what is represented as its foundation. He says to himself, I feel that I am bound not to rob or murder, betray or deceive; but why am I bound to promote the general happiness? If my own happiness lies in something else, why may I not give that the preference?

If the view adopted by the utilitarian philosophy of the nature of the moral sense be correct, this difficulty will always present itself, until the influences which form moral character have taken the same hold of the principle which they have taken of some of the consequences—until, by the improvement of education, the feeling of unity with our fellow creatures shall be (what it cannot be doubted that Christ intended it to be) as deeply rooted in our character, and to our own consciousness as completely a part of our nature, as the horror of crime is in an ordinarily well-brought up young person. In the meantime, however, the difficulty has no peculiar application to the doctrine of utility, but is inherent in every attempt to analyse morality and reduce it to principles; which, unless the principle is already in men's minds invested with as much sacredness as any of its applications, always seems to divest them of a part of their sanctity.

The principle of utility either has, nor there is no reason why it might not have, all the sanctions which belong to any other system of morals. Those sanctions are either external or internal. Of the external sanctions it is not necessary to speak at any length. They are the hope of favour and the fear of displeasure from our fellow creatures or from the Ruler of the Universe, along with whatever we may have of sympathy or affection for them or of love and awe of Him, inclining us to do his will independently of selfish consequences. There is evidently no reason why all these motives for observance should not attach themselves to the utilitarian morality, as completely and as powerfully as to any other. Indeed, those of them which refer to our fellow creatures are sure to do so, in proportion to the amount of general intelligence; for whether there be any other ground of moral obligation than the general happiness or not, men do desire happiness; and however imperfect may be their own practice, they desire and commend all conduct in others towards themselves, by which they think their happiness is promoted. With regard to the religious motive, if men believe, as most profess to do, in the goodness of God, those who think that conduciveness to the general happiness is the essence, or even only the criterion, of good, must necessarily believe that it is also that which God approves. The whole force therefore of external reward and punishment, whether physical or moral, and whether proceeding from God or from our fellow men, together with all that the capacities of human nature admit, of disinterested devotion to either, become available to enforce the utilitarian morality, in proportion as that morality is recognised; and the more powerfully, the more the appliances of education and general cultivation are bent to the purpose.

So far as to external sanctions. The internal sanction of duty, whatever our standard of duty may be is one and the same—a feeling in our own mind; a pain, more or less intense, attendant on violation of duty, which in properly-cultivated moral natures rises, in the more serious cases, into shrinking from it as an impossibility. This feeling, when disinterested, and connecting itself with the pure idea of duty, and not with some particular form of it, or with any of the merely accessory circumstances, is the essence of Conscience; though in that complex phenomenon as it actually exists, the simple fact is in general all encrusted over with collateral associations, derived from sympathy, from love, and still more from fear; from all the forms of religious feeling; from the recollections of childhood and of all our past life; from self-esteem, desire of the esteem of others, and occasionally even self-abasement. This extreme complication is, I apprehend, the origin of the sort of mystical character which, by a tendency of the human mind of which there are many other examples, is apt to be attributed to the idea of moral obligation, and which leads people to believe that the idea cannot possibly attach itself to any other objects than those which, by a supposed mysterious law, are found in our present experience to excite it. Its binding force, however, consists in the existence of a mass of feeling which must be broken through in order to do what violates our standard of right, and which, if we do nevertheless violate that standard, will probably have to be encountered afterwards in the form of remorse. Whatever theory we have of the nature or origin of conscience, this is what essentially constitutes it.

The ultimate sanction, therefore, of all morality (external motives apart) being a subjective feeling in our own minds, I see nothing embarrassing to those whose standard is utility, in the question, what is the sanction of that particular standard? We may answer, the same as of all other moral standards—the conscientious feelings of mankind. Undoubtedly this sanction has no binding efficacy on those who do not possess the feelings it appeals to; but neither will these persons be more obedient to any other moral principle than to the utilitarian one. On them morality of any kind has no hold but through the external sanctions. Meanwhile the feelings exist, a fact in human nature, the reality of which, and the great power with which they are capable of acting on those in whom they have been duly cultivated, are proved by experience. No reason has ever been shown why they may not be cultivated to as great intensity in connexion with the utilitarian, as with any other rule of morals.

There is, I am aware, a disposition to believe that a person who sees in moral obligation a transcendental fact, an objective reality belonging to the province of 'Things in themselves,' is likely to be more obedient to it than one who believes it to be entirely subjective, having its seat in human consciousness only. But whatever a person's opinion may be on this point of Ontology, the force he is really urged by is his own subjective feeling, and is exactly measured by its strength. No one's belief that Duty is an objective reality is stronger than the belief that God is so, yet the belief in God, apart from the expectation of actual reward and punishment, only operates on conduct through, and in proportion, to, the subjective religious feeling. The sanction, so far as it is disinterested, is always in the mind itself; and the notion therefore of the transcendental moralists must be, that this sanction will not exist in the mind unless it is believed to have its root out of the mind; and that if a person is able to say to himself, That which is restraining me, and which is called my conscience, is only a feeling in my own mind, he may possibly draw the conclusion that when the feeling ceases the obligation ceases, and that if he find the feeling inconvenient, he may disregard it, and endeavour to get rid of it. But is this danger confined to the utilitarian morality? Does the belief that moral obligation has its seat outside the mind make the feeling of it too strong to be got rid of? The fact is so far otherwise, that all moralists admit and lament the ease with which, in the generality of minds, conscience can be silenced or stifled. The question, Need I obey my conscience? is quite as often put to themselves by persons who never heard of the principle of utility, as by its adherents. Those whose conscientious feelings are so weak as to allow of their asking this question, if they answer it affirmatively, will not do so because they believe in the transcendental theory, but because of the external sanctions. . . .

CHAPTER IV: OF WHAT SORT OF PROOF THE PRINCIPLE OF UTILITY IS SUSCEPTIBLE

It has already been remarked, that questions of ultimate ends do not admit of proof, in the ordinary acceptation of the term. To be incapable of proof by reasoning is common to all first principles; to the first premises of our knowledge, as well as to those of our conduct. But the former, being matters of fact, may be the subject of a direct appeal to the faculties which judge of fact—namely, our senses, and our internal consciousness. Can an appeal be made to the same faculties on questions of practical ends? Or by what other faculty is cognizance taken of them?

Questions about ends are, in other words, questions about what things are desirable. The utilitarian doctrine is, that happiness is desirable, and the only thing desirable, as an end; all other things being only desirable as means to that end. What ought to be required of this doctrine—what conditions is it requisite that the doctrine should fulfil—to make good its claim to be believed?

The only proof capable of being given that an object is visible, is that people actually see it. The only proof that a sound is audible, is that people hear it: and so of the other sources of our experience. In like manner, I apprehend, the sole evidence it is possible to produce that anything is desirable, is that people do actually desire it. If the end which the utilitarian doctrine proposes to itself were not, in theory and in practice, acknowledged to be an end, nothing could ever convince any person that it was so. No reason can be given why the general happiness is desirable, except that each person, so far as he believes it to be attainable, desires his own happiness. This, however, being a fact, we have not only all the proof which the case admits of, but all which it is possible to require, that happiness is a good: that each person's happiness is a good to that person, and the general happiness, therefore, a good to the aggregate of all persons. Happiness has made out its title as *one* of the ends of conduct, and consequently one of the criteria of morality.

But it has not, by this alone, proved itself to be the sole criterion. To do that, it would seem, by the same rule, necessary to show, not only that people desire happiness, but that they never desire anything else. Now it is palpable that they do desire things which, in common language, are decidely distinguished from happiness. They desire, for example, virtue and the absence of vice, no less really than pleasure and the absence of pain. The desire of virtue is not as universal, but it is as authentic a fact, as the desire of happiness. And hence the opponents of the utilitarian standard deem that they have a right to infer that there are other ends of human action besides happiness, and that happiness is not the standard of approbation and disapprobation.

But does the utilitarian doctrine deny that people desire virtue, or maintain that virtue is not a thing to be desired? The very reverse. It maintains not only that virtue is to be desired, but that it is to be desired disinterestedly, for itself. Whatever may be the opinion of utilitarian moralists as to the original conditions by which virtue is made virtue; however, they may believe (as they do) that actions and dispositions are only virtuous because they promote another end than virtue; yet this being granted, and it having been decided, from considerations of this description, what *is* virtuous, they not only place virtue at the very head of the things which are good as means to ultimate end, but they also recognise as a psychological fact the possibility of its being, to the individual, a good in itself, without looking to any end beyond it; and hold, that the mind is not in a right state, not in a state comfortable to Utility, not in the state most conducive to the general happiness, unless it does love virtue in this manner—as a thing desirable in itself, even although, in the individual instance, it should not produce those other desirable consequences which it tends to produce, and on account of which it is held to be virtue. This opinion is not, in the smallest degree, a departure from the Happiness principle. The ingredients of happiness are very various, and each of them is desirable in itself, and not merely when considered as swelling an aggregate. The principle of utility does not mean that any given pleasure, as music, for instance, or any given exemption from pain, as for example health, are to be looked upon as a means to a collective something termed happiness, and to be desired on that account. They are desired and desirable in and for themselves; besides being means, they are a part of the end. Virtue, according to the utilitarian doctrine, is not naturally and originally part of the end, but it is capable of becoming so: and to those who love it disinterestedly it has become so, and is desired and cherished, not as a means to happiness, but as a part of their happiness.

To illustrate this farther, we may remember that virtue is not the only thing, originally a means, and which if it were not a means to anything else, would be and remain indifferent, but which by association with what it is a means to, comes to be desired for itself, and that too with the utmost intensity. What, for example, shall we say of the love of money? There is nothing originally more desirable about money than about any heap of glittering pebbles. Its worth is solely that of the things which it will buy; the desires for other things than itself, which it is a means of gratifying. Yet the love of money is not only one of the strongest moving forces of human life, but money is, in many cases, desired in and for itself; the desire to possess it is often stronger than the desire to use it, and goes on increasing when all the desires which point to ends beyond it, to be encompassed by it, are falling off. It may be then said truly, that money is desired not for the sake of an end, but as part of the end. From being a means to happiness, it has come to be itself a principal ingredient of the individual's conception of happiness. The same may be said of the majority of the great objects of human life—power, for example, or fame, except that to each of these there is a certain amount of immediate pleasure annexed, which has at least the semblance of being naturally inherent in them; a thing which cannot be said of money. Still, however, the strongest natural attraction, both of power and of fame, is the immense aid they give to the attainment of our other wishes; and it is the strong association thus generated between them and all our objects of desire, which gives to the direct desire of them the intensity it often assumes, so as in some characters to surpass in strength all other desires. In these cases the means have become a part of the end, and a more important part of it than any of the things which they are means to. What was once desired as an instrument for the attainment of happiness, has come to be desired for its own sake. In being desired for its own sake it is, however, desired as *part* of happiness. The person is made, or thinks he would be made, happy by its mere possession; and is made unhappy by failure to obtain it. The desire of it is not a different thing from the desire of happiness, any more than the love of music, or the desire of health. They are included in happiness. They are some of the elements of which the desire of happiness is made up. Happiness is not an abstract idea, but a concrete whole, and these are some of its parts. And the utilitarian standard sanctions and approves their being so. Life would be a poor thing, very ill provided with sources of happiness, if there were not this provision of nature, by which things originally indifferent, but conducive to, or otherwise associated with the satisfaction of our primitive desires, become in themselves sources of pleasure more valuable than the primitive pleasures, both in permanency, in the space of human existence that they are capable of covering, and even in intensity.

Virtue, according to the utilitarian conception, is a good of this description. There was no original desire of it, or motive to it, save its conduciveness to pleasure, and especially to protection from pain. But through the association thus formed, it may be felt a good in itself, and desired as such with as great intensity as any other good; and with this difference between it and the love of money, of power, or of fame, that all of these may, and often do, render the individual noxious to the other members of the society to which he belongs, whereas there is nothing which makes him so much a blessing to them as the cultivation of the disinterested love of virtue. And consequently, the utilitarian standard, while it tolerates and approves those other acquired desires, up to the point beyond which they would be more injurious to the general happiness than promotive of it, enjoins and requires the cultivation of the love of virtue up to the greatest strength possible, as being above all things important to the general happiness.

It results from the preceding considerations, that there is in reality nothing desired except happiness. Whatever is desired otherwise than as a means to some end beyond itself, and ultimately to happiness, is desired as itself a part of happiness, and is not desired for itself until it has become so. Those who desire virtue for its own sake, desire it either because the consciousness of it is a pleasure, or because the consciousness of being without it is a pain, or for both reasons united; as in truth the pleasure and pain seldom exist separately, but almost always together, the same person feeling pleasure in the degree of virtue attained, and pain in not having attained more. If one of these gave him no pleasure, and the other no pain, he would not love or desire virtue or would desire it only for the other benefits which it might produce to himself or to persons whom he cared for.

We have now, then, an answer to the question, of what sort of proof the principle of utility is susceptible. If the opinion which I have now stated is psychologically true—if human nature is so constituted as to desire nothing which is not either a part of happiness or a means of happiness, we can have no other proof, and we require no other, that these are the only things desirable. If so, happiness is the sole end of human action, and the promotion of it the test by which to judge of all human conduct; from whence it necessarily follows that it must be the criterion of morality, since a part is included in the whole.

And now to decide whether this is really so; whether mankind do desire nothing for itself but that which is a pleasure to them, or of which the absence is a pain; we have evidently arrived at a question of fact and experience, dependent, like all similar questions, upon evidence. It can only be determined by practised self-consciousness and self-observation, assisted by observation of others. I believe that these sources of evidence, impartially consulted, will declare that desiring a thing and finding it pleasant, aversion to it and thinking of it as painful, are phenomena entirely inseparable, or rather two parts of the same phenomenon; in strictness of language, two different modes of naming the same psychological fact: that to think of an object as desirable (unless for the sake of its consequences), and to think of it as pleasant, are one and the same thing; and that to desire anything, except in proportion as the idea of it is pleasant, is a physical and metaphysical impossibility. . . .

FOUNDATIONS OF THE METAPHYSICS OF MORALS

Immanuel Kant

Abridged by H. Gene Blocker

Library of Liberal Arts Archive

Nothing in the world—indeed nothing even beyond the world—can possibly be conceived which could be called good without qualification except a *GOOD WILL*. Intelligence, wit, judgment, and other talents of the mind however they maybe named, or courage, resoluteness, and perseverance as qualities of temperament, are doubtless in many respects good and desirable; but they can become extremely bad and harmful if the will, which is to make use of these gifts of nature and which in its special constitution is called character, is not good. It is the same with gifts of fortune. Power, riches, honor, even health, general well-being and the contentment with one's condition which is called happiness make for pride and even arrogance if there is not a good will to correct their influence on the mind and on its principle of action, so as to make it generally fitting to its entire end. It need hardly be mentioned that the sight of a being adorned with no feature of a pure and good will yet enjoying lasting good fortune can never give pleasure to an impartial rational observer. Thus the good will seems to constitute the indispensable condition even of worthiness to be happy.

Some qualities seem to be conducive to this good will and can facilitate its action, but in spite of that they have no intrinsic unconditional worth. They rather presuppose a good will, which limits the high esteem which one otherwise rightly has for them and prevents their being held to be absolutely good. Moderation in emotions and passions, self-control, and calm deliberation not only are good in many respects but seem even to constitute part of the inner worth of the person. But however unconditionally they were esteemed by the ancients, they are far from being good without qualification, for without the principles of a good will they can become extremely bad, and the coolness of a villain makes him not only far more dangerous but also more directly abominable in our eyes than he would have seemed without it.

The good will is not good because of what it effects or accomplishes or because of its competence to achieve some intended end; it is good only because of its willing (i.e., it is good in itself). And, regarded for itself, it is to be esteemed as incomparably higher than anything which could be brought about by it in favor of any inclination or even of the sum total of all inclinations. Even if it should happen that, by a particularly unfortunate fate or by the niggardly provision of a step-motherly nature, this will should be wholly lacking in power to accomplish its purpose, and if even the greatest effort should not avail it to achieve anything of its end, and if there remained only the good will—not as a mere wish, but as the summoning of all the means in our power—it would sparkle like a jewel all by itself, as something that had its full worth in itself. Usefulness or fruitlessness can neither diminish nor augment this worth. Its usefulness would be only its setting, as it were, so as to enable us to handle it more conveniently in commerce or to attract the attention of those who are not yet connoisseurs, but not to recommend it to those who are experts or to determine its worth.

But there is something so strange in this idea of the absolute worth of the will alone, in which no account is taken of any use, that, notwithstanding the agreement even of common sense, the suspicion must arise that perhaps only high-flown fancy is its hidden basis, and that we may have misunderstood the purpose of nature in appointing reason as the ruler of our will. We shall therefore examine this idea from this point of view.

In the natural constitution of an organized being (i.e., one suitably adapted to life), we assume as an axiom that no organ will be found for any purpose which is not the fittest and best adapted to that purpose. Now if its preservation, its welfare, in a word its happiness, were the real end of nature in a being having reason and will, then nature would have hit upon a very poor arrangement in appointing the reason of the creature to be the executor of this purpose. For all the actions which the creature has to perform with this intention of nature, and the entire rule of his conduct, would be dictated much more exactly by instinct, and the end would be far more certainly attained by instinct than it ever could be by reason. And if, over and above this, reason should have been granted to the favored creature, it would have served only to let him contemplate the happy constitution of his nature, to admire it, to rejoice in it, and to be grateful for it to its beneficent cause. But reason would not have been given in order that the being should subject his faculty of desire to that weak and delusive guidance and to meddle with the purpose of nature. In a word, nature would have taken care that reason did not break forth into practical use nor have the presumption, with its weak insight, to think out for itself the plan of happiness and the means of attaining it. Nature would have taken over the choice not only of ends but also of the means, and with wise foresight she would have entrusted both to instinct alone.

And, in fact, we find that the more a cultivated reason deliberately devotes itself to the enjoyment of life and happiness, the more the man falls short of true contentment. From this fact there arises in many persons, if only they are candid enough to admit it, a certain degree of misology, hatred of reason. This is particularly the case with those who are most experienced in its use. After counting all the advantages which they draw—I will not say from the invention of the arts of common luxury—from the sciences (which in the end seem to them to be also a luxury of the understanding), they nevertheless find that they have actually brought more trouble on their shoulders instead of gaining in happiness; they finally envy, rather than despise, the common run of men who are better guided by merely natural instinct and who do not permit their reason much influence on their conduct. And we must at least admit that a morose attitude or ingratitude to the goodness with which the world is governed is by no means found always among those who temper or refute the boasting eulogies which are given of the advantages of happiness and contentment with which reason is supposed to supply us. Rather, their judgment is based on the Idea of another and far more worthy purpose of their existence for which, instead of happiness, their reason is properly intended; this purpose, therefore, being the supreme condition to which the private purposes of men must, for the most part, defer.

Since reason is not competent to guide the will safely with regard to its objects and the satisfaction of all our needs (which it in part multiplies), to this end an innate instinct would have led with far more certainty. But reason is given to us as a practical faculty (i.e., one which is meant to have an influence on the will). As nature has elsewhere distributed capacities suitable to the functions they are to perform, reason's proper function must be to produce a will good in itself and not one good merely as a means, since for the former, reason is absolutely essential. This will need not be the sole and complete good, yet it must be the condition of all others, even of the desire for happiness. In this case it is entirely compatible with the wisdom of nature that the cultivation of reason, which is required for the former unconditional purpose, at least in this life restricts in many ways—indeed, can reduce to nothing—the achievement of the latter unconditional purpose, happiness. For one perceives that nature here does not proceed unsuitably to its purpose, because reason, which recognizes its highest practical vocation in the establishment of a good will, is capable of a contentment of its own kind (i.e., one that springs from the attainment of a purpose determined by reason), even though this injures the ends of inclination.

We have, then, to develop the concept of a will which is to be esteemed as good in itself without regard to anything else. It dwells already in the natural and sound understanding and does not need so much to be taught as only to be brought to light. In the estimation of the total worth of our actions it always takes first place and is the condition of everything else. In order to show this, we shall take the concept of duty. It contains the concept of a good will, though with certain subjective restrictions and hindrances, but these are far from concealing it and making it unrecognizable, for they rather bring it out by contrast and make it shine forth all the more brightly.

I here omit all actions which are recognized as opposed to duty, even though they may be useful in one respect or another, for with these the question does not arise as to whether they may be done *from* duty, since they conflict with it. I also pass over actions which are really in accord with duty and to which one has no direct inclination, rather doing them because impelled to do so by another inclination. For it is easily decided whether an action in accord with duty is done from duty or for some selfish purpose. It is far more difficult to note this difference when the action is in accord with duty and, in addition, the subject has a direct inclination to do it. For example, it is in accord with duty that a dealer should not overcharge an inexperienced customer, and wherever there is much trade the prudent merchant does not do so, but has a fixed price for everyone so that a child may buy from him as cheaply as any other. Thus the customer is honestly served, but this is far from sufficient to warrant the belief that the merchant has behaved in this way from duty and principles of honesty. His own advantage required this behavior, but it cannot be assumed that over and above that he had a direct inclination to his customers and that, out of love, as it were, he gave none an advantage in price over another. The action was done neither from duty nor from direct inclination but only for a selfish purpose.

On the other hand, it is a duty to preserve one's life, and moreover everyone has a direct inclination to do so. But for that reason, the often anxious care which most men take of it has no intrinsic worth, and the maxim of doing so has no moral import. They preserve their lives according to duty, but not from duty. But if adversities and hopeless sorrow completely take away the relish for life; if an unfortunate man, strong in soul, is indignant rather than despondent or dejected over his fate and wishes for death, and yet preserves his life without loving it and from neither inclination nor fear but from duty—then his maxim has moral merit.

To be kind where one can is a duty, and there are, moreover, many persons so sympathetically constituted that without any motive of vanity or selfishness they find an inner satisfaction in spreading joy and rejoice in the contentment of others which they have made possible. But I say that, however dutiful and however amiable it may be, that kind of action has no true moral worth. It is on a level with [actions done from] other inclinations, such as the inclination to honor, which, if fortunately directed to what in fact accords with duty and is generally useful and thus honorable, deserve praise and encouragement, but no esteem. For the maxim lacks the moral import of an action done not from inclination but from duty. But assume that the mind of that friend to mankind was clouded by a sorrow of his own which extinguished all sympathy with the lot of others, and though he still had the power to benefit others in distress their need left him untouched because he was preoccupied with his own. Now suppose him to tear himself, unsolicited by inclination, out of his dead insensibility and to do this action only from duty and without any inclination—then for the first time his action has genuine moral worth. Furthermore, if nature has put little sympathy into the heart of a man, and if he, though an honest man, is by temperament cold and indifferent to the sufferings of others perhaps because he is provided with special gifts of patience and fortitude and expects and even requires that others should have them too—and such a man would certainly not be the meanest product of nature—would not he find in himself a source from which to give himself a far higher worth than he could have got by having a good-natured temperament? This is unquestionably true even though nature did not make him philanthropic, for it is just here that the worth of character is brought out, which is morally the incomparably highest of all: he is beneficent not from inclination, but from duty.

To secure one's own happiness is at least indirectly a duty, for discontent with one's condition under pressure from many cares and amid unsatisfied wants could easily become a great temptation to transgress against duties. But, without any view to duty, all men have the strongest and deepest inclination to happiness, because in this Idea all inclinations are summed up. But the receipt of happiness is often so formulated that it definitely thwarts some inclinations, and men can make no definite and certain concept of the sum of satisfaction of all inclinations, which goes under the name of happiness. It is not to be wondered at, therefore, that a single inclination, definite as to what it promises and as to the time at which it can be satisfied, can outweigh a fluctuating idea and that, for example, a man with the gout can choose to enjoy what he likes and to suffer what he may, because according to his calculations at least on this occasion he has not sacrificed the enjoyment of the present moment to a perhaps groundless expectation of a happiness supposed to lie in health. But even in this case if the universal inclination to happiness did not determine his will, and if health were not at least for him a necessary factor in these calculations, there would still remain, as in all other cases, a law that he ought to promote his happiness not from inclination but from duty. Only from this law could his conduct have true moral worth.

It is in this way, undoubtedly, that we should understand those passages of Scripture which command us to love our neighbor and even our enemy, for love as an inclination cannot be commanded. But beneficence from duty, even when no inclination impels it and even when it is opposed by a natural and unconquerable aversion, is practical love, not pathological love; it resides in the will and not in the propensities of feeling, in principles of action and not in tender sympathy; and it alone can be commanded.

[Thus the first proposition of morality is that to have genuine moral worth, an action must be done from duty.] The second proposition is: An action done from duty does not have its moral worth in the purpose which is to be achieved through it but in the maxim whereby it is determined. Its moral value, therefore, does not depend upon the realization of the object of the action but merely on the principle of the volition by which the action is done irrespective of the objects of the faculty of desire. From the preceding discussion it is clear that the purposes we may have for our actions and their effects as ends and incentives of the will cannot give the actions any unconditional and moral worth. Wherein, then, can this worth lie, if it is not in the will in its relation to its hoped-for effect? It can lie nowhere else than in the principle of the will irrespective of the ends which can be realized by such action. For the will stands, as it were, at the crossroads halfway between its a priori principle which is formal and its posteriori incentive which is material. Since it must be determined by something, if it is done from duty it must be determined by the formal principle of volition as such, since every material principle has been withdrawn from it.

The third principle, as a consequence of the two preceding, I would express as follows: Duty is the necessity to do an action from respect for law.

I can certainly have an inclination to an object as an effect of the proposed action, but I can never have respect for it precisely because it is a mere effect and not an activity of a will. Similarly, I can have no respect for an inclination whatsoever, whether my own or that of another; in the former case I can at most approve of it and in the latter I can even love it (i.e., see it as favorable to my own advantage). But that which is connected with my will merely as ground and not as consequence, that which does not serve my inclination but overpowers it or at least excludes it from being considered in making a choice—in a word, law itself—can be an object of respect and thus a command. Now as an act from duty wholly excludes the influence of inclination and therewith every object of the will, nothing remains which can determine the will objectively except law and subjectively except pure respect for this practical law. This subjective element is the maxim that I should follow such a law even if it thwarts all my inclinations.

Thus the moral worth of an action does not lie in the effect which is expected from it or in any principle of action which has to borrow its motive from this expected effect. For all these effects (agreeableness of my own condition, indeed even the promotion of the happiness of others) could be brought about through other causes and would not require the will of a rational being, while the highest and unconditional good can be found only in such a will. Therefore the preeminent good can consist only in the conception of law in itself (which can be present only in a rational being) so far as this conception and not the hoped-for effect is the determining ground of the will. This preeminent good, which we call moral, is already present in the person who acts according to this conception, and we do not have to look for it first in the result.

But what kind of law can that be, the conception of which must determine the will without reference to the expected result? Under this condition alone can the will be called absolutely good without qualification. Since I have robbed the will of all impulses which could come to it from obedience to any law, nothing remains to serve as a principle of the will except universal conformity to law as such. That is, I ought never to act in such a way that I could not also will that my maxim should be a universal law. Strict conformity to law as such (without assuming any particular law applicable to certain actions) serves as the principle of the will, and it must serve as such a principle if duty is not to be a vain delusion and chimerical concept. The common sense of mankind (*gemeine Menschenvernunft*) in its practical judgments is in perfect agreement with this and has this principle constantly in view.

Let the question, for example, be: May I, when in distress, make a promise with the intention not to keep it? I easily distinguish the two meanings which the question can have, viz., whether it is prudent to make a false promise, or whether it conforms to duty. The former can undoubtedly be often the case, though I do see clearly that it is not sufficient merely to escape from the present difficulty by this expedient, but that I must consider whether inconveniences much greater than the present one may not later spring from this lie. Even with all my supposed cunning, the consequences cannot be so easily foreseen. Loss of credit might be far more disadvantageous than the misfortune I am now seeking to avoid, and it is hard to tell whether it might not be more prudent to act according to a universal maxim and to make it a habit not to promise anything without intending to fulfill it. But it is soon clear to me that such a maxim is based only on an apprehensive concern with consequences.

To be truthful from duty, however, is an entirely different thing from being truthful out of fear of untoward consequences, for in the former case the concept of the action itself contains a law for me, while in the latter I must first look about to see what results for me may be connected with it. To deviate from the principle of duty is certainly bad, but to be unfaithful to my maxim of prudence can sometimes be very advantageous to me, though it is certainly safer to abide by it. The shortest but most infallible way to find the answer to the question as to whether a deceitful promise is consistent with duty is to ask myself: Would I be content that my maxim of extricating myself from difficulty by a false promise should hold as a universal law for myself as well as for others? And could I say to myself that everyone may make a false promise when he is in a difficulty from which he otherwise cannot escape? Immediately I see that I could will the lie but not a universal law to lie. For with such a law there would be no promises at all, inasmuch as it would be futile to make a pretense of my intention in regard to future actions to those who would not believe this pretense or—if they overhastily did so— would pay me back in my own coin. Thus my maxim would necessarily destroy itself as soon as it was made a universal law.

I do not, therefore, need any penetrating acuteness to discern what I have to do in order that my volition may be morally good. Inexperienced in the course of the world, incapable of being prepared for all its contingencies, I only ask myself: Can I will that my maxim become a universal law? If not, it must be rejected, not because of any disadvantage accruing to myself or even to others, but because it cannot enter as a principle into a possible enactment of universal law, and reason extorts from me an immediate respect for such legislation. I do not as yet discern on what it is grounded (this is a question the philosopher may investigate), but I at least understand that it is an estimation of a worth which far outweighs all the worth of whatever is recommended by the inclinations, and that the necessity that I act from pure respect for the practical law constitutes my duty. To duty every other motive must give place because duty is the condition of a will good in itself, whose worth transcends everything.

Thus within the moral knowledge of ordinary human reason (*gemeine Menschenvernunft*) we have attained its principle. To be sure, ordinary human reason does not think this principle abstractly in such a universal form, but it always has the principle in view and uses it as the standard for its judgments. It would be easy to show how ordinary human reason, with this compass, knows well how to distinguish what is good, what is bad, and what is consistent or inconsistent with duty. Without in the least teaching common reason anything new, we need only to draw its attention to its own principle (in the manner of Socrates), thus showing that neither science nor philosophy is needed in order to know what one has to do in order to be honest and good, and even wise and virtuous. We might have conjectured beforehand that the knowledge of what everyone is obliged to do and thus also to know would be within the reach of everyone, even of the most ordinary man. Here we cannot but admire the great advantages which the practical faculty of judgment has over the theoretical in ordinary human understanding. In the theoretical, if ordinary reason ventures to go beyond the laws of experience and perceptions of the senses, it falls into sheer inconceivabilities and self-contradictions, or at least into a chaos of uncertainty, obscurity, and instability. In the practical, on the other hand, the power of judgment first shows itself to advantage when common understanding excludes all sensuous incentives from practical laws. It then even becomes subtle, quibbling with its own conscience or with other claims to what should be called right, or wishing to determine accurately, for its own instruction, the worth of certain actions. But the most remarkable thing about ordinary human understanding in its practical concern is that it may have as much hope as any philosopher of hitting the mark. In fact, it is almost more certain to do so than the philosopher, for while he has no principle which common understanding lacks, his judgment is easily confused by a mass of irrelevant considerations so that it easily turns aside from the correct way. Would it not, therefore, be wiser in moral matters to acquiesce in ordinary reasonable judgment and at most to call in philosophy in order to make the system of morals more complete and comprehensible and its rules more convenient for us (especially in disputation), than to steer the ordinary understanding from its happy simplicity in practical matters and to lead it through philosophy into a new path of inquiry and instruction?

Innocence is indeed a glorious thing, but it is very sad that it cannot well maintain itself, being easily led astray. For this reason, even wisdom—which consists more in acting than in knowing—needs science, not so as to learn from it but to secure admission and permanence to its precepts. Man feels in himself a powerful counterpoise against all commands of duty which reason presents to him as so deserving of respect. This counterpoise is his needs and inclinations, the complete satisfaction of which he sums up under the name of happiness. Now reason issues inexorable commands without promising anything to the inclinations. It disregards, as it were, and holds in contempt those claims which are so impetuous and yet so plausible, and which refuse to be suppressed by any command. From this a natural dialectic arises, i.e., a propensity to argue against the stern laws of duty and their validity, or at least to place their purity and strictness in doubt and, where possible, to make them more accordant with our wishes and inclinations. This is equivalent to corrupting them in their very foundations and destroying their dignity—a thing which even ordinary practical reason cannot finally call good.

In this way ordinary human reason is impelled to go outside its sphere and to take a step into the field of practical philosophy. But it is forced to do so not by any speculative need, which never occurs to it so long as it is satisfied to remain merely healthy reason; rather, it is impelled on practical grounds to obtain information and clear instruction respecting the source of its principle and the correct definition of this principle in its opposition to the maxims based on need and inclination. It seeks this information in order to escape from the perplexity of opposing claims and to avoid the danger of losing all genuine moral principles through the equivocation in which it is easily involved. Thus when ordinary practical reason cultivates itself, a dialectic surreptitiously ensues which forces it to seek aid in philosophy, just as the same thing happens in the theoretical use of reason. Ordinary practical reason, like theoretical reason, will find rest only in a complete critical examination of our reason.

• • •

Everything in nature works according to laws. Only a rational being has the capacity of acting according to the *conception* of laws (i.e., according to principles). This capacity is the will. Since reason is required for the derivation of actions from laws, will is nothing less than practical reason. If reason infallibly determines the will, the actions which such a being recognizes as objectively necessary are also subjectively necessary. That is, the will is a faculty of choosing only that which reason, independently of inclination, recognizes as practically necessary (i.e., as good). But if reason of itself does not sufficiently determine the will, and if the will is subjugated to subjective conditions (certain incentives) which do not always agree with the objective conditions—in a word, if the will is not of itself in complete accord with reason (which is the actual case with men), then the actions which are recognized as objectively necessary are subjectively contingent, and the determination of such a will according to objective laws is a constraint. That is, the relation of objective laws to a will which is not completely good is conceived as the determination of the will of a rational being by principles of reason to which this will is not by its nature necessarily obedient.

The conception of an objective principle, so far as it constrains a will, is a command (of reason), and the formula of this command is called an *imperative*.

All imperatives are expressed by an "ought" and thereby indicate the relation of an objective law of reason to a will which is not in its subjective constitution necessarily determined by this law. This relation is that of constraint. Imperatives say that it would be good to do or to refrain from doing something, but they say it to a will which does not always do something simply because the thing is presented to it as good to do. Practical good is what determines the will by means of the conception of reason and hence not by subjective causes but objectively, on grounds which are valid for every rational being as such. It is distinguished from the pleasant, as that which has an influence on the will only by means of a sensation from purely subjective causes, which hold for the senses only of this or that person and not as a principle of reason which holds for everyone.

A perfectly good will, therefore, would be equally subject to objective laws of the good, but it could not be conceived as constrained by them to accord with them, because it can be determined to act by its own subjective constitution only through the conception of the good. Thus no imperatives hold for the divine will or, more generally, for a holy will. The "ought" here is out of place, for the volition of itself is necessarily in unison with the law. Therefore imperatives are only formulas expressing the relation of objective laws of volition in general to the subjective imperfection of the will of this or that rational being, for example, the human will.

All imperatives command either *hypothetically* or *categorically*. The former present the practical necessity of a possible action as a means to achieving something else which one desires (or which one may possibly desire). The categorical imperative would be one which presented an action as of itself objectively necessary, without regard to any other end.

Since every practical law presents a possible action as good and thus as necessary for a subject practically determinable by reason, all imperatives are formulas of the determination of action which is necessary by the principle of a will which is in any way good. If the action is good only as a means to something else, the imperative is hypothetical; but if it is thought of as good in itself, and hence as necessary in a will which of itself conforms to reason as the principle of this will, the imperative is categorical.

The imperative thus says what action possible for me would be good, and it presents the practical rule in relation to a will which does not forthwith perform an action simply because it is good, in part because the subject does not always know that the action is good, and in part (when he does know it) because his maxims can still be opposed to the objective principles of a practical reason.

The hypothetical imperative, therefore, says only that the action is good to some purpose, possible or actual. In the former case, it is a problematical, in the latter an assertorical, practical principle. The categorical imperative, which declares the action to be of itself objectively necessary without making any reference to any end in view (i.e., without having any other purpose), holds as an apodictical practical principle.

We can think of what is possible only through the powers of some rational being as a possible end in view of any will. As a consequence, the principles of action thought of as necessary to attain a possible end in view which can be achieved by them, are in reality infinitely numerous. All sciences have some practical part consisting of problems which presuppose some purpose as well as imperatives directing how it can be reached. These imperatives can therefore be called, generally, imperatives of skill. Whether the purpose is reasonable and good is not in question at all, for the question concerns only what must be done in order to attain it. The precepts to be followed by a physician in order to cure his patient and by a poisoner to bring about certain death are of equal value in so far as each does that which will perfectly accomplish his purpose. Since in early youth we do not know what purposes we may have in the course of our life, parents seek to let their children learn a great many things and provide for skill in the use of means to all sorts of ends which they might choose, among which they cannot determine whether any one of them will become their child's actual purpose, though it may be that someday he may have it as his actual purpose. And this anxiety is so great that they commonly neglect to form and correct their children's judgment on the worth of the things which they may make their ends.

There is one end, however, which we may presuppose as actual in all rational beings so far as imperatives apply to them, that is, so far as they are dependent beings. There is one purpose which they not only *can* have but which we can presuppose that they all *do* have by a necessity of nature. This purpose is happiness. The hypothetical imperative which represents the practical necessity of an action as means to the promotion of happiness is an assertorical imperative. We may not expound it as necessary to a merely uncertain and merely possible purpose, but as necessary to a purpose which we can a priori and with assurance assume for everyone because it belongs to his essence. Skill in the choice of means to one's own highest well-being can be called prudence in the narrowest sense. Thus the imperative which refers to the choice of means to one's own happiness (i.e., the precept of prudence) is still only hypothetical, and the action is not commanded absolutely but commanded only as a means to another end in view.

Finally, there is one imperative which directly commands certain conduct without making its condition some purpose to be reached by it. This imperative is categorical. It concerns not the material of the action and its intended result, but the form and principle from which it originates. What is essentially good in it consists in the mental disposition, the result being what it may. This imperative may be called the imperative of morality.

Volition according to these three principles is plainly distinguished by the dissimilarity in the constraints by which they subject the will. In order to clarify this dissimilarity, I believe that they are most suitably named if one says that they are either rules of skill, counsels of prudence, or commands (laws) of morality, respectively. For law alone implies the concept of an unconditional and objective and hence universally valid necessity, and commands are laws which must be obeyed even against inclination. Counsels do indeed involve necessity, but a necessity that can hold only under a subjectively contingent condition (i.e., whether this or that man counts this or that as part of his happiness). The categorical imperative, on the other hand, is restricted by no condition. As absolutely, though practically, necessary it can be called a command in the strict sense. We could also call the first imperative *technical* (belonging to art), the second *pragmatic* (belonging to well-being), and the third *moral* (belonging to free conduct as such, i.e., to morals).

∙   ∙   ∙

If I think of a hypothetical imperative as such, I do not know what it will contain until the condition is stated [under which it is an imperative]. But if I think of a categorical imperative, I know immediately what it will contain. For since the imperative contains, besides the law, only the necessity of the maxim of acting in accordance with the law, while the law contains no condition to which it is restricted, nothing remains except the universality of law as such to which the maxim of the action should conform; and this conformity alone is what is represented as necessary by the imperative.

There is, therefore, only one categorical imperative. It is: Act only according to that maxim by which you can at the same time will that it should become a universal law.

Now if all imperatives of duty can be derived from this one imperative as a principle, we can at least show what we understand by the concept of duty and what it means, even though it remain undecided whether that which is called duty is an empty concept or not.

The universality of law according to which effects are produced constitutes what is properly called nature in the most general sense (as to form) (i.e., the existence of things so far as it is determined by universal laws). [By analogy], then, the universal imperative of duty can be expressed as follows: Act as though the maxim of your action were by your will to become a universal law of nature.

We shall now enumerate some duties, adopting the usual division of them into duties to ourselves and to others and into perfect and imperfect duties.

1. A man who is reduced to despair by a series of evils feels a weariness with life but is still in possession of his reason sufficiently to ask whether it would not be contrary to his duty to himself to take his own life. Now he asks whether the maxim of his action could become a universal law of nature. His maxim, however is: For love of myself, I make it my principle to shorten my life when by a longer duration it threatens more evil than satisfaction. But it is questionable whether this principle of self-love could become a universal law of nature. One immediately sees a contradiction in a system of nature whose law would be to destroy life by the feeling whose special office is to impel the improvement of life. In this case it would not exist as nature; hence that maxim cannot obtain as a law of nature, and thus it wholly contradicts the supreme principle of all duty.

2. Another man finds himself forced by need to borrow money. He well knows that he will not be able to repay it, but he also sees that nothing will

be lent him if he does not firmly promise to repay it at a certain time. He desires to make such a promise, but he has enough conscience to ask himself whether it is not improper and opposed to duty to relieve his distress in such a way. Now, assuming he does decide to do so, the maxim of his action would be as follows: When I believe myself to be in need of money, I will borrow money and promise to repay it, although I know I shall never be able to do so. Now this principle of self-love or of his own benefit may very well be compatible with his whole future welfare, but the question is whether it is right. He changes the pretension of self-love into a universal law and then puts the question: How would it be if my maxim became a universal law? He immediately sees that it could never hold as a universal law of nature and be consistent with itself; rather it must necessarily contradict itself. For the universality of a law which says that anyone who believes himself to be in need could promise what he pleased with the intention of not fulfilling it would make the promise itself and the end to be accomplished by it impossible; no one would believe what was promised to him but would only laugh at any such assertion as vain pretense.

3. A third finds in himself a talent which could, by means of some cultivation, make him in many respects a useful man. But he finds himself in comfortable circumstances and prefers indulgence in pleasure to troubling himself with broadening and improving his fortunate natural gifts. Now, however, let him ask whether his maxim of neglecting his gifts, besides agreeing with his propensity to idle amusement, agrees also with what is called duty. He sees that a system of nature could indeed exist in accordance with such a law, even though man (like the inhabitants of the South Sea Islands) should let his talents rust and resolve to devote his life merely to idleness, indulgence, and propagation—in a word, to pleasure. But he cannot possibly will that this should become a universal law of nature, or that it should be implanted in us by a natural instinct. For, as a rational being, he necessarily wills that all his faculties should be developed, inasmuch as they are given him and serve him for all sorts of purposes.

4. A fourth man, for whom things are going well, sees that others (whom he could help) have to struggle with great hardships, and he asks, "What concern of mine is it? Let each one be as happy as heaven wills, or as he can make himself; I will not take anything from him or even envy him; but to his welfare or to his assistance in time of need I have no desire to contribute." If such a way of thinking were a universal law of nature, certainly the human race could exist, and without doubt even better than in a state where everyone talks of sympathy and good will or even exerts himself occasionally to practice

them while, on the other hand, he cheats when he can and betrays or otherwise violates the right of man. Now although it is possible that a universal law of nature according to that maxim could exist, it is nevertheless impossible to will that such a principle should hold everywhere as a law of nature. For a will which resolved this would conflict with itself, since instances can often arise in which he would need the love and sympathy of others, and in which he would have robbed himself, by such a law of nature springing from his own will, of all hope of the aid he desires.

The foregoing are a few of the many actual duties, or at least of duties we hold to be actual, whose derivation from the one stated principle is clear. We must be able to will that a maxim of our action become a universal law; this is the canon of the moral estimation of our action generally. Some actions are of such a nature that their maxim cannot even be *thought* as a universal law of nature without contradiction, far from it being possible that one could will that it should be such. In others this internal impossibility is not found, though it is still impossible to *will* that that maxim should be raised to the universality of a law of nature, because such a will would contradict itself. We easily see that a maxim of the first kind conflicts with stricter or narrower (imprescriptable) duty, that of the latter with broader (meritorious) duty. Thus all duties, so far as the kind of obligation (not the object of their action) is concerned, have been completely exhibited by these examples in their dependence upon the same principle.

When we observe ourselves in any transgression of a duty, we find that we do not actually will that our maxim should become a universal law. That is impossible for us; rather, the contrary of this maxim should remain as a law generally, and we only take the liberty of making an exception to it for ourselves or for the sake of our inclination, and for this one occasion. Consequently, if we weighed everything from one and the same standpoint, namely, reason, we would come upon a contradiction in our own will, viz., that a certain principle is objectively necessary as a universal law and yet subjectively does not hold universally but rather admits exceptions. However, since we regard our action at one time from the point of view of a will wholly conformable to reason and then from that of a will affected by inclinations, there is actually no contradiction, but rather an opposition of inclination to the precept of reason (*antagonismus*). In this the universality of the principle (*universalitas*) is changed into mere generality (*generalitas*), whereby the practical principle of reason meets the maxim halfway. Although this cannot be justified in our own impartial judgment, it does show that we actually acknowledge the validity of the categorical imperative and allow ourselves (with all respect to it) only a few exceptions which seem to us to be unimportant and forced upon us.

• • •

The will is thought of as a faculty of determining itself to action in accordance with the conception of certain laws. Such a faculty can be found only in rational beings. That which serves the will as the objective ground of its self-determination is a purpose, and if it is given by reason alone it must hold alike for all rational beings. On the other hand, that which contains the ground of the possibility of the action, whose result is an end, is called the means. The subjective ground of desire is the incentive (*Triebfeder*) while the objective ground of volition is the motive (*Bewegungsgrund*). Thus arises the distinction between subjective purposes, which rest on incentives, and objective purposes, which depend on motives valid for every rational being. Practical principles are formal when they disregard all subjective purposes; they are material when they have subjective purposes and thus certain incentives as their basis. The purposes that a rational being holds before himself by choice as consequences of his action are material purposes and are without exception only relative, for only their relation to a particularly constituted faculty of desire in the subject gives them their worth. And this worth cannot afford any universal principles for all rational beings or any principles valid and necessary for every volition. That is, they cannot give rise to any practical laws. All these relative purposes, therefore, are grounds for hypothetical imperatives only.

But suppose that there were something the existence of which in itself had absolute worth, something which, as an end in itself, could be a ground of definite laws. In it and only in it could lie the ground of a possible categorical imperative (i.e., of a practical law).

Now, I say, man and, in general, every rational being exists as an end in himself and not merely as a means to be arbitrarily used by this or that will. In all his actions, whether they are directed toward himself or toward other rational beings, he must always be regarded at the same time as an end. All objects of inclination have only conditional worth, for if the inclinations and needs founded on them did not exist, their object would be worthless. The inclinations themselves as the source of needs, however, are so lacking in absolute worth that the universal wish of every rational being must be indeed to free himself completely from them. Therefore, the worth of any objects to be obtained by our actions is at times conditional. Beings whose existence does not depend on our will but on nature, if they are not rational beings, have only relative worth as means, and are therefore called "things"; rational beings, on the other hand, are designated "persons" because their nature indicates that they are ends in themselves (i.e., things which may not be used merely as means). Such a being is thus an object of respect, and as such restricts all [arbitrary] choice. Such beings are not merely subjective ends whose existence as a result of our action has a worth for us, but are objective ends (i.e., beings whose existence is an end in itself). Such an end is one in the place of which no other end, to which these beings should serve merely as means, can be put. Without them, nothing of absolute worth could be found, and if all worth is conditional and thus contingent, no supreme practice principle for reason could be found anywhere.

Thus if there is to be a supreme practical principle and a categorical imperative for the human will, it must be one that forms an objective principle of the will from the conception of that which is necessarily an end for everyone because it is an end in itself. Hence this objective principle can serve as a universal law. The ground of this principle is: rational nature exists as an end in itself. Man necessarily thinks of his own existence in this way, and thus far it is a subjective principle of human actions. Also every other rational being thinks of his existence on the same rational ground which holds also for myself; thus it is at the same time an objective principle from which, as a supreme practical ground, it must be possible to derive all laws of the will. The practical imperative, therefore, is the following: Act so that you treat humanity, whether in your own person or in that of another, always as an end and never as a means only. Let us now see whether this can be achieved. To return to our previous examples:

First, according to the concept of necessary duty to oneself, he who contemplates suicide will ask himself whether his action can be consistent with the idea of humanity as an end in itself. If in order to escape from burdensome circumstances he destroys himself, he uses a person merely as a means to maintain a tolerable condition up to the end of life. Man, however, is not a thing, and thus not something to be used merely as a means; he must always be regarded in all his actions as an end in himself. Therefore I cannot dispose of man in my own person so as to mutilate, corrupt, or kill him. (It belongs to ethics proper to define more accurately this basic principle so as to avoid all misunderstanding, e.g., as to amputating limbs in order to preserve myself, or to exposing my life to danger in order to save it; I must therefore omit them here.)

Second, as concerns necessary or obligatory duties to others, he who intends a deceitful promise to others sees immediately that he intends to use another man merely as a means, without the latter at the same time containing the end in himself. For he whom I want to use for my own purposes by means of such a promise cannot possibly assent to my mode of acting against him and thus share in the purpose of this action. This conflict with the principle of other men is even clearer if we cite examples of attacks on their freedom and property, for then it is clear that he who violates the rights of men intends to make use of the person of others merely as means, without considering that, as rational beings, they must always be esteemed at the same time as ends (i.e., only as beings who must be able to embody in themselves the purpose of the very same action).

Thirdly, with regard to contingent (meritorious) duty to oneself, it is not sufficient that the action not conflict with humanity in our person as an end in itself; it must also harmonize with it. In humanity there are capacities for greater perfection which belong to the purpose of nature with respect to humanity in our own person, and to neglect these might perhaps be consistent with the preservation of humanity as an end in itself, but not with the furtherance of that end.

Fourthly, with regard to meritorious duty to others, the natural purpose that all men have is their own happiness. Humanity might indeed exist if no one contributed to the happiness of others, provided he did not intentionally detract from it, but this harmony with humanity as an end in itself is only negative, not positive, if everyone does not also endeavor, as far as he can, to further the purposes of others. For the ends of any person, who is an end in himself, must as far as possible be also my ends, if that conception of an end in itself is to have its full effect on me.

This principle of humanity, and in general of every rational creature an end in itself, is the supreme limiting condition on the freedom of action of each man. It is not borrowed from experience, first, because of its universality, since it applies to all rational beings generally, and experience does not suffice to determine anything about them; and secondly, because in experience humanity is not thought of (subjectively) as the purpose of men (i.e., as an object which we of ourselves really make our purpose). Rather it is thought of as the objective end which ought to constitute the supreme limiting condition of all subjective ends whatever they may be. Thus this principle must arise from pure reason. Objectively the ground of all practical legislation lies (according to the first principle) in the rule and form of universality, which makes it capable of being a law (at least a natural law); subjectively it lies in the end. But the subject of all ends is every rational being as an end in itself (by the second principle); from this there follows the third practical principle of the will as the supreme condition of its harmony with universal practical reason, viz, the Idea of the will of every rational being as making universal law.

By this principle all maxims are rejected which are not consistent with the will's giving universal law. The will is not only subject to the law, but subject in such a way that it must be conceived also as itself prescribing the law, of which reason can hold itself to be the author; it is on this ground alone that the will is regarded as subject to the law.

•   •   •

ETHICAL RELATIVISM

H. Gene Blocker

IN THIS READING, the contemporary Ohio University philosopher Gene Blocker first tries to clarify precisely what ethical relativism is and then considers arguments for and against it. Unusual in Blocker's article is his claim that the ethical relativist cannot support the moral principle of tolerance. Why not? This would seem to be the relativist's strongest argument. Also questionable is Blocker's claim that the ethical relativist is often less tolerant than the ethical absolutist. Why does he hold that view, and do you agree? But surely, the strangest of all is Blocker's assertion that no one can (really, sincerely) be an ethical relativist! Surely, there are many ethical relativists in the world today. How can Blocker claim there can't be any?

———

E thics is the search for the most general and objectively valid moral principles. This assumes that there *are* such universal, objectively valid moral principles and, conversely, that if there are *not* such objectively valid moral principles, then ethics is strictly impossible. But it is precisely the existence of objective ethical standards which is denied by the popular view known as "ethical relativism."

What *is* ethical relativism? As we will see, that is not as easy to answer as it might seem at first. But the basic idea behind the theory is clear enough. It is based on the fact that different people hold different moral beliefs which are difficult, if not impossible, to reconcile. We are all familiar with the fact that different people believe in different moral principles. Today, for example, the debate rages concerning abortion; some people feel quite strongly that abortion in any form is simply murder, while others feel equally strongly that abortion is morally justifiable in certain circumstances, and that even where it is not morally defensible, the state has no right to interfere in a woman's personal decision in such a private matter.

We are also familiar with the fact that different societies hold different moral principles and standards. Polygamy is acceptable in Islamic societies although it is illegal in Judeo-Christian countries of Europe and North America. And we are equally familiar with differences in moral beliefs within the same society over time. Slavery was an acceptable practice in most societies of the world until fairly recently; it was morally approved in ancient Greece, for example, but occasional pockets of slavery discovered here and there in the world today are universally condemned.

Ethical relativism is a reflection of such differences in moral practices and beliefs around the world and throughout history, and the difficulty in resolving such differences to everyone's satisfaction. It is, most simply put, the view that different moral standards are right for different individuals and for different societies. What is right for one person or society is not necessarily right for another person or society. Polygamy is right in Saudi Arabia and wrong in the United States. Slavery used to be morally right, though it is now morally wrong.

In many ways ethical relativism is an attractive position and its widespread popularity today is not difficult to understand or explain. We live in a pluralistic society in which tolerance and respect for differing opinions are important, widely-shared, positive values. To reject ethical relativism would seem to be a form of dogmatic and intolerant "ethnocentrism," arbitrarily insisting that one's own particular brand of moral principles is the *only* correct one to adopt. If everyone in the world adopted such an ethnocentric position, we would all be constantly at each other's throats. Historically, the times we live in seem to call for greater understanding of and respect for the views of other people. What difference does it make whether we greet one another by shaking hands, kissing on both checks, embracing, or in some other way? How could any particular culture assume that its customs were morally superior to any other? Isn't that the rankest form of bigoted conceit which we would all want to avoid at all costs?

But there are problems with ethical relativism, too, which should make us reluctant to accept it too readily. First of all, it is not at all clear just what ethical relativism *means.* When the ethical relativist says that polygamy is right in Saudi Arabia and wrong in the United States, does be mean (1) that polygamy is *considered* or *thought to be* right by the Saudis and wrong by the Americans, or (2) that polygamy *is* morally correct in Saudi Arabia and morally wrong in the U. S. A.? The first is a purely *descriptive* statement, while the second is an evaluative, normative, or, as it is sometimes called, *prescriptive* statement. To say that polygamy is *thought to be* morally correct in Saudi Arabia is simply to state a matter of well-known and uncontested fact. The person making this statement is not expressing his or her own value judgement on polygamy. The speaker might be a Christian who disapproves of polygamy, but who can still truthfully report the polygamous practices and beliefs of the Saudis. As a matter of fact this is what they believe, whether we share that belief or not.

As such (1) is not a moral judgment, or normative statement at all and consequently does not belong to ethics. Only the second is a prescriptive, normative judgment belonging to ethics proper. The first is the kind of statement made by the value-free scientific inquiry of anthropology, sociology, or history, rather than a value-laden, normative judgment made by a moralist or a moral philosopher. And, while the second is highly controversial, the first is a mere statement of plain fact over which there can be no real disagreement.

But this crucial ambiguity is masked in ordinary English, where "Polygamy is morally right in Saudi Arabia" can mean *either* that the Saudis *think* that polygamy is morally right *or* that polygamy *is* morally right, at least within Saudi Arabia. Since only the second has any possible relevance as an ethical theory, we will consider only the second interpretation of the ethical relativist's statement to be ethical relativism proper. The problem is that the ethical relativist is himself often confused by this shift in meaning and his account of ethical relativism wavers back and forth between the first and the second interpretation, sometimes meaning the first and sometimes meaning the second, without any clear sense of the difference between them. The result is therefore apt to be confusing.

But assuming that ethical relativism proper can only be the second, normative and prescriptive claim above, how does the ethical relativist argue from the obviously true matters of fact in the descriptive claim of the first interpretation (that different people have different moral beliefs) to the more controversial normative, prescriptive claims involved in the second (that what is morally right varies from person to person, society to society), which we are here considering ethical relativism proper?

Because of the ambiguities and confusions mentioned above in the ethical relativist's claims, the difference between the descriptive and the prescriptive claims are sometimes simply not recognized, and so, evidence for the one is presumed to be evidence for the other.

But when the ethical relativist does recognize the difference between the two positions, he often tries to construct an argument from the first to the second, using the descriptive claims as evidence for the normative, prescriptive claim of ethical relativism. "Since the Saudis believe in polygamy, therefore it is right for them," "Because monogamy is practiced in the United States, it would be wrong to take a second wife (at least while living in the USA)." But can we ever argue legitimately from what *is* to what *ought to be*? This is the position known as "naturalism," which G. E. Moore called the "naturalistic fallacy." That is, according to Moore, it is a fallacy to argue from what *is* the case to what *ought to be* the case.

Did the fact that apartheid was the accepted policy of South Africa make it right? No more than slavery was morally correct in the United States when it was thought to be acceptable, or the Nazi's treatment of Jews and Gypsies during the Second World War. Other cases of naturalism include the argument that such and such is good because it is new or, alternatively, that it is bad because it is not traditional; that *X* is good because it is socially approved, or has stood the test of time—whenever, that is, we argue from what *is* the case to what *ought to be* the case. Arguments of this form are always fallacious, Moore held, since it is always possible for the facts used as evidence to be perfectly true and yet the conclusion to be false. For example, while it is certainly true that slavery was the accepted policy of the United States in the Eighteenth Century, most of us today would agree that it is *not* true that slavery was morally justified at that time. All such arguments are fallacious, the evidence simply does not establish the conclusion.

But there are further ambiguities and unclarities in the ethical relativist's position, and, in order to better analyse the relativist's claim, we should attempt to reconstruct the argument as carefully and in as much detail as we can. This will enable us to assess its strengths and weaknesses at each stage of the argument. The ethical relativist's argument seems to be something like this: because different people follow different moral practices they must hold different moral standards or principles, and because different people hold different moral standards or principles, different moral standards or principles are morally *right* for different people. The argument, in other words, seems to consist of two stages: the argument from different moral practices to different moral principles and another argument from different moral principles to the moral *correctness* of different moral principles. The ethical relativist's argument can therefore be schematised its follows.

1. Different people follow different moral practices. (Premise)

2. Therefore, different people hold different moral principles.

3. Therefore, different moral principles are morally right for different people. (Ethical Relativism)

There are really two arguments here, the argument from 1 to 2, and the argument from 2 to 3. We will examine each of the two separately beginning with the first. The first argument claims that it is always and necessarily true that different moral practices imply different moral principles, that is, that wherever different people *behave* differently, it must be because they believe in different moral principles or standards. Is that always or necessarily true? Sometimes, to be sure, the reason people act differently *is* that they have different moral principles, but is this always or necessarily so? Or are there other explantions for why people behave differently?

One obvious explanation why people who *share* the same moral princples behave differently is plain and simple lack of will power. Clearly, we do not always *do* what we believe we *ought* to do. The fact that one marital partner engages in extramarital sex while the other declines does not necessarily mean that the one believes in it and the other does not. More likely, they both believe it is wrong but one has momentarily yielded to temptation while the other has not, even, let us suppose, where there was ample opportunity. Here, then, is one counter-example to the first part of the relativist's argument. Are there others?

Some years ago a plane crashed high in the Andes and the passengers, starving to death, resorted to eating some of their fellow passengers who had died in the crash. These passengers therefore practiced what is known as cannibalism, which the passengers on other airlines do *not* practice, limited as they are to the usual inflight airline meals. But would we say that the reason these passengers followed different practices is that they hold different moral principles, the first group supporting cannibalism, and the second rejecting it? Obviously not. The only reasonable explanation for this difference in behavior is differences in *circumstances*. Once the first group of passengers were rescued they did not continue their cannibalism, and were the second group of passengers involved in similar circumstances, they too might well resort to the same emergency cannibalism as the Andes crash victims.

The same may be true generally of the differences in the practices of entire social groups. Some people are appalled when they hear about the traditional Eskimo practice of abandoning their aged parents to starve and freeze to death when thay are no longer able to contribute to the work of the group. This sounds horrible because it seems to imply a callous attitude toward human life and especially our elderly parents and grandparents who deserve our love and respect. But when we consider the extremely difficult conditions under which Eskimos lived, we may discover that they love their elders no less than we do. They do not allow them to starve and freeze to death because they lack humanistic moral principles, but simply out of harsh necessity. Like the Andes crash victims described above, the Eskimos behave differently from their American counterparts because they live in radically different circumstances—not because they hold radically different moral principles. As these conditions change we would expect their behavior to change, as indeed it has. And, by the same token if *we* were forced into such an extremely harsh environment, we might begin to act as the Eskimos traditionally behaved.

In general, then, differences in moral principles is *not* the only explanation for differences in moral practices. Now, consider a different sort of case. Some doctors perform abortions; others do not. Why? Is it due to differences in moral standards, as the relativist's argument suggests, or is there some other explanation? If we ask the doctors themselves, the first will probably tell us that he is willing to perform abortions because be does not feel that the fetus is a human being until birth, or at least until the "third trimester" after conception, while the second will most likely respond that he refuses to perform any abortion because he believes that the fetus is a human being from the moment of conception, or at least after the first trimester. Both of them seem to agree that deliberately killing a human being would be murder and that that is both legally and morally wrong. Where they differ, then, is in their beliefs concerning the metaphysical status of the fetus. Is it a human being or not? This is not itself a moral question, but a metaphysical issue on which moral practice greatly depends. The difference in the behavior of the doctors is not due, then, to differences in moral principles—both believe equally fervently in the sanctity of human life and the absolute moral injunction against murder. The difference consists in differences in their nonmoral beliefs about the world.

More generally, some societies burn suspected witches, others do not; some kill all human twins, others do not; and finally some social groups perform human sacrifices while others do not. How can we explain such radical differences in behavior? Societies burn witches because they *believe* in witches. That is, they believe in the existence of evil spirits which have the capacity to inhabit and control human beings and that the only way to get the evil spirit out of the human body is to burn the body, driving out the sprit. Certain groups traditionally killed twins because they believed twins would bring misfortune on the entire tribal group. And societies practice human sacrifice because they believe in the existence of gods who demand such sacrifices and who will bring great misfortune on the community which fails to provide such sacrifices.

What are the moral principles shared by all these groups? And do they differ from our own? They believe that it is their moral duty to do what is necessary to promote the welfare of the community. They believe that life is precious, indeed our most valuable possession. But these are very much the moral principles which we also hold. And, paradoxically, it is precisely because of these moral principles which they share with us that they do those things which we would *not* do—burn witches, kill twins, or engage in human sacrifice. All these things are done to *protect* and *preserve* life. The reason we do not engage in such activities is that we no longer believe in the power of evil spirits to inhabit a human body, or that God demands human sacrifices without which He will punish us.

To see that this is so, we can perform two related thought experiments, as we did above. What if *we* shared these nonmoral beliefs about the world? And what if *they* did *not*? If we believed that the universe was controlled by gods who demanded human sacrifices without which they would cause our crops to fail, disease and famine among our people, what would we do? We would reluctantly have to perform the occasional human sacrifice. Alternatively, what if these people who traditionally practiced human sacrifice became convinced that there were no such gods, or that they were more interested in our good deeds, animal sacrifices, or vegetable offerings than human sacrifices. Surely they would stop the practice of human sacrifice.

Once again, we find upon closer examination of all the facts involved that the degree of difference among people around the world and throughout history on moral issues has been greatly exaggerated and is in fact much less than we had been led to expect.

Sometimes differences in moral behavior are best explained in terms of differences in moral principles, but, as we have seen, these differences can also be explained in terms of differences in will power, differences in the circumstances involved and in terms of differences in the nonmoral beliefs held. Sometimes, too, people who share the same moral principles will act differently because they *interpert* those principles differently. For some people "Thou shalt not kill" includes capital punishment and warfare, while for others these are allowed as exceptions to the general rule.

In summary, we have considered four counterexamples to the first part of the ethical relativist's argument. The first part of the argument, you will remember, was that differences in moral behavior *always* and *necessarily* implied differences in the moral principles held. But we have seen that that is not the case. Since the second part of the argument leading to ethical relativism depends on the first part, this is enough to refute the argument as a whole. But let us go on and grant, for purposes of the argument, that differences in moral behavior *can* be explained in terms of differences in moral principles. After all, we do not want to deny that there are *any* differences in moral principles. Obviously, such differences exist. The question now is whether that logically implies the ethical relativist position that different moral principles are *right* for different people. Or, as we schematised this part of the argument earlier,

> *Different people hold different moral principles.*
>
> *Therefore, different moral principles are right for different people.*

Does it follow that because people *think* something is right that it *is* right? In general, this would seem to be obviously false. Is the world flat because some people think it is? People used to think that malaria was caused by damp air. Does the fact that this was believed make the belief true? Nor does such an inference seem any more plausible in the moral sphere. Was slavery morally right because people thought it was? In all areas of human thought we must recognize the possibility of error. Thinking can be either true or false, correct or incorrect, and if that is so, then it can never logically follow that just because someone *thinks* something is true that it *is* true.

Thus, the second part of the ethical relativist's argument also fails. It does not follow that because different people hold different moral principles that these different moral principles are therefore *right* for different people. But, of course, the fact that someone's argument is faulty doesn't mean that the position they are arguing for is wrong. Since the arguement we have just rejected is the primary argument in favor of ethical relativism, we can conclude that there is no good argument to date in favor of ethical relativism and ask whether there are any compelling reasons for *rejecting* it, that is, arguments *against* ethical relativism?

Certainly, there is something odd, if not downright contradictory in saying, as the ethical activist is prepared to say, that the same action can be both right and wrong, depending on which person or society you are considering. To say that abortion is morally wrong and not morally wrong doesn't seem to make any sense at all. As Aristotle pointed out, it amounts to saying *nothing*. But, of course, the relativist is not uttering such a blatant self-contradiction, for he is saying that abortion is morally wrong *for this particular person or this particular society* while it is morally right *for some other person or society.* An action is said to be right or wrong "relative" to a particular situation, hence the term ethical *relativism.* And, in general, we do allow that the same thing can be true in one situation and false in another. "Drive slowly in school areas" is applicable during the day but not at night. "Every human being should be free to make the major decisions affecting his or her life" may be valid for rational, sane adults, but does it apply to children, the mentally retarded, or the criminally insane? We say that everyone should pay income tax, though we exclude those below a certain income level.

Nonetheless, in each of these cases there is always a good reason why the rule applies in the one case but not in the other. We drive slowly in school zones to ensure the safety of school children, but since they are only in school during certain hours of the day, the rule is really only applicable during school hours and becomes irrelevant at night, during the weekends, and so on. We don't, generally, allow any and all exceptions, however—slow down if you feel like it, or have plenty of time, or have children of your own in that particular school. These exceptions are inadmissible, either because they are selfishly motivated or else because they have no rational basis whatever. We allow that those below a certain income level are not assessed income tax for what we consider a good reason, and that reason applies to everyone in that situation. We don't allow a person to skip IRS payments in a given year because he or she doesn't want to pay or prefers to use that money to purchase a new computer. The exception muse be based on a good reason which applies to everyone in that situation.

But when the ethical relativist argues that abortion is morally wrong in one situation and right in another, what sort of reason is given to justify the changing moral assessment? Generally, it is simply that in the one case the individual happens to believe that abortion is wrong and in the other the person thinks it is morally justifiable.

What is peculiar to ethical relativism is the allowance for differences in behavior for no other reason than differences in opinion concerning principles. Ethical relativism, in other words, is not simply the view, shared by all moral theories, that moral *behavoir* is contextually relative, depending on the application of moral principles, but that the moral principles themselves are culturally and contextually relative. It is simply that in the one case the individual believes abortion is wrong and in the other he thinks it is right. What kind of reason is that? It is true because I say or think it is true and false if I say or think it is false. If I say it is true today and tomorrow change my mind and say it is false, then it was true when I said it was true and false when I say it is false.

Sometimes the relativist speaks as though an action can be both morally right and morally wrong at the same time, but it is difficult to understand how slavery, for example, could be wrong for us today and right for the ancient Greeks. If we believe today that slavery is wrong then don't we have to say that the ancient Greeks were mistaken in their views on slavery, that it was wrong in ancient Greece though, unfortunately, they did not realize this. Sometimes, however, the relativist speaks as though he means that actions are neither right nor wrong, but that is also hard to understand. Of course, it is difficult to reach consensus on the morality of abortion, for example, but surely it is either morally right or wrong, one way or the other, and not both or neither.

So far, we have seen that the relativist's argument *for* his position is weak, and we have also considered some arguments *against* his position which seem fairly strong. Another kind of consideration often used to assess the strengths and weaknesses of a philosophical position is to see how well it accords with our other beliefs about the world. Whenever we are considering whether to accept a theory or to reject it, we have to consider how well it fits in with our other beliefs.

How well, then, does ethical relativism accord with our basic common sense assumptions? By accepting ethical relativism, how much would we have to give up, and is it worth it? First of all, as we have already seen, ethical relativism conflicts with our strongly held common sense belief that ethical disputes are genuine disagreements. If you hold abortion is morally wrong and I say it is morally justifiable, we both assume that there is a conflict between our two beliefs, and therefore a genuine disagreement and dispute between us. If abortion is wrong, then you are right and I am mistaken, and if abortion is right then I am correct in my belief and you are mistaken. For all our disagreement about abortion, we at least agree that abortion is either right or wrong, and that therefore only one of us can be correct. But, as we have seen, this is denied by ethical relativism, which holds that apparently contradictory moral beliefs are either both correct or that neither of them is correct. It is only in matters of subjective feelings and taste that different responses to the same object do not result in contradiction and conflicting disagreement. If you like chocolate ice cream and I do not, there is no real disagreement between us because we have not made contradictory claims about the same object. I did not claim that chocolate ice cream is bad;

I said something about myself, that I don't find it tasty. Nor have you said anything about the ice cream, but have also referred to yourself and your own reaction to chocolate ice cream, that you find it pleasing. But clearly between "I find it tasty" and "You do not find it tasty" there is no contradiction. Both these statements can be true at the same time.

If ethical relativism is true, it therefore follows that ethical disagreements must be understood on the analogy with differences of taste, on the model of liking or disliking chocolate ice cream. But this seems to contradict our most strongly held common sense beliefs about the nature of moral disputes. If you feel strongly that abortion is morally wrong, you do not imagine yourself to be asserting something about your own personal, subjective likes and dislikes; you imagine that you are saying something about the objective world, that killing the human fetus is murder and should be stopped. You feel that I am mistaken in my belief and would like to persuade me accordingly. When we interrogate our ordinary intuitions concerning disagreements on ethical issues, we find that they are ordinarily assumed to be much closer to disagreements we have about things in the objective world, where contradictory opinions cannot both be correct.

But from this, other conflicts emerge between ethical relativism and our ordinary common sense assumptions. If there are no right answers in ethics, then there can never be mistakes made by morals. Nor, by the same token, could we ever discover true or better moral standards, or feel that we had made progress in ethics. But this is contrary to what we ordinarily believe. We usually assume that people in the past were wrong to uphold slavery, and that progress was made when it came to be commonly accepted that slavery was morally wrong. But all these assumptions and ordinary beliefs would have to be given up were we to accept ethical relativism. Is this too high a price to pay?

A final argument against ethical relativism is that it is difficult, if not impossible, for anyone to actually *be* an ethical relativist. This wouldn't show that ethical relativism was *false*, but it would show that no human being could actually *be* a relativist, and that would surely undermine the doctrine considerably. Perhaps you have already anticipated part of this argument. When we speculate in the abstract concerning those rather more superficial standards of behavior which vary from country to country and which do not, therefore, directly or personally affect us in any way, it is easy to say "live and let live." What do we care, really, how the natives of Panga Panga greet one another? But when the issue is one which we take more seriously, and when the issue becomes one which affects us daily in a personal and direct way, then it is obviously much more difficult to be tolerant of others' moral views.

It is very difficult for someone suffering from sexual or racial discrimination to say or think with sincerity that those who support sexual or racial discrimination are just as correct in their views and should be allowed to practice those views just as much as those who oppose such forms of discrimination. Imagine you are the victim of such discrimination and you confront your oppressor who tells you that he has every moral right to oppress you since he is in a position of strength which he occupies precisely because he belongs to a superior race or sex. Now imagine yourself, replying, in all honesty and sincerity, "Well, although I hold a different view, your view is no better or worse than mine, and I certainly would not want to stand in the way of your carrying out what you feel is the morally right thing to do." Could you do it?

But one can go further and argue that it is impossible to ever be a consistent relativist because of the very assumptions on which ethical relativism depends. The ethical relativist argues that every human being has his or her own moral point of view which he or she feels is correct. This is the basis of the ethical relativist's plea for tolerance of other's moral views, for if each of us feels he or she is right and there is no way to resolve disagreements, then what can we do but agree to disagree, live and let live? But it is precisely for this reason that no one can be a sincere thoroughgoing relativist. If I feel that I am right and you take a contrary position, then I have to feel that you are wrong. If I feel that your discrimination against me is wrong and you believe it is morally justified, then, logically and psychologically, I must think that you are mistaken. Or to put it slightly differently, if I personally and emotionally dislike discrimination, especially as it is directed against me, then how can I feel anything but dislike and aversion to your attempts to discriminate against me. If I am a card-carrying Ethical Relativist I may feel deeply ashamed at my failure to carry out my belief in ethical relativism, but I will in practice find myself constantly sinning against my own doctrine. Will the real ethical relativist please stand up? If no one is able to stand up, who is left to defend the doctrine and against whom will we direct counter arguments?

Thus far we have examined the principle argument *for* ethical relativism, as well as major arguments *against* ethical relativism. The fact remains, however, that ethical relativism continues to be an extremely popular view, and we should say a word or two about the continued popularity of ethical relativism. If someone rejects ethical relativism, then what is he? An ethical "absolutist." That doesn't sound very nice, does it? Why not? An "absolutist" sounds like someone who is dogmatically certain that he is right and everyone else is wrong, someone who is absolutely sure of everything and therefore intolerant of the rights of others to their opinions. If it were true that the ethical relativist is more modest in how much he claims to know and how well he knows it and if he is more tolerant of other's views than the ethical absolutist, this would certainly be a point in the ethical relativist's favor. But is this really true?

A person who opposes ethical relativism need not believe that he or she *knows* what is right and wrong with complete certainty, but only that there *is* an objective right and wrong which we all try to discover. Similarly, a scientific *absolutist* need not believe that he or she knows all the answers to every scientific question with complete certainty, stubbornly refusing to consider new evidence or even to contemplate altering one's position. All the scientific absolutist holds is that scientific theories are either true or false and that there is evidence which at any given moment counts more toward one theory than another, so that it is possible for human beings to assess at any given moment which of several competing theories is the strongest and most convincing. The ethical absolutist may not be sure what to think about abortion, for example. Some arguments seem to weigh heavily against abortion, while other considerations make a convincing case for abortion. Nonetheless, unlike the ethical relativist, the ethical absolutist believes that abortion is either right or wrong, and is therefore committed to continuing the search for the correct answer to this perplexing moral dilemma.

In this respect the ethical relativist is ironically less flexible than the absolutist. The relativist is completely set in his ways, unbending, unchanging. He is convinced that there is no right or wrong answer, and so no amount of new information, reasons, arguments can possibly alter his fixed position. Of course, there are all kinds of ethical absolutists, and some of these may be just as rigid and inflexible as the ethical relativist. But at least it is possible for the ethical absolutist to adopt a more cautious, modest, wait-and-see approach, willing to listen to reasons, open to new information, which is not possible for the ethical relativist.

Nor need the ethical absolutist be less tolerant than the ethical relativist. Again, ethical absolutists *can* be, and some are, inflexible, intolerant, dogmatic bigots. The point is that the ethical absolutist *can* be and often is as tolerant as the relativist. The ethical absolutist is not logically committed to intolerance; his position is consistent with an attitude of tolerance. How so? We do not always or necessarily try to stop or dissuade people from doing what we believe is morally wrong. Suppose you are my neighbor and you see me constantly belittling and humiliating my wife and children. You feel quite clearly that this is wrong, but what do you do about it? Probably nothing. Why?

If you believe that what I am doing is wrong, then you not only think that I am mistaken in my moral beliefs, but that what I am doing is wrong. If you are sincere in your moral beliefs and if you feel that this is an important issue, then, to that extent, you would like me to stop what I am doing, and because you think it is wrong you would like to do what you can to bring these humiliating practices to a stop. And yet you do nothing. Why? Perhaps you are afraid. You don't want to get involved. But perhaps you have a better reason for not intervening. Perhaps you think that, however wrong I am to humiliate my family, it would be worse for you to interfere in my private life. It is not moral indifference or lack of will power which prevents you from interfering, but a conflict between *two* moral principles which you hold, one, to prevent the wrong of my humiliating my family and two, to respect my privacy within my own family affairs. In a pluralistic society like ours, we regard it as a positive virtue to allow people a large amount of autonomy over their private lives and within the family. So, now in weighing these conflicting moral obligations, you have decided that it would be better to respect my privacy than to try to prevent my humiliating treatment of my family, or to put it another way, you have decided that it would be *worse* to invade my privacy and that of my family than it would be to do nothing about my treatment of members of my family

Thus, in this case you have, at least within my example, taken the position of a tolerant ethical absolutist. You are firmly convinced that what I am doing is wrong, and being sincere and concerned, you would like to do what you can to stop this immoral activity on my part. Nonetheless, on balance, you respect my right within certain limits to do those things which you feel are immoral. In a similar way, some people feel that though abortion is morally wrong it should not be made illegal, that it is better to allow people to decide for themselves, even if they should then decide to do what is immoral and, putting it the other way round, that it would be worse to inhibit freedom of choice than it would be to prevent immoral actions.

But, of course, there are limits to such tolerant behavior. Suppose now that you observe me not only belittling and humiliating my wife and children, but brutally beating them as well, so severely in fact that they are on several occasions hospitalized. Now what do you do? This time to do nothing would be morally indefensible, that is, we would do nothing in this situation simply out of fear and indifference which are not very good reasons. But if you should now call in the police, it is not because you no longer respect my right of privacy within the family, but only that now the balance has tipped the other way. Unlike before, it is better to prevent harm than to avoid the wrong of interfering. In all conflicts of duties we have to weigh the lesser of two evils (and the better of two goods). In the first case when I was only belittling my family, most of us would agree that the greater good falls on the side of respecting the privacy of persons, even when he or she is doing what we think is wrong, whereas in the second case, things have gone too far, tipping the scales in favor of interference.

Tolerance, then, is a positive value, consistent with ethical absolutism, but, ironically, it is not for the ethical absolutist an *absolute* moral value. It is one value among others which must be weighed in each case to see whether it outweighs or is outweighed by other values. Ironically, it is the ethical relativist who is an "absolutist" when it comes to the principle of tolerance. For the relativist, a policy of tolerance must always be followed; there is nothing which can modify or offset that one "absolute". Pro-abortion, anti-abortion; pro-slavery, anti-slavery—all are equally correct and no one therefore has any right to impose his wishes on any other.

But *should* tolerance, important as it surely is, be an *absolute?* If you are convinced that child abuse or rape, for example, is morally wrong, then, as suggested before, can you honestly and sincerely say or believe that the person who believes in child abuse and rape is just as correct and as morally justified as you are? And if you feel that the person supporting rape or child abuse is wrong, don't you feel an obligation to do what you can to prevent that wrong? Thus, absolute tolerance is incompatible with morality and is not a value we would want to uphold. And can the ethical relativist accept any universal, absolute moral principle?

The alliance which the ethical relativist has tried to establish between ethical relativism and tolerance in what we claim to know ethically therefore appears to be misplaced. Tolerance is compatible with ethical absolutism and, in fact, in many ways, as we have seen, the relativist is ironically less tolerant and modest than the ethical absolutist.

Why Abortion Is Immoral
Don Marquis

Introduction, Arthur Zucker

MANY WOMEN WHO ARE SUBFERTILE and who choose not to adopt children utilize new reproductive techniques. These techniques often result in multiple gestational pregnancies—twins, triplets, sometimes as many as five or six fetuses. The chances of having a markedly premature infant are increased in these pregnancies. Therefore, the chances of having a normal baby unharmed by the problems of severe prematurity decrease as the number of fetuses increases. It has become relatively common to offer women in this situation what is termed "pregnancy reduction." Usually, all but two or three of the fetuses are aborted so that the remaining ones have a better chance of living. This is a very utilitarian view of justifying abortion.

This sort of case differs from the usual abortion scenarios where pregnancy was accidental or where the fetus is discovered to have a serious enough condition to "merit" being aborted. The word "merit" is in quotes because the central question is precisely what sorts of conditions justify abortion. This sort of case also highlights another question. Is being infertile or subfertile the sort of condition that medicine ought to treat? Put another way, are all desires serious enough needs so that it makes sense to harness the forces of medical science to answer them? Deciding on the legitimate goals of medicine is another way of determining what exactly are to be the obligations of the medical profession.

The ethical questions concerning abortion have to do with the justification of killing in a medical context. Medicine has always seen itself as a profession dedicated to helping, not killing. Of course, it is possible to see abortion as a help to the pregnant woman who wants the abortion. It is even possible to see abortion as a help to a fetus whose life, if not aborted, would be one of pain, degeneration, and death (for example: infants with Tay-Sachs disease). We must decide who is the patient, pregnant woman or fetus. We must also decide whether we should make quality of life decisions for the unborn, where a negative decision results in the death of the fetus.

What is the moral status of a fetus? Surely, a mother could not decide that her infant should be killed because it was, for example, mentally

91

retarded. Why is this so often an accepted reason for an abortion? This is another way to ask the central question about abortion. There is no way that an answer can be given here. But we can use the question to get clear on issues.

1. A fetus is a living thing. If it were not, then it would be spontaneously aborted (miscarried).

2. A fetus is human in the sense that it is a member of our species.

3. If by "human being" one means only a member of the species *Homo sapiens*, then a fetus is a human being.

4. If by "human being" one means a person invested with all the rights, obligations, and privileges of a normal adult, then it is not clear that a fetus is a human being in this sense.

What makes the abortion controversy so difficult is that there is no fact we can discover about fetuses that would make it clear that they are or are not persons in the sense of (4). Rather, we have to decide if they are to count as persons or not. Even this decision will not finish the issue for what we often find where abortion is a solution is a conflict. If the fetus were given full adult rights, we would still have a conflict between two equals. Such conflicts are not easily decided.

In his article "Why Abortion is Immoral," Don Marquis claims that " . . . the primary wrong-making feature of a killing is the loss to the victim of the value of its future. . . ." He goes on to say that the morally central category in understanding the wrongness of killing is "having a valuable future like ours." Marquis also notes, in defending his position against the reply that a fetus cannot value, that for a life to have value it need not be the value placed on it by the holder of that life. He uses a standard kind of example here of a young person who believes her life worthless but is saved from suicide by those who see through to her possible future; who see, in effect, better than she, that her life does have value. Marquis ends this rejoinder by saying, "A fetus's future can be valuable to it in the same way."

Marquis admits that his conclusion—"the serious presumptive wrongness of abortion"—is subject to the assumption that the fetus has a moral status such that killing it is presumptively wrong. Marquis thinks that one can make sense of the notion of a fetus's future having a value because there are others who will value the fetus. "It is, strictly speaking, the [positive] value of a human's future which makes killing wrong in this theory. This being so, killing does not necessarily wrong some persons who are sick and dying."

Marquis does not want to be committed to the view that all cases of active euthanasia must be immoral. This he says would be " . . . implausible, and it is a plus for the claim that the loss of a future of value is what makes killing wrong that it does not share this consequence." Marquis focuses on a future that might have been; a possible future without this or that serious disease. He appeals to self-conscious states of people to bolster his view that the loss of a future or kind of future is the wrong-making property.

As you read Marquis, consider the following questions: Must Marquis assume that fetuses have some degree of self-consciousness? What exactly does it mean to say that something is *prima facie* wrong? Marquis thinks he has avoided any appeal to rights talk. Has he really been successful in doing this?

———

The view that abortion is, with rare exceptions, seriously immoral has received little support in the recent philosophical literature. No doubt most philosophers affiliated with secular institutions of higher education believe that the anti-abortion position is either a symptom of irrational religious dogma or a conclusion generated by seriously confused philosophical argument. The purpose of this essay is to undermine this general belief. This essay sets out an argument that purports to show, as well as any argument in ethics can show, that abortion is, except possibly in rare cases, seriously immoral, that it is in the same moral category as killing an innocent adult human being.

The argument is based on a major assumption. Many of the most insightful and careful writers on the ethics of abortion—such as Joel Feinberg, Michael Tooley, Mary Anne Warren, H. Tristram Engelhardt, Jr., L. W. Sumner, John T. Noonan, Jr., and Philip Devine—believe that whether or not abortion is morally permissible stands or falls on whether or not a fetus is the sort of being whose life it is seriously wrong to end.[1] The argument of this essay will assume, but not argue, that they are correct.

Also, this essay will neglect issues of great importance to a complete ethics of abortion. Some anti-abortionists will allow that certain abortions, such as abortion before implantation or abortion when the life of a woman is

———

"Why Abortion Is Immoral," by Don Marquis, reprinted from *Journal of Philosophy*, 86, no. 4 (April 1989), pp. 183–202. Copyright © 1989 Journal of Philosophy, Inc.

threatened by a pregnancy or abortion after rape, may be morally permissible. This essay will not explore the casuistry of these hard cases. The purpose of this essay is to develop a general argument for the claim that the overwhelming majority of deliberate abortions are seriously immoral.

I

A sketch of standard anti-abortion and pro-choice arguments exhibits how those arguments possess certain symmetries that explain why partisans of those positions are so convinced of the correctness of their own positions, why they are not successful in convincing their opponents, and why, to others, this issue seems to be unresolvable. An analysis of the nature of this standoff suggests a strategy for surmounting it.

Consider the way a typical anti-abortionist argues. She will argue or assert that life is present from the moment of conception or that fetuses look like babies or that fetuses possess a characteristic such as a genetic code that is both necessary and sufficient for being human. Anti-abortionists seem to believe that (1) the truth of all of these claims is quite obvious, and (2) establishing any of these claims is sufficient to show that abortion is morally akin to murder.

A standard pro-choice strategy exhibits similarities. The pro-choicer will argue or assert that fetuses are not persons or that fetuses are not rational agents or that fetuses are not social beings. Pro-choicers seem to believe that (1) the truth of any of these claims is quite obvious, and (2) establishing any of these claims is sufficient to show that an abortion is not a wrongful killing.

In fact, both the pro-choice and the anti-abortion claims do seem to be true, although the "it looks like a baby" claim is more difficult to establish the earlier the pregnancy. We seem to have a standoff. How can it be resolved?

As everyone who has taken a bit of logic knows, if any of these arguments concerning abortion is a good argument, it requires not only some claim characterizing fetuses, but also some general moral principle that ties a characteristic of fetuses to having or not having the right to life or to some other moral characteristic that will generate the obligation or the lack of obligation not to end the life of a fetus. Accordingly, the arguments of the anti-abortionist and the pro-choicer need a bit of filling in to be regarded as adequate.

Note what each partisan will say. The anti-abortionist will claim that her position is supported by such generally accepted moral principles as "It is always prima facie seriously wrong to take a human life" or "It is always prima facie seriously wrong to end the life of a baby." Since these are generally accepted moral principles, her position is certainly not obviously wrong. The pro-choicer will claim that her position is supported by such plausible moral principles as "Being a person is what gives an individual intrinsic moral worth" or "It is only seriously prima facie wrong to take the life of a member of the human community." Since these are generally accepted moral principles, the pro-choice position is certainly not obviously wrong. Unfortunately, we have again arrived at a standoff.

Now, how might one deal with this standoff? The standard approach is to try to show how the moral principles of one's opponent lose their plausibility under analysis. It is easy to see how this is possible. On the one hand, the anti-abortionist will defend a moral principle concerning the wrongness of killing which tends to be broad in scope in order that even fetuses at an early stage of pregnancy will fall under it. The problem with broad principles is that they often embrace too much. In this particular instance, the principle "It is always prima facie wrong to take a human life" seems to entail that it is wrong to end the existence of a living human cancer-cell culture, on the grounds that the culture is both living and human. Therefore, it seems that the anti-abortionist's favored principle is too broad.

On the other hand, the pro-choicer wants to find a moral principle concerning the wrongness of killing which tends to be narrow in scope in order that fetuses will *not* fall under it. The problem with narrow principles is that they often do not embrace enough. Hence, the needed principles such as "It is prima facie seriously wrong to kill only persons" or "It is prima facie wrong to kill only rational agents" do not explain why it is wrong to kill infants or young children or the severely retarded or even perhaps the severely mentally ill. Therefore, we seem again to have a standoff. The anti-abortionist charges, not unreasonably, that pro-choice principles concerning killing are too narrow to be acceptable; the pro-choicer charges, not unreasonably, that anti-abortionist principles concerning killing are too broad to be acceptable.

Attempts by both sides to patch up the difficulties in their positions run into further difficulties. The anti-abortionist will try to remove the problem in her position by reformulating her principle concerning killing in terms of human beings. Now we end up with: "It is always prima facie seriously wrong to end the life of a human being." This principle has the advantage of avoiding the problem of the human cancer-cell culture counter-example. But this advantage is purchased at a high price. For although it is clear that a fetus is both human and alive, it is not at all clear that a fetus is a human being. There is at least something to be said for the view that something becomes a human being only after a process of development, and that therefore first trimester fetuses and perhaps all fetuses are not yet human beings. Hence, the anti-abortionist, by this move, has merely exchanged one problem for another.[2]

The pro-choicer fares no better. She may attempt to find reasons why killing infants, young children, and the severely retarded is wrong which are independent of her major principle that is supposed to explain the wrongness of taking human life, but which will not also make abortion immoral. This is no easy task. Appeals to social utility will seem satisfactory only to those who resolve not to think of the enormous difficulties with a utilitarian account of the wrongness of killing and the significant social costs of preserving the lives of the unproductive.[3] A pro-choice strategy that extends the definition of "person" to infants or even to young children seems just as arbitrary as an anti-abortion strategy that extends the definition of "human being" to fetuses. Again, we find symmetries in the two positions and we arrive at a standoff.

There are even further problems that reflect symmetries in the two positions. In addition to counterexample problems, or the arbitrary application problems that can be exchanged for them, the standard anti-abortionist principle "It is prima facie seriously wrong to kill a human being," or one of its variants, can be objected to on the grounds of ambiguity. If "human being" is taken to be a biological category, then the anti-abortionist is left with the problem of explaining why a merely biological category should make a moral difference. Why, it is asked, is it any more reasonable to base a moral conclusion on the number of chromosomes in one's cells than on the color of one's skin?[4] If "human being," on the other hand, is taken to be a *moral* category, then the claim that a fetus is a human being cannot be taken to be a premise in the anti-abortion argument, for it is precisely what needs to be established. Hence, either the anti-abortionist's main category is a morally irrelevant, merely biological category, or it is of no use to the anti-abortionist in establishing (noncircularly, of course) that abortion is wrong.

Although this problem with the anti-abortionist position is often noticed, it is less often noticed that the pro-choice position suffers from an analogous problem. The principle "Only persons have the right to life" also suffers from an ambiguity. The term "person" is typically defined in terms of psychological characteristics, although there will certainly be disagreement concerning which characteristics are most important. Supposing that this matter can be settled, the pro-choicer is left with the problem of explaining why *psychological* characteristics should make a *moral* difference. If the pro-choicer should attempt to deal with this problem by claiming that an explanation is not necessary, that in fact we do treat such a cluster of psychological properties as having moral significance, the sharp-witted anti-abortionist should have a ready response. We do treat being both living and human as having moral significance. If it is legitimate for the pro-choicer to demand that the anti-abortionist provide an explanation of the connection between the biological character of being a human being and the wrongness of being killed (even though people accept this connection), then it is legitimate for the anti-abortionist to demand that the pro-choicer provide an explanation of the connection between psychological criteria for being a person and the wrongness of being killed (even though that connection is accepted).[5]

Feinberg has attempted to meet this objection (he calls psychological personhood "commonsense personhood"):

> The characteristics that confer commonsense personhood are not arbitrary bases for rights and duties, such as race, sex, or species membership; rather they are traits that make sense out of rights and duties and without which those moral attributes would have no point or function. It is because people are conscious; have a sense of their personal identities; have plans, goals, and projects; experience emotions; are liable to pains, anxieties, and frustrations can reason and bargain, and so on—it is because of these attributes that people have values and interests, desires and expectations of their own, including a stake in their own futures, and a personal well-being of a sort we cannot ascribe to unconscious or nonrational beings. Because of their developed capacities they can assume duties and responsibilities and can have and make claims on one another. Only because of their sense of self, their life plans, the value hierarchies, and their stakes in their own futures can they be ascribe fundamental rights. There is nothing arbitrary about these linkages.[6]

The plausible aspects of this attempt should not be taken to obscure its implausible features. There is a great deal to be said for the view that being a psychological person under some description is a necessary condition for having duties. One cannot have a duty unless one is capable of behaving morally, and a being's capability of behaving morally will require having a certain psychology. It is far from obvious, however, that having rights entails consciousness or rationality, as Feinberg suggests. We speak of the rights of the severely retarded or the severely mentally ill, yet some of these persons are not rational. We speak of the rights of the temporarily unconscious. The New Jersey Supreme Court based their decision in the Quinlan case on Karen Ann Quinlan's right to privacy, and she was known to be permanently unconscious at that time. Hence, Feinberg's claim that having rights entails being conscious is, on its face, obviously false.

Of course, it might not make sense to attribute rights to a being that would never in its natural history have certain psychological traits. This modest connection between psychological personhood and moral person-hood will create a place for Karen Ann Quinlan and the temporarily unconscious. But then it makes a place for fetuses also. Hence, it does not serve Feinberg's pro-choice purposes. Accordingly, it seems that the pro-choicer will have as much difficulty bridging the gap between psychological person-hood and personhood in the moral sense as the anti-abortionist has bridging the gap between being a biological human being and being a human being in the moral sense.

Furthermore, the pro-choicer cannot any more escape her problem by making person a purely moral category than the anti-abortionist could escape by the analogous move. For if person is a moral category, then the pro-choicer is left without the resources for establishing (noncircularly, of course) the claim that a fetus is not a person, which is an essential premise in her argument. Again, we have both a symmetry and a standoff between pro-choice and anti-abortion views.

Passions in the abortion debate run high. There are both plausibilities and difficulties with the standard positions. Accordingly, it is hardly surprising that partisans of either side embrace with fervor the moral generalizations that support the conclusions they preanalytically favor, and reject with disdain the moral generalizations of their opponents as being subject to inescapable difficulties. It is easy to believe that the counterexamples to one's own moral principles are merely temporary difficulties that will dissolve in the wake of further philosophical research, and that the counterexamples to the principles of one's opponents are as straightforward as the contradiction between *A* and *O* propositions in traditional logic. This might suggest to an impartial observer (if there are any) that the abortion issue is unresolvable.

There is a way out of this apparent dialectical quandary. The moral generalizations of both sides are not quite correct. The generalizations hold for the most part, for the usual cases. This suggests that they are all accidental generalizations, that the moral claims made by those on both sides of the dispute do not touch on the *essence* of the matter.

This use of the distinction between essence and accident is not meant to invoke obscure metaphysical categories. Rather, it is intended to reflect the rather atheoretical nature of the abortion discussion. If the generalization a partisan in the abortion dispute adopts were derived from the reason why ending the life of a human being is wrong, then there could not be exceptions to that generalization unless some special case obtains in which there are even more powerful countervailing reasons. Such generalizations would not be merely accidental generalizations; they would point to, or be based upon, the essence of the wrongness of killing, what it is that makes killing wrong. All this suggests that a necessary condition of resolving the abortion controversy is a more theoretical account of the wrongness of killing. After all, if we merely believe, but do not understand, why killing adult human beings such as ourselves is wrong, how could we conceivably show that abortion is either immoral or permissible?

II

In order to develop such an account, we can start from the following unproblematic assumption concerning our own case: it is wrong to kill *us*. Why is it wrong? Some answers can be easily eliminated. It might be said that what makes killing us wrong is that a killing brutalizes the one who kills. But the brutalization consists of being inured to the performance of an act that is hideously immoral; hence, the brutalization does not explain the immorality. It might be said that what makes killing us wrong is the great loss others would experience as a result of our absence. Although such hubris is understandable, such an explanation does not account for the wrongness of killing hermits, or those whose lives are relatively independent and whose friends find it ease to make new friends.

A more obvious answer is better. What primarily makes killing wrong is neither its effect on the murderer nor its effect on the victim's friends and relatives, but its effect on the victim. The loss of one's life is one of the greatest losses one can suffer. The loss of one's life deprives one of all the experiences, activities, projects, and enjoyments that would otherwise have constituted one's future. Therefore, killing someone is wrong, primarily because the killing inflicts (one of) the greatest possible losses on the victim. To describe this as the loss of life can be misleading, however. The change in my biological state does not by itself make killing me wrong. The effect of the loss of my biological life is the loss to me of all those activities, projects, experiences, and enjoyments which would otherwise have constituted my future personal life. These activities, projects, experiences, and enjoyments are either valuable for their own sakes or are means to something else that is valuable for its own sake. Some parts of my future are not valued by me now, but will come to be valued by me as I grow older and as my values and capacities change. When I am killed, I am deprived both of what I now value which would have been part of my future personal life, but also of what I would come to value. Therefore, when I die, I am deprived of all of the value of my future. Inflicting this loss on me is ultimately what makes killing me wrong. This being the case, it would seem that what makes killing *any* adult human being prima facie seriously wrong is the loss of his or her future.[7]

How should this rudimentary theory of the wrongness of killing be evaluated? It cannot be faulted for deriving an "ought" from an "is," for it does not. The analysis assumes that killing me (or you, reader) is prima facie seriously wrong. The point of the analysis is to establish which natural property ultimately explains the wrongness of the killing, given that it is wrong. A natural property will ultimately explain the wrongness of killing, only if (1) the explanation fits with our intuitions about the matter and (2) there is no other natural property that provides the basis for a better explanation of the wrongness of killing. This analysis rests on the intuition that what makes killing a particular human or animal wrong is what it does to that particular human or animal. What makes killing wrong is some natural effect or other of the killing. Some would deny this. For instance, a divine-command theorist in ethics would deny it. Surely this denial is, however, one of those features of divine command theory which renders it so implausible.

The claim that what makes killing wrong is the loss of the victim's future is directly supported by two considerations. In the first place, this theory explains why we regard killing as one of the worst of crimes. Killing is especially wrong, because it deprives the victim of more than perhaps any other crime. In the second place, people with AIDS or cancer who know they are dying believe, of course, that dying is a very bad thing for them. They believe that the loss of a future to them that they would otherwise have experienced is what makes their premature death a very bad thing for them. A better theory of the wrongness of killing would require a different natural property associated with killing which better fits with the attitudes of the dying. What could it be?

The view that what makes killing wrong is the loss to the victim of the value of the victim's future gains additional support when some of its implications are examined. In the first place, it is incompatible with the view that it is wrong to kill only beings who are biologically human. It is possible that there exists a different species from another planet whose members have a future like ours. Since having a future like that is what makes killing someone wrong, this theory entails that it would be wrong to kill members of such a species. Hence, this theory is opposed to the claim that only life that is biologically human has great moral worth, a claim which many anti-abortionists have seemed to adopt. This opposition, which this theory has in common with personhood theories, seems to be a merit of the theory.

In the second place, the claim that the loss of one's future is the wrong-making feature of one's being killed entails the possibility that the futures of some actual nonhuman mammals on our own planet are sufficiently like ours that it is seriously wrong to kill them also. Whether some animals do have the same right to life as human beings depends on adding to the account of the wrongness of killing some additional account of just what it is about my future or the futures of other adult human beings which makes it wrong to kill us. No such additional account will be offered in this essay. Undoubtedly, the provision of such an account would be a very difficult matter. Undoubtedly, any such account would be quite controversial. Hence, it surely should not reflect badly on this sketch of an elementary theory of the wrongness of killing that it is indeterminate with respect to some very difficult issues regarding animal rights.

In the third place, the claim that the loss of one's future is the wrong-making feature of one's being killed does not entail, as sanctity-of-human-life theories do, that active euthanasia is wrong. Persons who are severely and incurably ill, who face a future of pain and despair, and who wish to die will not have suffered a loss if they are killed. It is, strictly speaking, the value of a human's future which makes killing wrong in this theory. This being so, killing does not necessarily wrong some persons who are sick and dying. Of course, there may be other reasons for a prohibition of active euthanasia, but that is another matter. Sanctity-of-human-life theories seem to hold that active euthanasia is seriously wrong even in an individual case where there seems to be good reason for it independently of public policy considerations. This consequence is most implausible, and it is a plus for the claim that the loss of a future of value is what makes killing wrong that it does not share this consequence.

In the fourth place, the account of the wrongness of killing defended in this essay does straightforwardly entail that it is prima facie seriously wrong to kill children and infants, for we do presume that they have futures of value. Since we do believe that it is wrong to kill defenseless little babies, it is important that a theory of the wrongness of killing easily account for this. Personhood theories of the wrongness of killing, on the other hand, cannot straightforwardly account for the wrongness of killing infants and young children.[8] Hence, such theories must add special ad hoc accounts of the wrongness of killing the young. The plausibility of such ad hoc theories seems to be a function of how desperately one wants such theories to work. The claim that the primary wrong-making feature of a killing is the loss to the victim of the value of its future accounts for the wrongness of killing young children and infants directly; it makes the wrongness of such acts as obvious as we actually think it is. This is a further merit of this theory. Accordingly, it seems that this value of a future-like-ours theory of the wrongness of killing shares strengths of both sanctity-of-life and personhood accounts while avoiding weaknesses of both. In addition, it meshes with a central intuition concerning what makes killing wrong.

The claim that the primary wrong-making feature of a killing is the loss to the victim of the value of its future has obvious consequences for the ethics of abortion. The future of a standard fetus includes a set of experiences, projects, activities, and such which are identical with the futures of adult human beings and are identical with the futures of young children. Since the reason that is sufficient to explain why it is wrong to kill human beings after the time of birth is a reason that also applies to fetuses, it follows that abortion is prima facie seriously morally wrong.

This argument does not rely on the invalid inference that, since it is wrong to kill persons, it is wrong to kill potential persons also. The category that is morally central to this analysis is the category of having a valuable future like ours; it is not the category of personhood. The argument to the conclusion that abortion is prima facie seriously morally wrong proceeded independently of the notion of person or potential person or any equivalent. Someone may wish to start with this analysis in terms of the value of a human future, conclude that abortion is, except perhaps in rare circumstances, seriously morally wrong, infer that fetuses have the right to life, and then call fetuses "persons" as a result of their having the right to life. Clearly, in this case, the category of person is being used to state the *conclusion* of the analysis rather than to generate the *argument* of the analysis.

The structure of this anti-abortion argument can be both illuminated and defended by comparing it to what appears to be the best argument for the wrongness of the wanton infliction of pain on animals. This latter argument is based on the assumption that it is prima facie wrong to inflict pain on me (or you, reader). What is the natural property associated with the infliction of pain which makes such infliction wrong? The obvious answer seems to be that the infliction of pain causes suffering and that suffering is a misfortune. The suffering caused by the infliction of pain is what makes the wanton infliction of pain on me wrong. The wanton infliction of pain on other adult humans causes suffering. The wanton infliction of pain on animals causes suffering. Since causing suffering is what makes the wanton infliction of pain wrong and since the wanton infliction of pain on animals causes suffering, it follows that the wanton infliction of pain on animals is wrong.

This argument for the wrongness of the wanton infliction of pain on animals shares a number of structural features with the argument for the serious prima facie wrongness of abortion. Both arguments start with an obvious assumption concerning what it is wrong to do to me (or you, reader). Both then look for the characteristic or the consequence of the wrong action which makes the action wrong. Both recognize that the wrong-making feature of these immoral actions is a property of actions sometimes directed at individuals other than postnatal human beings. If the structure of the argument for the wrongness of the wanton infliction of pain on animals is sound, then the structure of the argument for the prima facie serious wrongness of abortion is also sound, for the structure of the two arguments is the same. The structure common to both is the key to the explanation of how the wrongness of abortion can be demonstrated without recourse to the category of person. In neither argument is that category crucial.

This defense of an argument for the wrongness of abortion in terms of a structurally similar argument for the wrongness of the wanton infliction of pain on animals succeeds only if the account regarding animals is the correct account. Is it? In the first place, it seems plausible. In the second place, its a major competition is Kant's account. Kant believed that we do not have direct duties to animals at all, because they are not persons. Hence, Kant had to explain and justify the wrongness of inflicting pain on animals on the grounds that "he who is hard in his dealings with animals becomes hard also in his dealing with men."[9] The problem with Kant's account is that there seems to be no reason for accepting this latter claim unless Kant's account is rejected. If the alternative to Kant's account is accepted, then it is easy to understand why someone who is indifferent to inflicting pain on animals is also indifferent to inflicting pain on humans, for one is indifferent to what makes inflicting pain wrong in both cases. But if Kant's account is accepted, there is no intelligible reason why one who is hard in his dealings with animals (or crabgrass or stones) should also be hard in his dealings with men. After all, men are persons; animals are no more persons than crabgrass or stones. Persons are Kant's crucial moral category. Why, in short, should a Kantian accept the basic claim in Kant's argument?

Hence, Kant's argument for the wrongness of inflicting pain on animals rests on a claim that, in a world of Kantian moral agents, is demonstrably false. Therefore, the alternative analysis, being more plausible anyway, should be accepted. Since this alternative analysis has the same structure as the anti-abortion argument being defended here, we have further support for the argument for the immorality of abortion being defended in this essay.

Of course, this value of a future-like-ours argument, if sound, shows only that abortion is prima facie wrong, not that it is wrong in any and all circumstances. Since the loss of the future to a standard fetus, if killed, is, however, at least as great a loss as the loss of the future to a standard adult human being who is killed, abortion, like ordinary killing, could be justified only by the most compelling reasons. The loss of one's life is almost the greatest misfortune that can happen to one. Presumably abortion could be justified in some circumstances, only if the loss consequent on failing to abort would be at least as great. Accordingly, morally permissible abortions will be rare indeed unless, perhaps, they occur so early in pregnancy that a fetus is not yet definitely an individual. Hence, this argument should be taken as showing that abortion is presumptively very seriously wrong, where the presumption is very strong—as strong as the presumption that killing another adult human being is wrong.

III

How complete an account of the wrongness of killing does the value of a future-like-ours account have to be in order that the wrongness of abortion is a consequence? This account does not have to be an account of the necessary conditions for the wrongness of killing. Some persons in nursing homes may lack valuable human futures, yet it may be wrong to kill them for other reasons. Furthermore, this account does not obviously have to be the sole reason killing is wrong where the victim did have a valuable future. This analysis claims only that, for any killing where the victim did have a valuable future like ours, having that future by itself is sufficient to create the strong presumption that the killing is seriously wrong.

One way to overturn the value of a future-like-ours argument would be to find some account of the wrongness of killing which is at least as intelligible and which has different implications for the ethics of abortion. Two rival accounts possess at least some degree of plausibility. One account is based on the obvious fact that people value the experience of living and wish for that valuable experience to continue. Therefore, it might be said, what makes killing wrong is the discontinuation of that experience for the victim. Let us call this the *discontinuation account*.[10] Another rival account is based upon the obvious fact that people strongly desire to continue to live. This suggests that what makes killing us so wrong is that it interferes with the fulfillment of a strong and fundamental desire, the fulfillment of which is necessary for the fulfillment of any other desires we might have. Let us call this the *desire account*.[11]

Consider first the desire account as a rival account of the ethics of killing which would provide the basis for rejecting the anti-abortion position. Such an account will have to be stronger than the value of a future-like-ours account of the wrongness of abortion if it is to do the job expected of it. To entail the wrongness of abortion, the value of a future-like-ours account has only to provide a sufficient, but not a necessary condition for the wrongness of killing. The desire account, on the other hand, must provide us also with a necessary condition for the wrongness of killing in order to generate a pro-choice conclusion on abortion. The reason for this is that presumably the argument from the desire account moves from the claim that what makes killing wrong is interference with a very strong desire to the claim that abortion is not wrong because the fetus lacks a strong desire to live. Obviously, this inference fails if someone's having the desire to live is not a necessary condition of its being wrong to kill that individual.

One problem with the desire account is that we do regard it as seriously wrong to kill persons who have little desire to live or who have no desire to live or, indeed, have a desire not to live. We believe it is seriously wrong to kill the unconscious, the sleeping, those who are tired of life, and those who are suicidal. The value-of-a-human-future account renders standard morality intelligible in these cases; these cases appear to be incompatible with the desire account.

The desire account is subject to a deeper difficulty. We desire life, because we value the goods of this life. The goodness of life is not secondary to our desire for it. If this were not so, the pain of one's own premature death could be done away with merely by an appropriate alteration in the configuration of one's desires. This is absurd. Hence, it would seem that it is the loss of the goods of one's future, not the interference with the fulfillment of a strong desire to live, which accounts ultimately for the wrongness of killing.

It is worth noting that, if the desire account is modified so that it does not provide a necessary, but only a sufficient, condition for the wrongness of killing, the desire account is compatible with the value of a future-like-ours account. The combined accounts will yield an anti-abortion ethic. This suggests that one can retain what is intuitively plausible about the desire account without a challenge to the basic argument of this essay.

It is also worth noting that, if future desires have moral force in a modified desire account of the wrongness of killing, one can find support for an anti-abortion ethic even in the absence of a value of a future-like-ours account. If one decides that a morally relevant property, the possession of which is sufficient to make it wrong to kill some individual, is the desire at some future time to live—one might decide to justify one's refusal to kill suicidal teenagers on these grounds, for example—then, since typical fetuses will have the desire in the future to live, it is wrong to kill typical fetuses. Accordingly, it does not seem that a desire account of the wrongness of killing can provide a justification of a pro-choice ethic of abortion which is nearly as adequate as the value of a human-future justification of an anti-abortion ethic.

The discontinuation account looks more promising as an account of the wrongness of killing. It seems just as intelligible as the value of a future-like-ours account, but it does not justify an anti-abortion position. Obviously, if it is the continuation of one's activities, experiences, and projects, the loss of which makes killing wrong, then it is not wrong to kill fetuses for that reason, for fetuses do not have experiences, activities, and projects to be continued or discontinued. Accordingly, the discontinuation account does not have the anti-abortion consequences that the value of a future-like-ours account has. Yet it seems as intelligible as the value of a future-like-ours account, for when we think of what would be wrong with our being killed, it does seem as if it is the discontinuation of what makes our lives worthwhile which makes killing us wrong.

Is the discontinuation account just as good an account as the value of a future-like-ours account? The discontinuation account will not be adequate at all, if it does not refer to the *value* of the experience that may be discontinued. One does not want the discontinuation account to make it wrong to kill a patient who begs for death and who is in severe pain that cannot be relieved short of killing. (I leave open the question of whether it is wrong for other reasons.) Accordingly, the discontinuation account must be more than a bare discontinuation account. It must make some reference to the positive value of the patient's experiences. But, by the same token, the value of a future-like-ours account cannot be a bare future account either. Just having a future surely does not itself rule out killing the above patient. This account must make some reference to the value of the patient's future experiences and projects also. Hence, both accounts involve the value of experiences, projects, and activities. So far we still have symmetry between the accounts.

The symmetry fades, however, when we focus on the time period of the value of the experiences, etc., which has moral consequences. Although both accounts leave open the possibility that the patient in our example may be killed, this possibility is left open only in virtue of the utterly bleak future for the patient. It makes no difference whether the patient's immediate past contains intolerable pain, or consists in being in a coma (which we can imagine is a situation of indifference), or consists in a life of value. If the patient's future is a future of value, we want our account to make it wrong to kill the patient. If the patient's future is intolerable, whatever his or her immediate past, we want our account to allow killing the patient. Obviously, then, it is the value of that patient's future which is doing the work in rendering the morality of killing the patient intelligible.

This being the case, it seems clear that whether one has immediate past experiences or not does no work in the explanation of what makes killing wrong. The addition the discontinuation account makes to the value of a human future account is otiose. Its addition to the value-of-a-future account plays no role at all in rendering intelligible the wrongness of killing. Therefore, it can be discarded with the discontinuation account of which it is a part.

IV

The analysis of the previous section suggests that alternative general accounts of the wrongness of killing are either inadequate or unsuccessful in getting around the anti-abortion consequences of the value of a future-like-ours argument. A different strategy for avoiding these anti-abortion consequences involves limiting the scope of the value of a future argument. More precisely, the strategy involves arguing that fetuses lack a property that is essential for the value-of-a-future argument (or for any anti-abortion argument) to apply to them.

One move of this sort is based upon the claim that a necessary condition of one's future being valuable is that one values it. Value implies a valuer. Given this, one might argue that, since fetuses cannot value their futures, their futures are not valuable to them. Hence, it does not seriously wrong them deliberately to end their lives.

This move fails, however, because of some ambiguities. Let us assume that something cannot be of value unless it is valued by someone. This does not entail that my life is of no value unless it is valued by me. I may think, in a period of despair, that my future is of no worth whatsoever, but I may be wrong because others rightly see value—even great value—in it. Furthermore, my future can be valuable to me even if I do not value it. This is the case when a young person attempts suicide, but is rescued and goes on to significant human achievements. Such young people's futures are ultimately valuable to them, even though such futures do not seem to be valuable to them at the moment of attempted suicide. A fetus's future can be valuable to it in the same way. Accordingly, this attempt to limit the anti-abortion argument fails.

Another similar attempt to reject the anti-abortion position is based on Tooley's claim that an entity cannot possess the right to life unless it has the capacity to desire its continued existence. It follows that, since fetuses lack the conceptual capacity to desire to continue to live, they lack the right to life. Accordingly, Tooley concludes that abortion cannot be seriously prima facie wrong.[12]

What could be the evidence for Tooley's basic claim? Tooley once argued that individuals have a prima facie right to what they desire and that the lack of the capacity to desire something undercuts the basis of one's right to it.[13] This argument plainly will not succeed in the context of the analysis of this essay, however, since the point here is to establish the fetus's right to life on other grounds. Tooley's argument assumes that the right to life cannot be established in general on some basis other than the desire for life. This position was considered and rejected in the preceding section.

One might attempt to defend Tooley's basic claim on the grounds that, because a fetus cannot apprehend continued life as a benefit, its continued life cannot be a benefit or cannot be something it has a right to or cannot be something that is in its interest. This might be defended in terms of the general proposition that, if an individual is literally incapable of caring about or taking an interest in some X, then one does not have a right to X or X is not a benefit or X is not something that is in one's interest.[14]

Each member of this family of claims seems to be open to objections. As John C. Stevens has pointed out, one may have a right to be treated with a certain medical procedure (because of a health insurance policy one has purchased), even though one cannot conceive of the nature of the procedure.[15] And, as Tooley himself has pointed out, persons who have been indoctrinated, or drugged, or rendered temporarily unconscious may be literally incapable of caring about or taking an interest in something that is in their interest or is something to which they have a right, or is something that benefits them. Hence, the Tooley claim that would restrict the scope of the value of a future-like-ours argument is undermined by counterexamples.[16]

Finally, Paul Bassen has argued that even though the prospects of an embryo might seem to be a basis for the wrongness of abortion, an embryo cannot be a victim and therefore cannot be wronged.[17] An embryo cannot be a victim, he says, because it lacks sentience. His central argument for this seems to be that even though plants and the permanently unconscious are alive, they clearly cannot be victims. What is the explanation of this? Bassen claims that the explanation is that their lives consist of mere metabolism, and mere metabolism is not enough to ground victimizability. Mentation is required.

The problem with this attempt to establish the absence of victimizability is that both plants and the permanently unconscious clearly lack what Bassen calls "prospects" or what I have called "a future life like ours." Hence, it is surely open to one to argue that the real reason we believe plants and the permanently unconscious cannot be victims is that killing them cannot deprive them of a future life like ours; the real reason is not their absence of present mentation.

Bassen recognizes that his view is subject to this difficulty, and he recognizes that the case of children seems to support this difficulty, for "much of what we do for children is based on prospects." He argues, however, that in the case of children and in other such cases, "potentiality comes into play only where victimizability has been secured on other grounds."[18]

Bassen's defense of his view is patently question-begging, since what is adequate to secure victimizability is exactly what is at issue. His examples do not support his own view against the thesis of this essay. Of course, embryos can be victims: when their lives are deliberately terminated, they are deprived of their futures of value, their prospects. This makes them victims, for it directly wrongs them.

The seeming plausibility of Bassen's view stems from the fact that paradigmatic cases of imagining someone as a victim involve empathy, and empathy requires mentation of the victim. The victims of flood, famine, rape, or child abuse are all persons with whom we can empathize. That empathy seems to be part of seeing them as victims.[19]

In spite of the strength of these examples, the attractive intuition that a situation in which there is victimization requires the possibility of empathy is subject to counterexamples. Consider a case that Bassen himself offers: "Posthumous obliteration of an author's work constitutes a misfortune for him only if he had wished his work to endure."[20] The conditions Bassen wishes to impose upon the possibility of being victimized here seem far too strong. Perhaps this author, due to his unrealistic standards of excellence and his low self-esteem, regarded his work as unworthy of survival, even though it possessed genuine literary merit. Destruction of such work would surely victimize its author. In such a case, empathy with the victim concerning the loss is clearly impossible.

Of course, Bassen does not make the possibility of empathy a necessary condition of victimizability; he requires only mentation. Hence, on Bassen's actual view, this author, as I have described him, can be a victim. The problem is that the basic intuition that renders Bassen's view plausible is missing in the author's case. In order to attempt to avoid counterexamples, Bassen has made his thesis too weak to be supported by the intuitions that suggested it.

Even so, the mentation requirement on victimizability is still subject to counterexamples. Suppose a severe accident renders me totally unconscious for a month, after which I recover. Surely killing me while I am unconscious victimizes me, even though I am incapable of mentation during that time. It follows that Bassen's thesis fails. Apparently, attempts to restrict the value of a future-like-ours argument so that fetuses do not fall within its scope do not succeed.

V

In this essay, it has been argued that the correct ethic of the wrongness of killing can be extended to fetal life and used to show that there is a strong presumption that any abortion is morally impermissible. If the ethic of killing adopted here entails, however, that contraception is also seriously immoral, then there would appear to be a difficulty with the analysis of this essay.

But this analysis does not entail that contraception is wrong. Of course, contraception prevents the actualization of a possible future of value. Hence, it follows from the claim that futures of value should be maximized that contraception is prima facie immoral. This obligation to maximize does not exist, however; furthermore, nothing in the ethics of killing in this paper entails that it does. The ethics of killing in this essay would entail that contraception is wrong only if something were denied a human future of value by contraception. Nothing at all is denied such a future by contraception, however.

Candidates for a subject of harm by contraception fall into four categories: (1) some sperm or other, (2) some ovum or other, (3) a sperm and an ovum separately, and (4) a sperm and an ovum together. Assigning the harm to some sperm is utterly arbitrary, for no reason can be given for making a sperm the subject of harm rather than an ovum. Assigning the harm to some ovum is utterly arbitrary, for no reason can lie given for making an ovum the subject of harm rather than a sperm. One might attempt to avoid these problems by insisting that contraception deprives both the sperm and the ovum separately of a valuable future like ours. On this alternative, too many futures are lost. Contraception was supposed to be wrong because it deprived us of one future of value, not two. One might attempt to avoid this problem by holding that contraception deprives the combination of sperm and ovum of a valuable future like ours. But here the definite article misleads. At the time of contraception, there are hundreds of millions of sperm, one (released) ovum, and millions of possible combinations of all of these. There is no actual combination at all. Is the subject of the loss to be a merely possible combination? Which one? This alternative does not yield an actual subject of harm either. Accordingly, the immorality of contraception is not entailed by the loss of a future-like-ours argument, simply because there is no nonarbitrarily identifiable subject of the loss in the case of contraception.

VI

The purpose of this essay has been to set out an argument for the serious presumptive wrongness of abortion subject to the assumption that the moral permissibility of abortion stands or falls on the moral status of the fetus. Since a fetus possesses a property, the possession of which in adult human beings is sufficient to make killing an adult human being wrong, abortion is wrong.

This way of dealing with the problem of abortion seems superior to other approaches to the ethics of abortion, because it rests on an ethics of killing which is close to self-evident, because the crucial morally relevant property clearly applies to fetuses, and because the argument avoids the usual equivocations on "human life," "human being," or "person." The argument rests neither on religious claims nor on papal dogma. It is not subject to the objection of "speciesism." Its soundness is compatible with the moral permissibility of euthanasia and contraception. It deals with our intuitions concerning young children.

Finally, this analysis can be viewed as resolving a standard problem—indeed, the standard problem—concerning the ethics of abortion. Clearly, it is wrong to kill adult human beings. Clearly, it is not wrong to end the life of some arbitrarily chosen single human cell. Fetuses seem to be like arbitrarily chosen human cells in some respects and like adult humans in other respects. The problem of the ethics of abortion is the problem of determining the fetal property that settles this moral controversy. The thesis of this essay is that the problem of the ethics of abortion, so understood, is solvable.

ENDNOTES

[1] Joel Feinberg, "Abortion," in *Matters of Life and Death: New Introductory Essays in Moral Philosophy*, ed. Tom Regan (New York: Random House, 1986), pp. 256–93; Michael Tooley, "Abortion and Infanticide," *Philosophy and Public Affairs*, 11, no. 1 (1972), pp. 37–65, idem, *Abortion and Infanticide* (New York: Oxford University Press, 1984); Mary Anne Warren, "On the Moral and Legal Status of Abortion," *The Monist* 57, no. 1 (1973), pp. 43–61; H. Tristram Engelhardt Jr., "The Ontology of Abortion," *Ethics* 84, no. 3 (1974), pp. 217–34; L. W. Sumner, *Abortion and Moral Theory* (Princeton: Princeton University Press, 1981); John T. Noonan Jr., "An Almost Absolute Value in History," in *The Morality of Abortion: Legal and Historical Perspectives*, ed. Noonan (Cambridge: Harvard University Press, 1970); and Philip Devine, *The Ethics of Homicide* (Ithaca: Cornell University Press, 1978).

[2] For interesting discussions of this issue, see Warren Quinn, "Abortion: Identity and Loss," *Philosophy and Public Affairs* 13, no. 1 (1984), pp. 24–54; and Lawrence C. Becker, "Human Being: The Boundaries of the Concept," *Philosophy and Public Affairs* 4, no. 1 (1975), pp. 334–59.

[3] See, e.g., Don Marquis, "Ethics and the Elderly: Some Problems," in *Aging and the Elderly: Humanistic Perspectives in Gerontology*, ed. Stuart Spicker, Kathleen Woodward, and David Van Tassel (Atlantic Highlands, N. J.: Humanities Press, 1978), pp. 341–55.

[4] See Warren, "Moral and Legal Status"; and Tooley, "Abortion and Infanticide."

[5] This seems to be the fatal flaw in Warren's treatment of this issue.

[6] Feinberg, "Abortion," p. 270.

[7] I have been most influenced on this matter by Jonathan Glover, *Causing Death and Saving Lives* (New York: Penguin, 1977), chap. 3; and Robert Young, "What Is So Wrong with Killing People?" *Philosophy* 54, no. 210 (1979), pp. 515–28.

[8] Feinberg, Tooley, Warren, and Engelhardt have all dealt with this problem.

[9] Immanuel Kant, "Duties to Animals and Spirits," in *Lectures on Ethics*, trans. Louis Infeld (New York: Harper, 1963), p. 239.

[10] I am indebted to Jack Bricke for raising this objection.

[11] Presumably a preference utilitarian would press such an objection. Tooley once suggested that his account has such a theoretical underpinning; "Abortion and Infanticide," pp. 44–45.

[12] Tooley, "Abortion and Infanticide," pp. 46–47.

[13] Ibid., pp. 44–45.

[14] Donald VanDeVeer seems to think this is selfevident; see his "Whither Baby Doe?" in Regan, *Matters of Life and Death*, p. 233.

[15] John C. Stevens, "Must the Bearer of a Right Have the Concept of That to Which He Has a Right?" *Ethics* 95, no. 1 (1984), pp. 68–74.

[16] See Tooley, "Abortion and Infanticide," pp. 47–49.

[17] Paul Bassen, "Present Sakes and Future Prospects: The Status of Early Abortion," *Philosophy and Public Affairs* 11, no. 4 (1982), pp. 322–26.

[18] Ibid., p. 333.

[19] Note carefully the reasons he gives on the bottom of ibid., p. 316.

[20] Ibid., p. 318.

A DEFENSE OF ABORTION
Judith Jarvis Thompson

Introduction, Arthur Zucker

IN "A DEFENSE OF ABORTION," Judith Jarvis Thompson begins by accepting as a hypothesis that a fetus is a person from the moment of conception. She tries to show that even with this starting point, it is not at all clear that abortion is always wrong. Her argument comes via an example, an example that is now one of the most famous in contemporary ethics: the violinist. Her example of being kidnapped to help save the life of a violinist and the many odd ones that follow are meant to appeal to our moral intuitions about what is right and wrong. She thinks that her examples will make it plain to us that there are cases where killing a fetus would be justified. Thompson never claims that such killing is a happy event, nor does she claim that all abortions are morally permissible.

As you read Thompson's article, consider the following questions: As a strategy, are Thompson's examples so strange that they just fail to be convincing? Thompson refers to the killing of Kitty Genovese in New York City. We think that those who did nothing to help were wrong. Opponents of abortion might say, "That is why we try to interfere with abortions at abortion clinics so that we don't have to live with our not having done the right thing." How would Thompson reply?

═══════

M ost opposition to abortion relies on the premise that the fetus is a human being, a person, from the moment of conception. The premise is argued for, but, as I think, not well. Take, for example, the most common argument. We are asked to notice that the development of a human being from conception through birth into childhood is continuous; then it is said that to draw a line, to choose a point in this development and say "before this point the thing is not a person, after this point it is a person" is to make an arbitrary choice, a choice for which in the nature of things no good rea-

"A Defense of Abortion," by Judith Jarvis Thompson, reprinted from *Philosophy and Public Affairs* 1, no. 1 (1971), pp. 47–66. Copyright © 1971 Princeton University Press.

son can be given. It is concluded that the fetus is, or anyway that we had better say it is, a person from the moment of conception. But this conclusion does not follow. Similar things might be said about the development of an acorn into an oak tree, and it does not follow that acorns are oak trees, or that we had better say they are. Arguments of this form are sometimes called "slippery slope arguments"—the phrase is perhaps self-explanatory—and it is dismaying that opponents of abortion rely on them so heavily and uncritically.

I am inclined to agree, however, that the prospects for "drawing a line" in the development of the fetus look dim. I am inclined to think also that we shall probably have to agree that the fetus has already become a human person well before birth. Indeed, it comes as a surprise when one first learns how early in its life it begins to acquire human characteristics. By the tenth week, for example, it already has a face, arms and legs, fingers and toes; it has internal organs, and brain activity is detectable.[1] On the other hand, I think that the premise is false, that the fetus is not a person from the moment of conception. A newly fertilized ovum, a newly implanted clump of cells, is no more a person than an acorn is an oak tree. But I shall not discuss any of this. For it seems to me to be of great interest to ask what happens if, for the sake of argument, we allow the premise. How, precisely, are we supposed to get from there to the conclusion that abortion is morally impermissible? Opponents of abortion commonly spend most of their time establishing that the fetus is a person, and hardly any time explaining the step from there to the impermissibility of abortion. Perhaps they think the step too simple and obvious to require much comment. Or perhaps instead they are simply being economical in argument. Many of those who defend abortion rely on the premise that the fetus is not a person, but only a bit of tissue that will become a person at birth; and why pay out more arguments than you have to? Whatever the explanation, I suggest that the step they take is neither easy nor obvious, that it calls for closer examination than it is commonly given, and that when we do give it this closer examination we shall feel inclined to reject it.

I propose, then, that we grant that the fetus is a person from the moment of conception. How does the argument go from here? Something like this, I take it. Every person has a right to life. So the fetus has a right to life. No doubt the mother has a right to decide what shall happen in and to her body; everyone would grant that. But surely a person's right to life is stronger and more stringent than the mother's right to decide what happens in and to her body, and so outweighs it. So the fetus may not be killed; an abortion may not be performed.

It sounds plausible. But now let me ask you to imagine this. You wake up in the morning and find yourself back to back in bed with an unconscious violinist. A famous unconscious violinist. He has been found to have a fatal kidney ailment, and the Society of Music Lovers has canvassed all the available medical records and found that you alone have the right blood type to help. They have therefore kidnapped you, and last right the violinist's circulatory system was plugged into yours, so that your kidneys can be used to extract poisons from his blood as well as your own. The director of the hospital now tells you, "Look, we're sorry the Society of Music Lovers did this to you—we would never have permitted it if we had known. But still, they did it, and the violinist now is plugged into you. To unplug you would be to kill him. But never mind, it's only for nine months. By then he will have recovered from his ailment, and can safely be unplugged from you." Is it morally incumbent on you to accede to this situation? No doubt it would be very nice of you if you did, a great kindness. But do you have to accede to it? What if it were not nine months, but nine years? Or longer still? What if the director of the hospital says, "Tough luck, I agree, but you've now got to stay in bed, with the violinist plugged into you, for the rest of your life. Because remember this. All persons have a right to life, and violinists are persons. Granted you have a right to decide what happens in and to your body, but a person's right to life outweighs your right to decide what happens in and to your body. So you cannot ever be unplugged from him." I imagine you would regard this as outrageous, which suggests that something really is wrong with that plausible-sounding argument I mentioned a moment ago.

In this case, of course, you were kidnapped; you didn't volunteer for the operation that plugged the violinist into your kidneys. Can those who oppose abortion on the ground I mentioned make an exception for a pregnancy due to rape? Certainly. They can say that persons have a right to life only if they didn't come into existence because of rape; or they can say that all persons have a right to life, but that some have less of a right to life than others, in particular, that those who came into existence because of rape have less. But these statements have a rather unpleasant sound. Surely the question of whether you have a right to life at all, or how much of it you have, shouldn't turn on the question of whether or not you are the product of a rape. And in fact the people who oppose abortion on the ground I mentioned do not make this distinction, and hence do not make an exception in case of rape.

116

Nor do they make an exception for a case in which the mother has to spend the nine months of her pregnancy in bed. They would agree that would be a great pity, and hard on the mother; but all the same, all persons have a right to life, the fetus is a person, and so on. I suspect, in fact, that they would not make an exception for a case in which, miraculously enough, the pregnancy went on for nine years, or even the rest of the mother's life.

Some won't even make an exception for a case in which continuation of the pregnancy is likely to shorten the mother's life; they regard abortion as impermissible even to save the mother's life. Such cases are nowadays very rare, and many opponents of abortion do not accept this extreme view. All the same, it is a good place to begin: a number of points of interest come out in respect to it.

1. Let us call the view that abortion is impermissible even to save the mother's life "the extreme view." I want to suggest first that it does not issue from the argument I mentioned earlier without the addition of some fairly powerful premises. Suppose a woman has become pregnant, and now learns that she has a cardiac condition such that she will die if she carries the baby to term. What may be done for her? The fetus, being a person, has a right to life, but as the mother is a person too, so has she a right to life. Presumably they have an equal right to life. How is it supposed to come out that an abortion may not be performed? If mother and child have an equal right to life, shouldn't we perhaps flip a coin? Or should we add to the mother's right to life her right to decide what happens in and to her body, which everybody seems to be ready to grant—the sum of her rights now outweighing the fetus' right to life?

The most familiar argument here is the following. We are told that performing the abortion would be directly killing the child,[2] whereas doing nothing would not be killing the mother, but only letting her die. Moreover, in killing the child, one would be killing an innocent person, for the child has committed no crime, and is not aiming at his mother's death. And then there are a variety of ways in which this might be continued. (1) But as directly killing an innocent person is always and absolutely impermissible, an abortion may not be performed. Or, (2) is directly killing an innocent person is murder, and murder is always and absolutely impermissible, an abortion may not be performed.[3] Or, (3) as one's duty to refrain from directly killing an innocent person is more stringent than one's duty to keep a person from dying, an abortion may not be performed. Or, (4) if one's only options are directly killing an innocent person or letting a person die, one must prefer letting the person die, and thus an abortion may not be performed.[4]

Some people seem to have thought that these are not further premises which must be added if the conclusion is to be reached, but that they follow from the very fact that an innocent person has a right to life.[5] But this seems to me to be a mistake, and perhaps the simplest way to show this is to bring out that while we must certainly grant that innocent persons have a right to life, the theses in (1) through (4) are all false. Take (2), for example. If directly killing an innocent person is murder, and thus is impermissible, then the mother's directly killing the innocent person inside her is murder, and thus is impermissible. But it cannot seriously be thought to be murder if the mother performs an abortion on herself to save her life. It cannot seriously be said that she *must* refrain, that she *must* sit passively by and wait for her death. Let us look again at the case of you and the violinist. There you are, in bed with the violinist, and the director of the hospital says to you, "It's all most distressing, and I deeply sympathize, but you see this is putting an additional strain on your kidneys, and you'll be dead within the month. But you *have* to stay where you are all the same. Because unplugging you would be directly killing an innocent violinist, and that's murder, and that's impermissible." If anything in the world is true, it is that you do not commit murder, you do not do what is impermissible, if you reach around to your back and unplug yourself from that violinist to save your life.

The main focus of attention in writings on abortion has been on what a third party may or may not do in answer to a request from a woman for an abortion. This is in a way understandable. Things being as they are, there isn't much a woman can safely do to abort herself. So the question asked is what a third party may do, and what the mother may do, if it is mentioned at all, is deduced, almost as an afterthought, from what it is concluded that third parties may do. But it seems to me that to treat the matter in this way is to refuse to grant to the mother that very status of person which is so firmly insisted on for the fetus. For we cannot simply read off what a person may do from what a third party may do. Suppose you find yourself trapped in a tiny house with a growing child. I mean a very tiny house, and a rapidly growing child—you are already up against the hall of the house and in a few minutes you'll be crushed to death. The child on the other hand won't be crushed to death; if nothing is done to stop him from growing he'll be hurt, but in the end he'll simply burst open the house and walk out a free man. Now I could well understand it if a bystander were to say, "There's nothing we can do for you. We cannot choose between your life and his, we cannot be the ones to decide who is to live, we cannot intervene." But it cannot be concluded that you too can do nothing, that you cannot attack it to save your life. However innocent the child may be, you do not have to wait passively while it crushes you to death. Perhaps a pregnant woman is vaguely felt to have the status of house, to which we don't allow the right of self-defense. But if the woman houses the child, it should be remembered that she is a person who houses it.

I should perhaps stop to say explicitly that I am not claiming that people have a right to do anything whatever to save their lives. I think, rather, that there are drastic limits to the right of self-defense. If someone threatens you with death unless you torture someone else to death, I think you have not the right, even to save your life, to do so. But the case under consideration here is very different. In our case there are only two people involved, one whose life is threatened, and one who threatens it. Both are innocent: the one who is threatened is not threatened because of any fault, the one who threatens does not threaten because of any fault. For this reason we may feel that we bystanders cannot intervene. But the person threatened can.

In sum, a woman surely can defend her life against the threat to it posed by the unborn child, even if doing so involves its death. And this shows not merely that the theses in (1) through (4) are false; it shows also that the extreme view of abortion is false, and so we need not canvass any other possible ways of arriving at it from the argument I mentioned at the outset.

2. The extreme view could of course be weakened to say that while abortion is permissible to save the mother's life, it may not be performed by a third party, but only by the mother herself. But this cannot be right either. For what we have to keep in mind is that the mother and the unborn child are not like two tenants in a small house which has, by an unfortunate mistake, been rented to both: the mother *owns* the house. The fact that she does adds to the offensiveness of deducing that the mother can do nothing from the supposition that third parties can do nothing. But it does more than this: it casts a bright light on the supposition that third parties can do nothing. Certainly it lets us see that a third party who says "I cannot choose between you" is fooling himself if he thinks this is impartiality. If Jones has found and fastened on a certain coat, which he needs to keep him from freezing, but which Smith also needs to keep him from freezing, then it is not impartiality that says "I cannot choose between

you" when Smith owns the coat. Women have said again and again "This body is *my* body!" and they have reason to feel angry, reason to feel that it has been like shouting into the wind. Smith, after all, is hardly likely to bless us if we say to him, "Of course it's your coat, anybody would grant that it is. But no one may choose between you and Jones who is to have it."

We should really ask what it is that says "no one may choose" in the face of the fact that the body that houses the child is the mother's body. It may be simply a failure to appreciate this fact. But it may be something more interesting, namely the sense that one has a right to refuse to lay hands on people, even where it would be just and fair to do so, even where justice seems to require that somebody do so. Thus justice might call for somebody to get Smith's coat back from Jones, and yet you have a right to refuse to be the one to lay hands on Jones, a right to refuse to do physical violence to him. This, I think, must be granted. But then what should be said is not "no one may choose," but only "*I* cannot choose," and indeed not even this, but "*I* will not *act*," leaving it open that somebody else can or should, and in particular that anyone in a position of authority, with the job of securing people's rights, both can and should. So this is no difficulty. I have not been arguing that any given third party must accede to the mother's request that he perform an abortion to save her life, but only that he may.

I suppose that in some views of human life the mother's body is only on loan to her, the loan not being one which gives her any prior claim to it. One who held this view might well think it impartiality to say "I cannot choose." But I shall simply ignore this possibility. My own view is that if a human being has any just, prior claim to anything at all, he has a just, prior claim to his own body. And perhaps this needn't be argued for here anyway, since, as I mentioned, the arguments against abortion we are looking at do grant that the woman has a right to decide what happens in and to her body.

But although they do grant it, I have tried to show that they do not take seriously what is done in granting it. I suggest the same thing will reappear even more clearly when we turn away from cases in which the mother's life is at stake, and attend, as I propose we now do, to the vastly more common cases in which a woman wants an abortion for some less weight, reason than preserving her own life.

3. Where the mother's life is not at stake, the argument I mentioned at the onset seems to have a much stronger pull. "Everyone has a right to

life, so the unborn person has a right to life." And isn't the child's
right to life weightier than anything other than the mother's own right
to life, which she might put forward as ground for an abortion?

This argument treats the right to life as if it were unproblematic. It is
not, and this seems to me to be precisely the source of the mistake.

For we should now, at long last, ask what it comes to, to have a right to
life. In some views having a right to life includes having a right to be given at
least the bare minimum one needs for continued life. But suppose that what
in fact *is* the bare minimum a man needs for continued life is something he
has no right at all to be given? If I am sick unto death, and the only thing that
hill save my life is the touch of Henry Fonda's cool hand on my fevered
brow, then all the same, I have no right to be given the touch of Henry
Fonda's cool hand on my fevered brow. It would be frightfully nice of him to
fly in from the West Coast to provide it. It would be less nice, though no
doubt well meant, if my friends flew out to the West Coast and carried Henry
Fonda back with them. But I have no right at all against anybody that he
should do this for me. Or again, to return to the story I told earlier, the fact
that for continued life that violinist needs the continued use of your kidneys
does not establish that he has a right to be given the continued use of your
kidneys. He certainly has no right against you that *you* should give him continued use of your kidneys. For nobody has any right to use your kidneys
unless you give him such a right; and nobody has the right against you that
you shall give such a right; and nobody has the right against you that you
shall give him this right—if you do allow him to go on using your kidneys,
this is a kindness on your part, and not something he can claim from you as
his due. Nor has he any right against anybody else that *they* should give him
continued use of your kidneys. Certainly he had no right against the Society
of Music Lovers that they should plug him into you in the first place. And if
you now start to unplug yourself, having learned that you will otherwise
have to spend nine years in bed with him, there is nobody in the world who
must try to prevent you, in order to see to it that he is given something he has
a right to be given.

Some people are rather stricter about the right to life. In their view, it
does not include the right to be given anything, but amounts to, and only to,
the right not to be killed by anybody. But here a related difficulty arises. If
everybody is to refrain from killing that violinist, then everybody must
refrain from doing a great many different sorts of things. Everybody must
refrain from slitting his throat, everybody must refrain from shooting him—

and everybody must refrain from unplugging you from him. But does he have a right against everybody that they shall refrain from unplugging you from him? To refrain from doing this is to allow him to continue to use your kidneys. It could be argued that he has a right against us that *we* should allow him to continue to use your kidneys. That is, while he had no right against us that we should give him the use of your kidneys, it might be argued that he anyway has a right against us that we shall not now intervene and deprive him of the use of your kidneys. I shall come back to third-rate interventions later. But certainly the violinist has no right against you that *you* shall allow him to continue to use your kidneys. As I said, if you do allow him to use them, it is a kindness on your part, and not something you owe him.

The difficulty I point to here is not peculiar to the right to life. It reappears in connection with all the other natural rights; and it is something which an adequate account of rights must deal with. For present purposes it is enough just to draw attention to it. But I would stress that I am not arguing that people do not have a right to life—quite to the contrary, it seems to me that the primary control we must place on the acceptability of an account of rights is that it should turn out in that account to be a truth that all persons have a right to life. I am arguing only that having a right to life does not guarantee having either a right to be given the use of or a right to be allowed continued use of another person's body—even if one needs it for life itself. So the right to life will not serve the opponents of abortion in the very simple and clear way in which they seem to have thought it would.

4. There is another way to bring out the difficulty. In the most ordinary sort of case, to deprive someone of what he has a right to is to treat him unjustly. Suppose a boy and his small brother are jointly given a box of chocolates for Christmas. If the older boy takes the box and refuses to give his brother any of the chocolates, he is unjust to him, for the brother has been given a right to half of them. But suppose that, having learned that otherwise it means nine years in bed with that violinist, you unplug yourself from him. You surely are not being unjust to him, for you gave him no right to use your kidneys, and no one else can have given him any such right. But we have to notice that in unplugging yourself, you are killing him; and violinists, like everybody else, have a right to life, and thus in the view we were considering just now, the right not to be killed. So here you do what he supposedly has a right you shall not do, but you do not act unjustly to him in doing it.

The emendation which may be made at this point is this: the right to life consists not in the right not to be killed, but rather in the right not to be killed unjustly. This runs a risk of circularity, but never mind: it would enable us to square the fact that the violinist has a right to life with the fact that you do not act unjustly toward him in unplugging yourself, thereby killing him. For if you do not kill him unjustly, you do not violate his right to life, and so it is no wonder you do him no injustice.

But if this emendation is accepted, the gap in the argument against abortion stares us plainly in the face: it is by no means enough to show that the fetus is a person, and to remind us that all persons have a right to life—we need to be shown also that killing the fetus violates its right to life, i.e., that abortion is unjust killing. And is it?

I suppose we may take it as a datum that in a case of pregnancy due to rape the mother has not given the unborn person a right to the use of her body for food and shelter. Indeed, in what pregnancy could it be supposed that the mother has given the unborn person such a right? It is not as if there were unborn persons drifting about the world, to whom a woman who wants a child says "I invite you in."

But it might be argued that there are other ways one can have acquired a right to the use of another person's body than by having been invited to use it by that person. Suppose a woman voluntarily indulges in intercourse, knowing of the chance it will issue in pregnancy, and then she does become pregnant; is she not in part responsible for the presence, in fact the very existence, of the unborn person inside her? No doubt she did not invite it in. But doesn't her partial responsibility for its being there itself give it a right to the use of her body?[6] If so, then her aborting it would be more like the boy's taking away the chocolates, and less like your unplugging yourself from the violinist—doing so would be depriving it of what it does have a right to, and thus would be doing it an injustice.

And then, too, it might be asked whether or not she can kill it even to save her own life: If she voluntarily called it into existence, how can she now kill it, even in self-defense?

The first thing to be said about this is that it is something new. Opponents of abortion have been so concerned to make out the independence of the fetus, in order to establish that it has a right to life, just as its mother does, that they have tended to overlook the possible support they might gain from making out that the fetus is *dependent* on the mother, in order to establish that she has a special kind of responsibility for it, a responsibility that gives it rights against her which are not possessed by any independent person—such as an ailing violinist who is a stranger to her.

On the other hand, this argument would give the unborn person a right to its mother's body only if her pregnancy resulted from a voluntary act, undertaken in full knowledge of the chance a pregnancy might result from it. It would leave out entirely the unborn person whose existence is due to rape. Pending the availability of some further argument, then, we would be left with the conclusion that unborn persons whose existence is due to rape have no right to the use of their mothers' bodies, and thus that aborting them is not depriving them of anything they have a right to and hence is not unjust killing.

And we should also notice that it is not at all plain that this argument really does go even as far as it purports to. For there are cases and cases, and the details make a difference. If the room is stuffy, and I therefore open a window to air it, and a burglar climbs in, it would be absurd to say, "Ah, now he can stay, she's given him a right to the use of her house—for she is partially responsible for his presence there, having voluntarily done what enabled him to get in, in full knowledge that there are such things as burglars, and that burglars burgle." It would be still more absurd to say this if I had had bars installed outside my windows, precisely to prevent burglars from getting in, and a burglar got in only because of a defect in the bars. It remains equally absurd if we imagine it is not a burglar who climbs in, but an innocent person who blunders or falls in. Again, suppose it were like this: people-seeds drift about in the air like pollen, and if you open your windows, one may drift in and take root in your carpets or upholstery. You don't want children, so you fix up your windows with fine mesh screens, the very best you can buy. As can happen, however, and on very, very rare occasions does happen, one of the screens is defective; and a seed drifts in and takes root. Does the person plant who now develops have a right to the use of your house? Surely not—despite the fact that you voluntarily opened your windows, you knowingly kept carpets and upholstered furniture, and you knew that screens were sometimes defective. Someone may argue that you are responsible for its rooting, that it does have a right to your house, because after all you *could* have lived out your life with bare floors and furniture, or with sealed windows and doors. But this won't do—for by the same token anyone can avoid a pregnancy due to rape by having a hysterectomy, or anyway by never leaving home without a (reliable!) army.

It seems to me that the argument we are looking at can establish at most that there are *some* cases in which the unborn person has a right to the use of its mother's body, and therefore *some* cases in which abortion is unjust killing. There is room for much discussion and argument as to precisely which, if any. But I think we should sidestep this issue and leave it open, for at any rate the argument certainly does not establish that all abortion is unjust killing.

5.   There is room for yet another argument here, however. We surely must a rant that there may be cases in which it would be morally indecent to detach a person from your body at the cost of his life. Suppose you learn that what the violinist needs is not nine years of your life, but only one hour: all you need do to save his life is to spend one hour in that bed with him. Suppose also that letting him use your kidneys for that one hour would not affect your health in the slightest. Admittedly you were kidnapped. Admittedly you did not give anyone permission to plug him into you. Nevertheless it seems to me plain you *ought* to allow him to use your kidneys for that hour—it would be indecent to refuse.

Again, suppose pregnancy lasted only an hour, and constituted no threat to life or health. And suppose that a woman becomes pregnant as a result of rape. Admittedly she did not voluntarily do anything to bring about the existence of a child. Admittedly she did nothing at all which would give the unborn person a right to the use of her body. All the same it might well be said, as in the newly emended violinist story, that she *ought* to allow it to remain for that hour—that it would be indecent in her to refuse.

Now some people are inclined to use the term "right" in such a way that it follows from the fact that you ought to allow a person to use your body for the hour he needs, that he has a right to use your body for the hour he needs, even though he has not been given that right by any person or act. They may say that it follows also that if you refuse, you act unjustly toward him. This use of the term is perhaps so common that it cannot be called wrong; nevertheless it seems to me to be an unfortunate loosening of what we would do better to keep a tight rein on. Suppose that box of chocolates I mentioned earlier had not been given to both boys jointly, but was given only to the older boy. There he sits, stolidly eating his way through the box, his small brother watching enviously. Here we are likely to say "You ought not to be so mean. You ought to give your brother some of those chocolates." My own view is that it just does not follow from the truth of this that the brother has any right to any of the chocolates. If the boy refuses to give his brother any, he is greedy, stingy, callous—but not unjust. I suppose that the people I have in mind will say it does follow that the brother has a right to some of the chocolates, and thus that the boy does act unjustly if he refuses to give his brother any. But the effect of saving this is to obscure what we should keep distinct, namely the difference between the boy's refusal in this case and the boy's refusal in the earlier case, in which the box was given to both boys jointly, and in which the small brother thus had what was from any point of view clear title to half.

A further objection to so using the term "right" that from the fact that A ought to do a thing for B, it follows that B has a right against A that A do it for him, is that it is going to make the question of whether or not a man has a right to a thing turn on how easy it is to provide him with it; and this seems not merely unfortunate, but morally unacceptable. Take the case of Henry Fonda again. I said earlier that I had no right to the touch of his cool hand on my fevered brow, even though I needed it to save my life. I said it would be frightfully nice of him to fly in from the West Coast to provide me with it, but that I had no right against him that he should do so. But suppose he isn't on the West Coast. Suppose he has only to walk across the room, place a hand briefly on my brow—and lo, my life is saved. Then surely he ought to do it, it would be indecent to refuse. Is it to be said "Ah, well, it follows that in this case she has a right to the touch of his hand on her brow, and so it would be an injustice in him to refuse"? So that I have a right to it when it is easy for him to provide it, though no right when it's hard? It's rather a shocking idea that anyone's rights should fade away and disappear as it gets harder and harder to accord them to him.

So my own view is that even though you ought to let the violinist use your kidneys for the one hour he needs, we should not conclude that he has a right to do so—we should say that if you refuse, you are, like the boy who owns all the chocolates and will give none away, self-centered and callous, indecent in fact, but not unjust. And similarly, that even supposing a case in which a woman pregnant due to rape ought to allow the unborn person to use her body for the hours he needs, we should not conclude that he has a right to do so; we should conclude that she is self-centered, callous, indecent, but not unjust, if she refuses. The complaints are no less grave; they are just different. However, there is no need to insist on this point. If anyone does wish to deduce "he has a right" from "you ought," then all the same he must surely grant that there are cases in which it is not morally required of you that you allow that violinist to use your kidneys, and in which he does not have a right to use them, and in which you do not do him an injustice if you refuse. And so also for mother and unborn child. Except in such cases as the unborn person has a right to demand it—and we were leaving open the possibility that there may be such cases—nobody is morally *required* to make large sacrifices, of health, of all other interests and concerns, of all other duties and commitments, for nine years, or even for nine months, in order to keep another person alive.

6. We have in fact to distinguish between two kinds of Samaritan: the Good Samaritan and what we might call the Minimally Decent Samaritan. The story of the Good Samaritan, you will remember, goes like this (Luke 10:30–35):

> A certain man went down from Jerusalem to Jerico, and fell among thieves, which stripped him of his raiment, and wounded him, and departed, leaving him half dead.
>
> And by chance there came down a certain priest that way; and when he saw him, he passed by on the other side.
>
> And likewise a Levite, when he was at the place, came and looked on him, and passed by on the other side.
>
> But a certain Samaritan, as he journeyed, came where he was; and when he saw him he had compassion on him.
>
> And went to him, and bound up his wounds, pouring in oil and wine, and set him on his own beast, and brought him to an inn, and took care of him.
>
> And on the morrow, when he departed, he took out two pence, and gave them to the host, and said unto him, "Take care of him; and whatsoever thou spendest more, when I come again, I will repay thee."

The Good Samaritan went out of his way, at some cost to himself, to help one in need of it. We are not told what the options were, that is, whether or not the priest and the Levite could have helped by doing less than the Good Samaritan did, but assuming they could have, then the fact they did nothing at all shows they were not even Minimally Decent Samaritans, not because they were not Samaritans, but because they were not even minimally decent.

These things are a matter of degree, of course, but there is a difference, and it comes out perhaps most clearly in the story of Kitty Genovese, who, as you will remember, was murdered while thirty-eight people watched or listened, and did nothing at all to help her. A Good Samaritan would have rushed out to give direct assistance against the murderer. Or perhaps we had better allow that it would have been a Splendid Samaritan who did this, on the ground that it would have involved a risk of death for himself. But the thirty-eight not only did not do this, they did not even trouble to pick up a phone to call the police. Minimally Decent Samaritanism would call for doing at least that, and their not having done it was monstrous.

After telling the story of the Good Samaritan, Jesus said "Go, and do thou likewise." Perhaps he meant that we are morally required to act as the Good Samaritan did. Perhaps he was urging people to do more than is morally required of them. At all events it seems plain that it was not morally required of any of the thirty-eight that he rush out to give direct assistance at the risk of his own life, and that it is not morally required of anyone that he give long stretches of his life—nine years or nine months—to sustaining the life of a person who has no special right (we were leaving open the possibility of this) to demand it.

Indeed, with one rather striking class of exceptions, no one in any country in the world is *legally* required to do anywhere near as much as this for anyone else. The class of exceptions is obvious. My main concern here is not the state of the law in respect to abortion, but it is worth drawing attention to the fact that in no state in this country is any man compelled by law to be even a Minimally Decent Samaritan to any person; there is no law under which charges could be brought against the thirty-eight who stood by while Kitty Genovese died. By contrast, in most states in this country women are compelled by law to be not merely Minimally Decent Samaritans, but Good Samaritans to unborn persons inside them. This doesn't by itself settle anything one way or the other, because it may well be argued that there should be laws in this country—as there are in many European countries—compelling at least Minimally Decent Samaritanism.[7] But it does show that there is a gross injustice in the existing state of the law. And it shows also that the groups currently working against liberalization of abortion laws, in fact working toward having it declared unconstitutional for a state to permit abortion, had better start working for the adoption of Good Samaritan laws generally, or earn the charge that they are acting in bad faith.

I should think, myself, that Minimally Decent Samaritan laws would be one thing, Good Samaritan laws quite another, and in fact highly improper. But we are not here concerned with the law. What we should ask is not whether anybody should be compelled by law to be a Good Samaritan, but whether we must accede to a situation in which somebody is being compelled—by nature, perhaps—to be a Good Samaritan. We have, in other words, to look now at third-rate interventions. I have been arguing that no person is morally required to make large sacrifices to sustain the life of another who has no right to demand them, and this even where the sacrifices do not include life itself; we are not morally required to be Good Samaritans or anyway Very Good Samaritans to one another. But what if a man cannot extricate himself from such a situation? What if he appeals to us to extricate him? It seems to me plain that there are cases in which we can, cases in which a Good Samaritan would extricate him. There you are, you were kidnapped, and nine years in bed with that violinist lie ahead of you. You have your own life to lead. You are sorry, but you simply cannot see giving up so much of your life to the sustaining of his. You cannot extricate yourself, and ask us to do so. I should have thought that—in light of his having no right to the use of your body—it was obvious that we do not have to accede to your being forced to give up so much. We can do what you ask. There is no injustice to the violinist in our doing so.

7. Following the lead of the opponents of abortion, I have throughout been speaking of the fetus merely as a person, and what I have been asking is whether or not the argument we began with, which proceeds only from the fetus being a person, really does establish its conclusion. I have argued that it does not.

But of course there are arguments and arguments, and it may be said that I have simply fastened on the wrong one. It may be said that what is important is not merely the fact that the fetus is a person, but that it is a person for whom the woman has a special kind of responsibility issuing from the fact that she is its mother. And it might be argued that all my analogies are therefore irrelevant—for you do not have that special kind of responsibility for that violinist, Henry Fonda does not have that special kind of responsibility for me. And our attention might be drawn to the fact that men and women both *are* compelled by law to provide support for their children.

I have in effect dealt (briefly) with this argument in section 4 above; but a (still briefer) recapitulation now may be in order. Surely we do not have any such "special responsibility" for a person unless we have assumed it, explicitly or implicitly. If a set of parents do not try to prevent pregnancy, do not obtain an abortion, and then at the time of birth of the child do not put it out for adoption, but rather take it home with them, then they have assumed responsibility for it, they have given it rights, and they cannot *now* withdraw support from it at the cost of its life because they now find it difficult to go on providing for it. But if they have taken all reasonable precautions against having a child, they do not simply by virtue of their biological relationship to the child who comes into existence have a special responsibility for it. They may wish to assume responsibility for it, or they may not wish to. And I am suggesting that if assuming responsibility for it would require large sacrifices, then they may refuse. A good Samaritan would not refuse—or anyway, a Splendid Samaritan, if the sacrifices that had to be made were enormous. But then so would a Good Samaritan assume responsibility for that violinist; so would Henry Fonda, if he is a Good Samaritan, fly in from the West Coast and assume responsibility for me.

8. My argument will be found unsatisfactory on two counts by many of those who want to regard abortion as morally permissible. First, while I do argue that abortion is not impermissible, I do not argue that it is always permissible. There may well be cases in which carrying the child to term requires only Minimally Decent Samaritanism of the mother, and this is a standard we must not fall below. I am inclined to think it a merit of my account precisely that it does *not* give a general yes or a general no. It allows for and supports our sense that, for example, a sick and desperately frightened fourteen-year-old schoolgirl, pregnant due to rape, may *of course* choose abortion, and that any law which rules this out is an insane law. And it also allows for and supports our sense that in other cases resort to abortion is even positively indecent. It would be indecent in the woman to request an abortion, and indecent in a doctor to perform it, if she is in her seventh month, and wants the abortion just to avoid the nuisance of postponing a trip abroad. The very fact that the arguments I have been drawing attention to treat all cases of abortion, or even all cases of abortion in which the mother's life is not at stake, as morally on a par ought to have made them suspect at the outset.

Secondly, while I am arguing for the permissibility of abortion in some cases, I am not arguing for the right to secure the death of the unborn child. It is easy to confuse these two things in that up to a certain point in the life of the fetus it is not able to survive outside the mother's body; hence removing it from her body guarantees its death. But they are importantly different. I have argued that you are not morally required to spend nine months in bed, sustaining the life of that violinist; but to say this is by no means to say that if, when you unplug yourself, there is a miracle and he survives, you then have a right to turn round and slit his throat. You may detach yourself even if this costs him his life; you have no right to be guaranteed his death, by some other means, if unplugging yourself does not kill him. There are some people who will feel dissatisfied by this feature of my argument. A woman may be utterly devastated by the thought of a child, a bit of herself, put out for adoption and never seen or heard of again. She may therefore want not merely that the child be detached from her, but more, that it die. Some opponents of abortion are inclined to regard this as beneath contempt—thereby showing insensitivity to what is surely a powerful source of despair. All the same, I agree that the desire for the child's death is not one which anybody may gratify, should it turn out to be possible to detach the child alive.

At this place, however, it should be remembered that we have only been pretending throughout that the fetus is a human being from the moment of conception. A very early abortion is surely not the killing of a person, and so is not dealt with by anything I have said here.

ENDNOTES

[1] Daniel Callahan, *Abortion: Law, Choice, and Morality* (New York, 1970), p. 373. This book gives a fascinating survey of the available information on abortion. The Jewish tradition is surveyed in David M. Feldman, *Birth Control in Jewish Law* (New York, 1968), part 5; and the Catholic tradition in John T. Noonan Jr., "An Almost Absolute Value in History," in *The Morality of Abortion*, ed. John T. Noonan Jr. (Cambridge Mass., 1970).

[2] The term "direct" in the arguments I refer to is a technical one. Roughly, what is meant by "direct killing" is either killing as an end in itself or killing as a means to some end, for example, the end of saving someone else's life. See note 5 below for an example of its use.

[3] Cf. *Encyclical Letter of Pope Pius XI on Christian Marriage* (Boston, n.d.), p. 32: "however much we may pity the mother whose health and even life is gravely imperiled in the performance of the duty allotted to her by nature, nevertheless what could ever be a sufficient reason for excusing in any way the direct murder of the innocent? This is precisely what we are dealing with here." Noonan ("An Almost Absolute Value," p. 43) reads this as follows: "What cause can ever avail to excuse in any way the direct killing of the innocent? For it is a question of that."

[4] The thesis in (4) is in an interesting way weaker than those in (1), (2), and (3): they rule out abortion even in cases in which both mother *and* child will die if the abortion is not performed. By contrast, one who held the view expressed in (4) could consistently say that one needn't prefer letting two persons die to killing one.

[5] Cf. the following passage from Pope Pius XU, *Address to the Italian Catholic Society of Midwives*: "The baby in the maternal breast has the right to life immediately from God.—Hence there is no man, no human authority, no science, no medical, eugenic, social, economic or moral 'indication' which can establish or grant a valid juridical ground for a direct deliberate disposition of an innocent human life, that is a disposition which looks to its destruction either as an end or as a means to another end perhaps in itself not illicit. The baby, still not born, is a man in the same degree and for the same reason as the mother" (quoted in Noonon, "An Almost Absolute Value," p. 45).

[6] The need for a discussion of this argument was brought home to me by members of the Society for Ethical and Legal Philosophy, to whom this paper was originally presented.

[7] For a discussion of the difficulties involved and a survey of the European experience with such laws, see James M. Ratcliffe, ed., *The Good Samaritan and the Law* (New York, 1966).

Affirmative Action

AN INTRODUCTION

Albert Mosley

From the introduction of Africans into the American colonies through the first half of the twentieth century, the practice of denying people of African descent privileges and rights granted to members of other groups was the norm in both social custom and law. After the abolition of slavery, most labor union locals explicitly prohibited membership to African Americans. And the establishment of union shops in private and public enterprises typically resulted in the expulsion of African Americans from skilled labor positions. Federal support of labor unionization through the National Labor Relations Board contributed substantially to the marginalization of African American workers. Only with the threat of a march on Washington in the midst of World War II did President Franklin D. Roosevelt relent and issue Executive Order 8802 banning employment discrimination by the federal government and defense contractors. But the ban against discrimination required no special effort to include members of the groups previously excluded.

The first directive aimed at encouraging inclusiveness was Executive Order 10952, issued by President John F. Kennedy in 1961. This order directed that contractors on projects receiving federal funds "take affirmative action to ensure that applicants are employed, and employees are treated during their employment, without regard to race, creed, color, or national origin." To monitor this Kennedy established the Equal Employment Opportunity Commission (EEOC).

Under pressure from increasing civil disobedience, a Congress dominated by southern Democrats reluctantly passed the *Civil Rights Act of 1964,* which prohibited discrimination on the basis of race, color, or national origin in the distribution of benefits in any federally assisted programs (Title VII) and prohibited employers (of at least fifteen people), employment agencies, and labor organizations from using race, color, religion, sex, or national origin to exclude individuals from the full benefits offered by those agencies (unless the use of such factors served a bona fide occupational qualification). Title VII also prohibited employment practices that perpetuated the effects of past discrimination (except where this might result from a bona fide seniority or merit system) but did not require preferential treatment to achieve racial balance.

In 1965 President Lyndon Johnson issued Executive Order 11246, which established the Office of Federal Contract Compliance (OFFCC) under the Department of Labor. Because local unions (especially of the AFL) were rigidly segregated and rabidly opposed to making jobs available to minorities, OFFCC required that prospective contractors to the federal government show that they had proactive plans to ensure the inclusion of minorities in their workforce. In 1970 under President Nixon, OFFCC instituted the Philadelphia Plan, requiring that the highly segregated construction contractors and labor unions of Philadelphia employ more minority workers. The Plan was extended in Order 4, requiring employers with at least fifty employees and $50,000 in government business to develop "specific goals and timetables" to correct for the underutilization of minority workers or face the loss of government business.

In 1971 a Revised Order 4 was extended to include women as well as minority workers. Major corporations (Bethlehem Steel, AT&T) and universities (Columbia University) were forced to end discriminatory practices and initiate affirmative action plans to employ and promote more women and minorities. And the Supreme court, in *Griggs v. Duke Power Co.* (1971), extended the prohibition against discrimination from disparate treatment (intentionally treating one individual different from another individual on the basis of irrelevant factors such as race, sex, national origin, or religion) to disparate impact (whereby a practice, procedure, or test that on face value is neutral nonetheless produces an underrepresentation of a group formerly excluded from such positions and is unnecessary for the performance of the duties required by the position in question).

Thus, requiring a high school diploma for jobs that could be performed without need of such would disproportionately affect blacks and other groups who historically had been denied equal educational benefits. By outlawing irrelevant "colorblind" requirements and recruitment based on personal networks, affirmative action has made it possible for more people—both black and white, men and women—to have opportunities that otherwise would have been reserved for a privileged few.

Because of continued resistance to the inclusion of minorities by universities and housing authorities, in 1971 the Department of Health, Education and Welfare required recipients of federal funds to "take affirmative action to overcome the effects of prior discrimination" and "even in the absence of such prior discrimination, a recipient in administering a program may take affirmative action to overcome the effects of conditions which resulted in limiting participation of a particular race, color, or national origin." To illustrate, "where a university is not adequately serving members of a particular racial or nationality group, it may establish special recruitment policies to make its program better known and more readily available to such group, and take other steps to provide that group with more adequate service."

After the abolition of slavery many states continued to deny African Americans the equal protection of the law, and to remedy this, the Fourteenth Amendment to the U.S. Constitution was passed prohibiting state and local governments from denying persons within their jurisdiction equal protection of the law. Although designed to outlaw invidious discrimination against African Americans, it has in recent times been used equally to challenge benign discrimination. Despite many differences among the Justices on this issue, the Supreme Court has remained consistent in allowing benign discrimination as a remedy for official findings of continuing invidious discrimination and in cases of voluntary remedy.

A case of voluntary remedy is illustrated by *Kaiser & United Steelworkers v. Weber,* in which the Supreme Court upheld a voluntary agreement between a union (the United Steelworkers of America) and a corporation (Kaiser Aluminum and Chemical Corporation) to correct the discrepancy between the percentage of blacks in skilled craft positions (0%) and the percentage of blacks in the local labor force (39%). This agreement required reserving for minorities 50% of the openings in a training program (sponsored by the corporation) until the discrepancy was eliminated. Both the union and the corporation tacitly acknowledged that each had engaged in years of racial discrimination against black workers to exclude them from such positions.

And in 1986, the Supreme Court upheld an order requiring that Sheet Metal Workers Union, Local 28 admit 29% of new members from minority groups. The union was founded in 1888 with an "all-white" requirement for membership. In 1964 the State of New York initiated a suit that led to a state court's ordering the use of a race-neutral testing procedure for selecting apprentices for membership. Because of numerous "bad-faith" attempts to evade and delay the admission of nonwhites, the union was ordered to cease discriminating and to admit 29% minorities (the percentage of nonwhites in the relevant labor pool in New York City) by July 1981. The union was found in contempt of court in 1982 and 1983, and again ordered to admit 29% of new members from minority groups. The union appealed to the Supreme Court, arguing that the numerical goal amounted to a quota and rewarded individuals who had not been the specific victims of past discrimination by the union. The EEOC under the Reagan administration (directed by Clarence Thomas) supported the union's brief.

The Supreme Court upheld the hiring goal and rejected the contention that Title VII limited relief only to direct victims of discrimination. For the majority, Justice Brennan stated: "The purpose of affirmative action is not to make identified victims whole but rather to dismantle prior patterns of employment discrimination and to prevent discrimination in the future" (478 US 474; Greene, pp. 126–7). Because union membership was typically the result of sponsorship by existing union members, it was necessary that the union admit a substantial number of minority members to insure that its past discriminatory practices no longer served to discourage minority applications. Numerical goals were not a means to ensure a racial balance but were intended only as a "benchmark against which the court could gauge petitioners' efforts to remedy past discrimination" (478 US 474; Greene, p. 127).

Because of widespread resistance to the inclusion of women and minorities in the workplace, the Department of Labor was aggressive in requiring goals, timetables, and good faith efforts on the part of federal contractors. This plus the use of quotas in cases of egregious discrimination established a climate in which many white males felt their chances for success were being diminished unfairly. This has encouraged the view that affirmative action is synonymous with programs that use race and sex to meet a quota.

The debate about affirmative action has accordingly centered primarily around policies that are interpreted as giving preferential treatment to women and minorities. Unfortunately, this has shifted attention from affirmative action programs emphasizing outreach and recruitment (special efforts to make employment opportunities known to women and minorities), development (skill enhancement, diversity management, mentoring), and support (child care, flexible working hours).

Since *Baake*, affirmative action has been recognized as a legitimate means of increasing diversity in higher education. Institutions of higher learning should provide a forum where many points of view can be presented and discussed. Soon over 50% of the working force in the United States will be of non-European origin. It is in everyone's interest that all segments of the population be provided with sound education. This forward-looking orientation is meant to help prepare us for a future in a global, multicultural world.

The other justification for affirmative action is backward-looking, seeking to ensure that those discriminated against do not bequeath their disadvantages to their progeny. Most African Americans see banishing slavery, segregation, and the unequal application of law as necessary but not sufficient to offset the accumulated effects of racist practices over the last hundred years.

For critics of affirmative action, making it illegal to discriminate against individuals on the basis of sex or race makes it illegal to correct for racism and sexism by taking race and sex into account. But for supporters of affirmative action, making a special effort to include women and minorities is what the legacy of racism and sexism requires. If A unjustly pushes B down, then A is obligated to pull B up. If one group harms another, it has an obligation to repair the harm caused. Such examples reflect a general moral principle of restitution. It is absurd to condemn acts of corrective justice as if they were malicious attempts to exclude young white males.

Although the primary rationale of the Fourteenth Amendment, the *Civil Rights Act of 1964,* and its subsequent extensions was to end policies and practices aimed at excluding African Americans, the remedies they provide have been extended to other groups historically discriminated against: women, the elderly, the disabled, Hispanic, Asian, and Native Americans. This means that alleviating injustices to African Americans has helped alleviate injustices to many other groups as well. But the belief that antidiscrimnination laws and policies need not be supplemented with aggressive outreach engenders a policy of benign neglect that perpetuates the effects of the past. It is not enough for A to cease pushing B down. A must actively work to pull B up. This is the spirit of affirmative action.

In the selections presented, many argue that actively working to include members of historically excluded groups amounts to little less than reverse discrimination in which white males are denied opportunities because of their sex and race. Others defend the need to take race and gender into consideration in order to compensate for the continuing effects of racism and sexism. The historical legacy, they claim, creates a need to exhibit blacks, women, and other historically maligned groups in positive roles that challenge historical stereotypes.

Questions and issues to consider: Do individuals or groups suffer the ills and reap the benefits of racism and sexism? Does taking race and sex into account mean that those who benefit most will have been harmed least, and those who have been harmed most will benefit least? Is taking race into consideration precluded by the Fourteenth Amendment and the *1964 Civil Rights Act?* Did African Americans suffer a loss as a result of slavery and segregation? If so, is compensation owed to members of the current generation of African Americans? Did European Americans reap a benefit as a result of slavery and segregation? If so, are younger European Americans morally required to relinquish unjustly acquired advantages? Is the goal of affirmative action proportional representation? Should there be any attempt to compensate for societal and institutional discrimination, where there is often no intent to cause harm to any particular individual? Is diversity a legitimate goal for taking race and sex into consideration in granting employment, educational, and investment opportunities? Do policies that take race and gender into consideration incorporate a form of reverse discrimination? Is being a member of the white race and the male gender grounds for being denied educational, employment, and investment opportunities?

SUGGESTED FURTHER READING

Boxill, Bernard. "The Morality of Reparation." *Social Theory and Practice.* 1972; 2, 113–123.

Fullinwider, Robert K. "The Life and Death of Racial Preferences." *Philosophical Studies* 85 (1997): 173–80.

Gomberg, Paul. "Against Competitive Equal Opportunity." *Journal of Social Philosophy* 26:3 (Winter 1995): 59–74.

Hall, Pamela. "From Justified Discrimination to Responsive Hiring: The Role Model Argument and Female Equity Hiring in Philosophy." *Journal of Social Philosophy.* (Spring 1993): 23–45.

Jaggar, Allison M. "Gender, Race, and Difference: Individual Consideration versus Group-based Affirmative Action in Admission to Higher Education." *The Southern Journal of Philosophy* 35 (1966): Supplement.

Katzner, Louis. "Is the Favoring of Women and Blacks in Employment and Educational Opportunities Justified?" *Philosophy of Law.* Ed. Feinber and Gross (Belmont, Calif.: Wadsworth 1980).

Mosley, Albert. "Policies of Straw or Policies of Inclusion: A Review of Pojman's 'The Case Against Affirmative Action.'" *International Journal of Applied Philosophy* 12:2. 161–68.

Mosley, Albert & Nicholas Capaldi. *Affirmative Action—Social Justice or Unfair Preference* (Lanham, Md.: Rowman & Littlefield, 1996).

Pluhar, Evelyn. "Preferential Hiring and Unjust Sacrifice." *The Philosophical Forum* 12:3 (Spring 1981): 214–24.

Pojman, Louis. "The Case Against Affirmative Action." *International Journal of Applied Philosophy* 12:1, 97–115.

Purdy, Laura. "Why Do We Need Affirmative Action?" *Journal of Social Philosophy* 25:1 (Spring 1994): 133–43.

Thompson, Judith Jarvis. "Preferential Hiring." *Philosophy and Public Affairs* 2:4 (Summer 1973): 364–84.

Van Dyke, Vernon. "Collective Entities and Moral Rights: Problems in Liberal-Democratic Thought." *The Journal of Politics* 44:1 (February 1982): 21–40.

Wasserstrom, Richard. "The University and the Case for Preferential Treatment." *American Philosophical Quarterly* 13:2 (April 1976): 165–70.

Principles of Justice: Rights and Needs
Larry Churchill

Introduction, Arthur Zucker

In "Principles of Justice: Rights and Needs," Larry Churchill challenges H. T. Engelhardt's conception of rights as defined in his article "Allocating Scarce Medical Resources and the Availability of Organ Transplantation." Where Engelhardt sees rights embedded in individual freedom, Churchill argues that justice demands that rights be understood in terms of social relationships. What good are liberties, Churchill would ask, if I lack the ability because of disease to take advantage of them? I may be free to decide to go to the park to hear a band concert but what good is that freedom if I am deaf and there are no provisions for my getting a hearing aid? Churchill stresses that Engelhardt's view leads to hollow rights. According to Churchill, these are no rights at all. Indeed, the social relationships engendered by such a system of allocation would in time be self-destructive.

While reading Churchill's article, consider the following questions: What do you think a hollow right would be? What would Churchill's position be on hollow rights? Where would the right to health care end, especially given what might soon be our ability to change our very genetic make-up?

A sense of ourselves as social creatures is a beginning, but it is not sufficient. So far the arguments have been largely negative—ruling out certain individualistic concepts of self and society—and illustrative—in the sense of pointing and appealing to a sense of moral selfhood that is socially grounded. At best, these observations can orient our thinking, but they do not make the case for any policy of distributive justice. To do this principled argument is required to show why we should accept some principles of justice over others as we ration health care resources. Perceptions of justice without principles are like blind motives or good intentions without a sense

"Principles of Justice: Rights and Needs," by Larry Churchill, reprinted from *Rationing Health Care in America,* 1987, University of Notre Dame Press, pp. 70–86.

of direction. Principles of justice which are not grounded in perceptions and moral sensibilities are empty formalisms. Affirming principles will deepen our perceptions, just as perceptions will be honed through their expression as principles.

Rights Language: Problems and Prospects

Sooner or later all considerations of justice in health care must consider the question of whether health care is a right, and if so, what that means. Rights language has become the favored way to address the issue, and this is hardly surprising, for all of our moral language seems to have been taken over by this idiom. In the recent past all proponents of social change have employed rights rhetoric to couch their claims. Civil rights, women's rights, and gay rights have been some of the most visible instances, but the extension of such claims has reached a considerable distance into health care as well. The Hospital Patients' "Bill of Rights," the rights of children, of psychiatric patients, of those who refuse treatment, and of the dying are examples but do not exhaust the list. Physicians have claimed their rights as well, most notably the right to choose whom they will serve. So it is not surprising that in this atmosphere of a banquet of rights, the right to health care should become the focus of questions about justice.

This obsession with rights language is unfortunate, primarily because it feeds the individual and private notion of self. In many instances those who claim rights neglect its rich, moral legacy in favor of a notion of rights as quasi-legal absolutes. Holders of rights are frequently conceived as having overriding claims, to which no opposition or abridgment can be tolerated. Too often, as in the abortion debate, rights claims are thought to have such a preeminence over all other moral considerations that to wield a right is to apply the *coup de grace* in moral argument. Some (though not all) feminists claim total "reproductive rights," while "pro-lifers" put forward a "right-to-life" for the unborn. Both seem to be acting on the assumption that they hold unassailable ground.

Ronald Dworkin captures the tone of such rhetoric nicely in calling rights "political trumps held by individuals." In the current climate rights seem to function as truncheons. In either case, rights have taken on an absolutist flavor and are tools of moral debate (or castigation) wielded by individuals as claims against others. Recourse to an individualized and absolute notion of rights is frequently used as a conversation-stopper and as an excuse against further probing. The idea of rights as trumps held by individuals is only one dimension of the moral significance of rights. When taken by itself it distorts other key notions of social life, such as responsibility, and more generally, the role of the person in a larger communal order of living.

The reason why rights language has lost its deeper social reference is, of course, easy to see in the legacy bequeathed to us from political philosophies and cultural traditions. An ethos of individualism which is innately skeptical about, and believes it has sovereignty over, social relationships dovetails with a notion of rights as negative absolutes—immunities from interference by others and defenses of individual liberties and entitlements. What is needed is a notion of rights that incorporates individual liberties with a lively sense of social interdependence.

While it is true that rights, when inscribed into law, can and do entail specific claims and duties, the moral notion of rights is more complex. Neglect of this complexity cripples the debate about a right to health care.

For H. L. A. Hart, a moral right is something to be taken into account, not an obligation to undertake or refrain from a specific action. Joel Feinberg says that rights are the grounds of obligation. Rights do generally imply correlative duties, yet it would be naive to think that the mere assertion of a right somehow settles an issue like access to health care. Ascribing rights is only a first step in moral discernment; a second and necessary step is deciding what ascribing rights to persons amounts to and what actions, if any, licitly follow.

Rights are never conclusive until their range of application is specified. The task is to delineate carefully the scope of a right as it is brought into play in particular instances. This is precisely what is foreclosed by the absolutist doctrine of rights.

To say that rights are not absolutes is not to say that rights are relative or that they can be upheld only when it seems convenient. Indeed, the allegation of relativism simply misses the point. Absolutist and relativist doctrines of rights both presuppose a private and possessive individualism.

Rights are also distorted if they are treated as private possessions. The claim "I have a right to . . ." is often thought to be a claim of a sovereignty over a range of choice and action. Such an interpretation is adversarial and anticommunal, precisely because conflicting absolute claims do not acknowledge, and tend to erode, the social foundations on which any rights claim can be made.

The claim "I have a right to do X" stated absolutely indicates a need for moral certainty, that is, the need to guarantee the rightness of a choice in advance and irrespective of context and history. Doing "X" may, of course, turn out to be good or evil, but it is—on this reading—one to which I am entitled and in this way, a choice beyond reproach. Such purity and security of choice, however, is a manipulation of individual prerogatives beyond any common sense of morality.

THE SOCIAL ETHOS OF RIGHTS

Personal rights and social interdependence are inseparable aspects of human life. Individual freedom is a social reality. Individual rights are rooted in a social reality that antedates them and gives them meaning. Each of us can exercise rights in a meaningful way only so long as these rights are recognized and respected by others. Rights are social in the sense that a social context must exist for them to have any meaningful range of application. But the social meaning of rights has a deeper sense.

Rights for individuals make sense at all only within a social ethos. Just as there is no freedom without a field of action, there are no individual rights outside a social ambiance. A convivial order is the condition for the possibility of a rights claim. Assertions of rights are claims for recognition within the moral commons. Acknowledgment of rights claims are recognition that others are also members of the commons. Every notion of natural or human rights implies mutuality within a social order, that is, the recognition of others who are equals in moral prerogative and agency.

The social ethos of rights indicates that rights claims are ways of displaying our humanity. Rights define us, delineate our moral agency, symbolize our mutual self-regard. Natural or human rights apply to persons irrespective of class, economic condition, race, religion, or other contingent conditions. Such rights are anterior to particular social contracts and are not abolished by political revolutions because they are based in a social sense of self that antedates formal governments and institutions. Indeed, in Western democracies, governments are thought to derive their just powers from their fidelity to a more primordial social order in which the rights of all individuals are respected.

Natural or human rights are, therefore, not individual but social in character, or better, individual only because they are social. The social dimension is not a human creation constituted by choice for the convenience of individuals, nor is it merely an aggregate of individuals. Sociality is a given and inalienable state of affairs. We are innately social, not social by choice, and rights are one expression of the meaning of our sociality.

The human being is individual and social. Acknowledging this deep reciprocity between the individual and the social dimensions of human life supports neither individualism nor socialism as political ideologies. Rather it indicates the need for a sense of morality in which individual rights and social obligations are seen as mutually critical and interpretive dimensions of a single moral phenomenon.

It is the institutions and roles of social life that give to individual rights their purpose and completeness. Without our social lineaments, rights are empty formalisms, lacking a historical context or a political meaning. The choice between individual rights and social obligations is not one between conflicting alternatives but between complementary dimensions. Neither makes sense without the other. If the social ethos of rights is neglected, moral disputes will continue to be jousting matches for individual superiority in an antagonistic commons.

There is a right to health care, but it is a right which must be carefully defined within, and responsive to, the social ambiance. This refinement must wait, however, until we have examined the claims of those who deny that there is such a right at all.

The Right to Health Care vs. Prior Rights

Acknowledging the social character of rights points to the difficulties in Robert Nozick's denial of a right to health care. Libertarians such as Nozick are fond of the notion of "rights as trumps held by individuals" because they believe that any scheme of distributive justice wrongly presupposes allocative prerogatives and violates individuals' entitlements to their holdings. In *Anarchy, State and Utopia*, Nozick compares doctors to barbers, claiming that there is no more reason to distribute doctors according to need than to distribute barbers according to need. In both cases the redistribution would do violence to the prior claims doctors and barbers have to control their own actions. We may believe that because doctors perform a more socially valued service that we can control their actions, but Nozick asserts that doctors, just like anyone else, have a prior right of entitlement.

The flaw in his argument is, again, to view rights from an individualistic and not a social perspective. The fatal move is to assume at the outset that entitlement rights exist logically prior to (and, in the state-of-nature hypothetical schema, historically prior to) the existence of society, so that the social order can be viewed as having emerged out of a wish to protect the rights that people have in the state of nature and that they bring with them into the social compact. But this is like saying that trumps existed prior to the game of bridge, and that from some earlier state, the game of bridge evolved because people had these trumps lying around. Here bridge is just the (dispensable) occasion to use trumps. The analogy drives home the point that rights exist, and have both meaning and substance, only if one presupposes a social context, just as trumps make no sense outside of bridge.

An argument similar to Nozick's, but couched more in terms of laissez-faire economics, is made by Robert Sade. In a well-known article in the *New England Journal of Medicine* in 1972, Sade claims that there is no right to health care. His position is that since a physician owns his professional skills, he is entitled to dispense with them as he pleases. As bread belongs to the baker who made it, to sell at whatever price he wishes, so medical services belong to the physician. To force the physician into a fee schedule or to oblige him to see patients he does not choose or make him a government employee (in, say, a National Health Service) is to violate the physician's liberty and his right to practice as he sees fit.

Sade believes that justice is served when the free market is preserved because the market is the least restrictive and most respectful of individual rights. So if a physician chooses to serve those who cannot pay, it is a charitable act, but not one which is in any sense obligated. The patient has no right to care, but can purchase it if he or she is able.

Critics of the laissez-faire model of justice, or "market justice" argue that it is flawed in three ways:

The first flaw is that persons are not in a bargaining position when they are ill or injured. Persons seek a physician when they are compromised—functionally, physically, and psychologically. They are therefore not free, rational or their corporate employers) who would prey on the sick for personal profit (or corporate survival). The patient as free agent is largely a fiction.

The second flaw in the market model of justice is the idea that physicians constitute a supply and demand market. The classic laws of supply and demand do not operate in medical care. The evidence shows that just the reverse occurs. The greater the supply of physicians, the greater the demands and the greater the cost for medical services. This is so because physicians largely generate their own business. They are simultaneously the experts who decide *who needs care, how much care, and what kind of care* patients need (gatekeepers), and the recipients of the financial rewards. This dual role provides no incentives for cost control and exacerbates the market difficulties. Moreover, physicians are largely bound to each other by noncompetitive, fraternal ties, exemplified in the traditional prohibition of advertising.

The third argument against market justice is that it contains a tacit and unacceptable merit criterion for access to care. "To each according to ability to pay" functions on the (largely unspoken) premise that those who can afford health services are deserving, while those who cannot afford them may not be. While the poor are rarely explicitly said to be unworthy of care, tacit negative assumptions about the indigent are correlate of letting market forces dictate access. (Consider recent debates about just who constitutes the "deserving" poor.) Market justice rewards those with financial resources and disenfranchises further those who lack such resources. Market justice follows, and accepts as normative, the economic disparities that already exist in society. Market justice says that disparities of wealth can legitimately translate into disparities of health care. It sees the financial barriers to health care as unfortunate, but not unfair.

Thus there are a number of problems underlying the market model for health care which disqualify it as the primary principle of distribution. Yet the fundamental problem is not with the market *per se*, but with the individualism of Sade's vision of the market. The market can be adjusted to accommodate the objections raised against it; by providing advisors and education for patients, by changing incentives for cost control, and/or by providing funds for the poor to enter the medical market. Some of these measures have been tried, with modest results. But none of these adjustments would change the fundamental individualism that underlies Sade's position. For his basic commitments are not to the market as a distributional device, but to a concept of rights. The core notion is, like Nozick's, one of private entitlements, garnered anterior to any social relationship, and without obligation, which it is the primary duty of society to protect. But, as we have seen, this image of self and society is gravely distorted. And this is no less true of physicians than for others in society. In fact, the doctor's route for coming into possession of and exercising his or her skills is far more socially supported than other positions or professions.

For example, over half the cost of medical education and about forty percent of the cost of health care services are paid out of public funds. This does not close the case, as Victor Sidel believes, in favor of a right to health care, but it does at least move us beyond a naive notion of Lockean ownership of professional skills. Physicians do not acquire their knowledge and skills or apply them by independently realized labor from a state of nature.

146

Older traditions of professionalism are clear on this, seeing the holding of expert skills not as a piece of private property but as a public trust. The religious term for this is "stewardship." But even outside of religious contexts, professionals have borrowed the religious language of fiduciary relationships to express their status and press their claims.

James Childress correctly points out that although physicians in training and in practice accept public funds, there is no explicit contract, nor even an explicit expectation of obligation, at the time the funds are offered and accepted. Indeed, many medical students are, no doubt, unaware of this assistance. Childress argues, therefore, that there should be considerable discretion about how any such obligation to the public should be met. But Sade's premises are fictional for, in Nozick's words, we must look not only to allocation outcomes but to "where the things or actions to be allocated and distributed come from." And at least a *prima facie* case can be made, on Nozick's own terms—on the basis of historical entitlements—for turning a portion of physicians' skills toward the public which helped them acquire those skills.

A variety of other measures by which health professionals are supported by public actions and assisted by regulations could also be discussed here— licensing laws, accreditation practices, and other means by which the professional mandate is vested in providers because of the public good that is thought to accrue. Traditionally, professional self-regulation has been given to medicine in exchange for services society needs and values. All of these are ways in which physicians, both individually and collectively, profess to be a part of the larger social order.

This is not to say that health professionals have no rights, or that there may not be times when the rights of individual practitioners need to be asserted against the inflated expectations and demands of individual patients or a dubious agenda of the state. The efforts to enlist physicians in the execution of criminals or in some military operations may be legitimate occasions for physicians to protect their professional integrity by evocation of prior rights of refusal or noninvolvement. But here the appeal to prior rights is grounded simply in different sets of social obligations rather than individual entitlements. Prior rights always imply a social context, and while this recognition does not make the case for a right to health care, it removes the libertarian impediments frequently erected against it.

The Right to Health Care vs. Freedom

A position in some ways similar to Nozick's but with greater stress on freedom is that of H. Tristram Engelhardt. He begins with an assumption of society as secular and pluralistic, in which a variety of different communities must peaceably resolve their differences. Such a society, he argues, will be unwilling to impose on its diverse citizenry a single concept of the good life and will tolerate the freedom of its members to pursue their own goals as they see fit with minimal interference, so long as the similar freedoms of others are not abridged. This tolerance and freedom must also mark definitions of health and health care, so that "rights to health care are more created than discovered," owing to pluralistic definitions of health itself. There is, Engelhardt claims, no morally compelling reason for any particular health care system. Such a system cannot be discovered in the nature of persons, their association, or in the practices of medicine. All these are culturally relative, subject to human priorities and perceptions of what is valuable, and contingent across time and space. So whatever health care system and health priorities are devised must be created by the will of the moral communities which compose society. The only constraint is the minimal condition necessary for moral dialogue—respect for the freedom of others. All else is based on aesthetic choice, emotional preference, custom, etc., but not on anything inherent in the nature of things. Thus, in Engelhardt's view, a society could decide to spend all its health resources on rhinoplasty and hip reductions and neglect cancer research or infectious diseases, and this may seem an odd set of priorities, but it would not be necessarily wrong. Moreover, health care could be ignored altogether. "The choice of art over health care may, thus, be a bizarre, but not an intrinsically immoral choice." Why? Because "the provision for health care, unlike respect for the freedom of moral agents, is not essential for the possibility of the moral life."

The result is that rights to health care, unless derived from a special contractual agreement, depend on the principle of beneficence, and therefore, are likely to conflict with the stronger principle of autonomy. So like Nozick, Engelhardt's version of self and society begins with the assumption that whatever resources exist are private, rather than common. Inequities in these resources, so that the wealthy, the well-placed, those with media-appeal, or good insurance get, say, liver transplants while others do not, are "unfortunate but not unfair." In sum, there is no right to have corrections made for, or protections against, the exigencies of the natural or social lottery.

In his new book *The Foundations of Bioethics*, Engelhardt discusses what he takes to be the root tension at the heart of ethics between autonomy and beneficence. Autonomy is more basic, he claims, because beneficence is always contingent on some notion of the good, and ultimately, definitions of the good have to be agreed upon commonly and freely. So "the principle of beneficence is exhortatory, while the principle of autonomy is constitutive." It is for this reason that Engelhardt prefers Nozick over Rawls. Nozick embodies what he calls a freedom-based system of justice which sets limits to the goals a society can pursue constrained by freedom and property rights, while Rawls espouses a goal-based system of justice which presumes to define the desirable outcomes in advance.

Several objections can be raised to Engelhardt's view of the person, of health, and of social life. To some extent his assumptions about the relationship between the self and society mirror those of Nozick, Rawls, Locke, and others. Like his predecessors, he has no place for a moral self which is constitutively formed by life in a social world. Although he does accredit life in particularistic communities as valid, he does not seem to lend theoretical weight to this fact. It is worth noting that advocacy for individualism is frequently connected with a conviction that freedom, or autonomy, is the highest value, and, in liberalism, the notion that tolerance is the greatest virtue. The pairing of autonomy with beneficence as the root tension of ethics indicates that the freedom denoted here is largely a negative one which sees coercion as the greatest evil, even for beneficent ends. In a universe devoid of intrinsic notions of right and wrong or good and evil, freedom becomes not only the greatest value but the condition of all other values.

Objection could also be made to Engelhardt's relativism, and Leon Kass, among others, has done much to persuade us that nature (hence disease, health, well-being) is not just what we choose. But to dwell on this would distract us from the major points on which Engelhardt's thesis runs aground: (1) that freedom is itself contingent in many cases upon the provision of health care, and (2) that the structure of social life contributes heavily to the differences which mark the natural lottery.

(1). The relationship between freedom and access to health care is of great importance, potentially for many of us, and actually for some of us. Most considerations of distributive justice highlight the *tension* between liberty and equitable access to needed care. Providing equitable care for all in need will invariably restrict the liberties of some (notably physicians and other health professionals) and a granting of maximal liberty (to physicians) is not conducive to meeting a goal of equitable access (for patients). This is a standard interpretation of the problem and one which Engelhardt shares.

While this tension is real, to focus on it exclusively as *the* problem of justice overlooks a more fundamental relationship between access to health care and freedom. Harold Laski, in a quote attributed to L. T. Hobbhouse, said "Liberty without equality is a name of noble sound and squalid result." A liberty which does not recognize the material conditions necessary for liberty is as good as no liberty at all. My freedom is empty if my disease or disability prevents me from acting, or forecloses the real possibility of choosing from the start.

Freedom as a goal requires a minimal level of health care as a means. To the extent that we value the freedom of others, to that extent we must be committed to access to the health care necessary to achieve their freedom. Otherwise a commitment to their freedom is empty. Any moral system which values autonomy over beneficence must also realize that beneficence is sometimes necessary to achieve autonomy. Our ability to act as relatively free and independent agents is contingent upon a vast array of previous beneficent acts toward us that supported and nurtured our achievement of that autonomy.

So while at one level of analysis, liberty and equity are at odds, at a more primitive level of human functioning, liberty (in any meaningful sense) is dependent upon a range of action and reflection only possible for the healthy, or those who are reasonably confident that their ill health, present or anticipated, will not become a barrier to their lifeplans. For many people in this country the choice to seek medical attention is bought at the price of sacrifice of another of life's necessities. This is a poor freedom indeed, a caricature of liberty, which not only makes liberty the supreme value but also makes it merely an abstract ideal.

Thus, the problem here is the notion that freedom is a natural state which requires little or nothing to be realized. In reality when we are hungry, hurt, or disenfranchised we realize how radically contingent and fragile our freedom is and how interdependent we are on others to help us achieve and maintain our personal autonomy.

We can agree with Engelhardt that autonomy is a high value, in the absence of which other goods of life are diminished in meaning, but focusing on the tension between autonomy and the beneficence meeting of needs will distort and confine the notion of autonomy too severely. Autonomy is more

more an achievement of just communities than a given or natural condition of individuals.

We will finally have to choose between limiting the freedom of some or undermining the *conditions* of freedom for others, and this is, to be sure, not a simple choice. If the sick poor are to have freedom at all, some freedoms of health professionals will have to be bounded. But to leave it at this is fundamentally to misunderstand the point. An unlimited, individual freedom is a mistaken concept to begin with and not a right anyone can claim. Moreover, freedom can be served in a variety of ways. It is not self-evident, even from a conviction that autonomy is the prime value in the moral life, that beneficence and equity take a back seat. For our values reside, not in independence from each other in some hierarchical ranking, but in a moral symbiosis. Libertarians are fond of pointing out that a secure life marked by lack of personal freedom is not worth having. But they neglect the converse of this, that a personal liberty or autonomous life is not even possible when physical necessity reduces our choices to the meager and brutal options of a Hobbesian survival ethics. To claim that we prize and protect the freedoms of the disenfranchised while failing to act materially for the welfare which would provide their freedom is naive at best.

(2). The structure of social life frequently exacerbates, and sometimes even causes, differences in the natural lottery. Fifty years ago Henry Sigerist claimed "the chief cause of disease is poverty." Research on the relationship between race, class, poverty, and health consistently shows the same pattern. Economic and social conditions play a role not only in health care, but in overall health. Some are in ill health because they are poor; some are poor because they are in ill health. Most researchers assume that the effects of poor health and low socioeconomic status are circular. Whatever the precise relationship, it is sufficiently clear that class differences contribute to the etiology of disease, so that disease is not just a natural component of the human genetic lottery, not just a chance and uncontrollable occurrence for which no one is responsible. George Silver puts it graphically:

> The air we breathe, the water we drink, the food we eat are poisoned, contaminated with carcinogens and heavily pathogenic, so that we all suffer the consequences. But not equally. The poor live in areas of cities where air is dirtier and concentration of lead is greater, so children of the poor are poisoned more quickly than suburban children. The water of the poor is piped from foul faucets in decaying slum dwellings where typhoid and salmonella thrive. . . . Factory workers, not the managerial

and executive class, are the ones exposed to poisons and hazards and carcinogens of the ill-protected workers.

The idea of a natural lottery (the phrase is Rawls') is one which obscures social complicity in disease occurrence and fits nicely with an individualism which considers persons as essentially complete in the state of nature. If all disease can be attributed to original patterns in the genetic pool, rather than to our historical existence in social patterns, then all obligations to alter or be responsive to these social patterns are optional and gratuitous responses of charity. The "natural lottery" concept functions here to reinforce the myth of innocence and disclaimers of responsibility. If social class has nothing to do with disease and health, we can say that inequities in access to health care are unfortunate, but not unfair. But this is not the case. All diseases are not socially determined, but the social structure in which we live plays a part in if, when, how often, and with what malady we fall ill. Not all our health problems relate to social conditions, but, more than it is comfortable to think about, many of them do. So we cannot agree with Engelhardt's conclusion that "the differences in need, both medical and fnancial, must be recognized as unfortunate . . . but not unfair." Sometimes the unfairness results precisely from our participation in the social nexus which contributed to those differences, both medical and financial. The natural lottery turns out to be not so natural as it appeared.

For all there is to admire in Engelhardt's espousal of freedom, it finally does not serve us well. Emphasizing the theoretical conditions for moral agency rather than the material conditions for real choice, Engelhardt defines autonomy too narrowly. A more fulsome view should recognize the social involvement in the distribution of ill health. These dimensions must inform our thinking about a right to health care. While rights claims restrict the freedoms of some, they are materially necessary to the freedom of others. But the argument should not be over freedom vs. some other value, but degrees of freedom, and the meaning of freedom. The individualist, atomic freedom claimed by Nozick, Sade, and Engelhardt does not accurately reflect the human situation and is untenable as a premise. The basic temptation is to suppose that individual freedom is "for free," without cost or effort, and not a goal which communities and just societies must achieve for their members through strenuous efforts. Getting past that sort of naiveté is essential to thinking about justice in health care.

Allocating Scarce Medical Resources and the Availability of Organ Transplantation

H. Tristram Engelhardt Jr.

Introduction, Arthur Zucker

SUPPOSE THAT WE HAD DECIDED exactly what the medical profession ought to be. Given that resources—time and money, as well as organs, fetal tissue, hospitals, operating rooms, etc.—are limited, it would still be difficult to decide how to distribute health care in a just manner. Why should some people get more and better health care than others? It certainly does happen. Is it due to planning or is it just "the luck of the draw"? Should something so important as health care be left to luck?

In the recent literature we see two different answers to these questions. Larry Churchill and H. T. Engelhardt agree that rationing is both a reality and a necessity. The question is how to deal with the reality and the necessity.

H. T. Engelhardt addresses the need for a program of allocation based on autonomy, in other words, the freedom of individuals to make their own decisions. Engelhardt discusses organ transplants in particular but is actually facing the general issue of macro-allocation. He mentions three important values. Force should not be used to impose a concept of the good life. We ought to respect the values of others. My body and its parts are mine; if I have a right to anything I have a right to my body and its parts.

Engelhardt points out that in a free, pluralistic society there will be occasions where some people are harmed by the fact that individual freedom must be respected because this is the only way to ensure the social good, the good of all. Notice how he uses two distinctions: between the natural and the social lottery, and between the unfortunate and the unfair.

SOME MORAL PRESUPPOSITIONS

THE PROBLEM

Some controversies have a staying power because they spring from unavoidable moral and conceptual puzzles. The debates concerning transplantation are a good example. To begin with, they are not a single controversy. Rather, they are examples of the scientific debates with heavy political and ethical overlays that characterize a large area of public-policy discussions.[1] The determination of whether public-policy not heart or liver transplantation is an experimental or nonexperimental procedure for which it is reasonable and necessary to provide reimbursement is not simply a determination on the basis of facts regarding survival rates or the frequency with which the procedure is employed. Nor is it a purely moral issue.[2]

It is an issue similar to that raised regarding the amount of pollutants that ought to be considered safe in the work place. The question cannot be answered simply in terms of scientific data, unless one presumes that there will be a sudden inflection in the curve expressing the relationship of decreasing parts per billion of the pollutant and the incidence of disease or death, after which very low concentrations do not contribute at all to an excess incidence of disability or death. If one assumes that there is always some increase in death and disability due to the pollutant, one is not looking for an absolutely safe level but rather a level at which the costs in lives and health do not outbalance the costs in jobs and societal vexation that most more stringent criteria would involve. Such is not a purely factual judgment but requires a balancing of values. Determinations of whether a pollutant is safe at a particular level, of whether a procedure is reasonable and necessary, of whether a drug is safe, of whether heart and liver transplantations should be regarded as nonexperimental procedures are not simply factual determinations. In the background of those determinations is a set of moral judgments regarding equity, decency, and fairness, cost-benefit tradeoffs, individual rights, and the limits of state authority.

Since such debates are structured by the intertwining of scientific, ethical, and political issues, participants appeal to different sets of data and rules of inference, which leads to a number of opportunities for confusion. The questions that cluster around the issue of providing for the transplantation of organs have this distracting heterogeneity. There are a number of questions with heavy factual components, such as, "Is the provision of liver transplants an efficient use of healthcare resources?" and "Will the cost of care in the absence of a transplant approximate the costs involved in the transplant?" To answer such questions, one will need to continue to acquire data concerning the long-term survival rates of those receiving transplants.[3–8] There are, as well, questions with major moral and political components, which give public policy direction to the factual issues. "Does liver or heart transplantation offer a proper way of using our resources, given other available areas of investment?" "Is there moral authority to use state force to redistribute financial resources so as to provide transplantations for all who would benefit from the procedure?" "How ought one fairly to resolve controversies in this area when there is important moral disagreement?"

These serious questions have been engaged in a context marked by passion, pathos, and publicity. George Deukmejian, governor of California, ordered the state to pay for liver transplantation for Koren Crosland, and over $265,000 was raised through contributions from friends and strangers to support the liver transplantation of Amy Hardin of Cahokia, Illinois.[9] Charles and Marilyn Fiske's testimony to the Subcommittee on Investigations and Oversight of the House Committee on Science and Technology provided an example of how fortuitous publicity can lead to treatment[10]—in this case, to their daughter Jamie's receiving payment through Blue Cross of Massachusetts by agreement on October 1, 1982,[11] along with contingency authorization for coverage for liver-transplantation expenses through the Commonwealth of Massachusetts on October 29, 1982.[12] The proclamation by President Reagan of a National Organ Donation Awareness Week, which ran from April 22 through 28, further underscored the public nature of the issues raised.[13] In short, several serious and difficult moral and political dilemmas have been confronted under the spotlight of media coverage and political pressures.[14–17] What is needed is an examination of the moral and conceptual assumptions that shape the debate, so that one can have a sense of where reasonable answers call be sought.

WHY DEBATES ABOUT ALLOCATING RESOURCES GO ON AND ON

The debates concerning the allocation of resources to the provision of expensive, life-saving treatment such as transplantation have recurred repeatedly over the past two decades and show no promise of abating.[18–21] To understand why that is the case, one must recall the nature of the social and moral context within which such debates are carried on. Peaceable, secular, pluralist societies are by definition ones that renounce the use of force to impose a particular ideology or view of the good life, though they include numerous communities with particular, often divergent, views of the ways in which men and women should live and use their resources. Such peaceable, secular societies require at a minimum a commitment to the resolution of disputes in ways that are not fundamentally based on force.[22] There will thus be greater clarity regarding how peaceably to discuss the allocation of resources for transplantation than there will be regarding the importance of the allocation of resources itself.[23] The latter requires a more concrete view of what is important to pursue through the use of our resources than can be decisively established in general secular terms. As a consequence, it is clearer that the public has a right to determine particular expenditures of common resources than that any particular use of resources, as for the provision of transplantation, should be embraced.

This is a recurring situation in large-scale, secular, pluralist states. The state as such provides a relatively neutral bureaucracy that transcends the particular ideological and religious commitments of the communities it embraces, so that its state-funded health-care service (or its postal service) should not be a Catholic, Jewish, or even Judeo-Christian service. This ideal of a neutral bureaucracy is obviously never reached. However, the aspiration to this goal defines peaceable, secular; pluralist societies and distinguishes them from the political vision that we inherited from Aristotle and which has guided us and misguided us over the past two millennia. Aristotle took as his ethical and political ideal the city-state with no more than 100,000 citizens, who could then know each other, know well whom they should elect, and create a public consensus.[24, 25] It is ironic that Aristotle fashioned this image as lie participated in the fashioning of the first large-scale Greek state.

We do not approach the problems of the proper allocations of scarce resources within the context of a citystate, with a relatively clear consensus of the ways in which scarce resources ought to be used. Since the Reformation and the Renaissance, the hope for a common consensus has dwindled, and with good cause. In addition, the Enlightenment failed to provide a fully satisfactory secular surrogate. It failed to offer clearly convincing moral arguments that would have established a particular view of the good life and of the ways in which resources ought to be invested. One is left only with a general commitment to peaceable negotiation as the cardinal moral canon of large-scale peaceable, secular, pluralist states.[26]

As a result, understandings about the proper use of scarce resources tend to occur on two levels in such societies. They occur within particular religious bodies, political and ideological communities, and interest groups, including insurance groups. Then take place as well within the more procedurally oriented vehicles and structures that hold particular communities within a state. The more one addresses issues such as the allocation of scarce resource in the context of a general secular, pluralist society, the more one will be pressed to create all answer in some procedurally fair fashion, rather than hope to discover a proper pattern for the distribution of resources to meet medical needs. However, our past has left us with the haunting and misguided hope that the answer can be discovered.

There are difficulties as well that stem from a tension within morality itself: a conflict between respecting freedom and pursuing the good. Morality as an alternative to force as the basis for the resolution of disputes focuses on the mutual respect of persons. This element of morality, which is autonomy-directed, can be summarized in the maxim, Do not do unto others what they would not have done unto themselves. In the context of secular pluralist ethics, this element has priority, in that it call more clearly be specified and justified. As a result, it sets limits to the moral authority of others to act and thus conflicts with that dimension of morality that focuses on beneficence, on achieving the good for others. This second element of morality may be summarized in the maxim, Do to others their good. The difficulty is that the achievement of the good will require the cooperation of others who may claim a right to be respected in their nonparticipation. It will require as well deciding what goods are to be achieved and how they are to be ranked. One might think here of the conflict between investing communal resources in liver and heart transplantations and providing adequate general medical care to the indigent and near indigent. The more one respects freedom, the more difficult it will be for a society to pursue a common view of the good. Members will protest that societal programs restrict their freedom of choice, either through restricting access to programs or through taxing away their disposable income.

The problem of determining whether and to what extent resources should be invested in transplantation is thus considerable. The debate must be carried on in a context in which the moral guidelines are more procedural than supplied with content. Moreover, the debate will be characterized by conflicting views of what is proper to do, as well as by difficulties in showing that there is state authority to force the participation of unwilling citizens. Within these vexing constraints societies approach the problem of allocating scarce medical resources and in particular of determining the amount of resources to be diverted to transplantation. This can be seen as a choice among possible societal insurance mechanisms. As with the difficulty of determining a safe level of pollutants, the answer with respect to the correct level of insurance will be as much created as discovered.

INSURANCE AGAINST THE NATURAL AND SOCIAL LOTTERIES

Individuals are at a disadvantage or an advantage as a result of the outcomes of two major sets of forces that can be termed the natural and social lotteries.[27, 28] By the natural lottery I mean those forces of nature that lead some persons to be healthy and others to be ill and disabled through no intention or design of their own or of others. Those who win the natural lottery do not need transplantations. They live long and healthy a lives and die peacefully. By the social lottery I mean the various interventions, compacts, and activities of persons that, with luck, lead to making some rich and others poor. The natural lottery surely influences the social lottery. However, the natural lottery need not conclusively determine one's social and economic power, prestige, and advantage. Thus, those who lose at the natural lottery and who are in need of heart and liver transplantation may still have won at the social lottery by having either inherited or earned sufficient funds to pay for a transplantation. Or they may have such a social advantage because their case receives sufficient publicity so that others contribute to help shoulder the costs of care.

An interest in social insurance mechanisms directed against losses at the natural and social lotteries is usually understood as an element of beneficence-directed justice. The goal is to provide the amount of coverage that is due to all persons. The problem in such societal insurance programs is to determine what coverage is due. Insofar as societies provide all citizens with a minimal protection against losses at the natural and the social lotteries, they give a concrete understanding of what is due through public funds. At issue here is whether coverage must include transplantation for those who cannot pay.

However, there are moral as well as financial limits to a society's protection of its members against such losses. First and foremost, those limits derive from the duty to respect individual choices and to recognize the limits of plausible state authority in a secular, pluralist society. If claims by society to the ownership of the resources and services of persons have limits, then there will always be private property that individuals will have at their disposal to trade for the services of others, which will create a second tier of health care for the affluent. Which is to say, the more it appears reasonable that property is owned neither totally societally nor only privately, and insofar as one recognizes limits on society's right to constrain its members, two tiers of health-care services will by right exist: those provided as a part of the minimal social guarantee to all and those provided in addition through the funds of those with an advantage in the social lottery who are interested in investing those resources in health care.

In providing a particular set of protections against loses at the social and natural lotteries, societies draw one of the most important societal distinctions—namely, between outcomes that will be socially recognized as unfortunate and unfair and those that will not be socially recognized as unfair, no matter how unfortunate they may be. The Department of Health and Human Services, for instance, in not recognizing heart transplantation as a nonexperimental procedure, removed the provision of such treatment from the social insurance policy. The plight of persons without private funds for heart transplantation, should they need heart transplantation, would be recognized as unfortunate but not unfair.[29-31] Similarly, proposals to recognize liver transplantation for children and adults as nonexperimental are proposals to alter the socially recognized boundary between losses at the natural and social lotteries that will be understood to be unfortunate and unfair and those that will simply be lamented as unfortunate but not seen as entitling the suffering person to a claim against societal resources.[32]

The need to draw this painful line between unfortunate and unfair outcomes exists in great measure because the concerns for beneficence do not exhaust ethics. Ethics is concerned as well with respecting the freedom of individuals. Rendering to each his or her due also involves allowing individuals the freedom to determine the use of their private energies and resources. In addition, since secular pluralist arguments for the authority of peaceable states most clearly establish those societies as means for individuals peaceably to negotiate the disposition of their communally-owned resources, difficulties may arise in the allocation of scarce resources to health care in general and to transplantation in particular. Societies may decide to allocate the communal resources that would have been available for liver and heart transplantation to national defense or the building of art museums and the expansion of the national park system. The general moral requirement to respect individual choice and procedurally fair societal decisions will mean that there will be a general secular, moral right for individuals to dispose of private resources, and for societies to dispose of communal resources, in ways that will be wrong from a number of moral perspectives. As a result, the line between outcomes that will count as unfortunate and those that will count as unfair will often be at variance with the moral beliefs and aspirations of particular ideological and moral communities encompassed by any large-scale secular society.

Just as one must create a standard of safety for pollutants in the work place by negotiations between management and labor and through discussions in public forums one will also need to create a particular policy for social insurance to cover losses at the natural and social lotteries. This will mean that one will not be able to discover that any particular investment in providing health care for those who cannot pay is morally obligatory. One will not be able to show that societies such as that of the United Kingdom, which do not provide America's level of access to renal dialysis for endstage renal disease, have made a moral mistake.[33, 34] Moral criticism will succeed best in examining the openness of such decisions to public discussion and control.

It is difficulties such as these that led the President's Commission for the Study of Ethical Problems in Medicine and Biomedical and Behavioral Research to construe equity in health care neither as equality in health care nor as access to whatever would benefit patients or meet their needs. The goal of equality in health care runs aground on both conceptual and moral difficulties. There is the difficulty of understanding whether equality would embrace equal amounts of health care or equal amounts of funds for health care. Since individual health needs differ widely, such interpretations of equality are fruitless. Attempting to understand equality as providing health care only from a predetermined list of services to which all would have access conflicts with the personal liberty to use private resources in the acquisition of additional care not on the list. Construing equity as providing all with any health care that would benefit them would threaten inordinately to divert resources to health care. It would conflict as well with choices to invest resources in alternative areas. Substituting "need" for "benefit" leads to similar difficulties unless one can discover, among other things, a notion of need that would not include the need to have one's life extended, albeit at considerable cost.

The commission, as a result, construed equity in health care as the provision of an "adequate level of health care." The commission defined adequate care as "enough care to achieve sufficient welfare, opportunity, information, and evidence of interpersonal concern to facilitate a reasonably full and satisfying life."[35] However, this definition runs aground on the case of children needing liver transplants and other such expensive health-care interventions required to secure any chance of achieving "a reasonably full and satisfying life." There is a tension in the commission's report between an acknowledgment that a great proportion of one's meaning of "adequate health care" must be created and a view that the lineaments of that meaning can be discovered. Thus, the commission states that "[i]n a democracy, the appropriate values to be assigned to the consequences of policies must ultimately be determined by people expressing their values through social and political processes as well as in the marketplace."[36] On the other hand, the commission states that "adequacy does require that everyone receive care that meets standards of sound medical practice."[37] The latter statement may suggest that one could discover what would constitute sound medical practice. In addition, an appeal to a notion of "excessive burdens" will not straightforwardly determine the amount of care due to individuals, since a notion of "excessiveness" requires choosing a particular hierarchy of costs and benefits.[38] Neither will an appeal to excessive burdens determine the amount of the tax burden that others should bear,[39] since there will be morally determined upper limits to taxation set by that element of property that is not communal. People, insofar as they have private property in that sense, have the secular moral right, no matter how unfeeling and uncharitable such actions may appear to others, not to aid those with excessive burdens, even if the financial burdens of those who could be taxed would not be excessive.

Rather, it would appear, following other suggestions from the commission, that "adequate care" will need to be defined by considering, among other things, professional judgments of physicians, average current use, lists of services that health-maintenance organizations and others take to be a part of decent care, as well as more general perceptions of fairness.[40] Such factors influence what is accepted generally in a society as a decent minimal or adequate level of health care. As reports considering the effects of introducing expensive new technology suggest, there is a danger that treatments may be accepted as part of "sound medical practice" before the full financial and social consequences of that acceptance are clearly understood. Much of the caution that has surrounded the development of liver and heart transplantation has been engendered by the experience with renal dialysis, which was introduced with overly optimistic judgments regarding the future costs that would be involved.

Even if, as I have argued, the concrete character of "rights to health care" is more created as an element of societal insurance programs than discovered and if the creation is properly the result of the free choice of citizens, professional and scientific bodies will need to aid in the assessment of the likely balance of costs and benefits to be embraced with the acceptance of any new form of treatment as standard treatment, such as heart and liver transplantation. A premature acceptance may lead to cost pressures on services that people will see under mature consideration to be more important. At that point it may be very difficult to withdraw the label of "standard treatment" from a technologic approach that subsequent experience shows to be too costly, given competing opportunities for the investment of resources. On the other hand, new technologic developments may offer benefits worth the cost they will entail, such as the replacement by computerized tomography of pneumoencephalography. But in any event, there is no reason to suppose that there is something intrinsically wrong with spending more than 10.5 percent of the gross national product on health care.

IS TRANSPLANTATION SPECIAL?

All investments in expensive life-saving treatment raise a question of prudence: Could the funds have been better applied elsewhere? Will the investment in expensive life-saving treatment secure an equal if not greater decrease in morbidity and mortality than an investment in improving the health care of the millions who lack health-care insurance or have only marginal coverage? If the same funds were invested in prenatal health care or the treatment of hypertension, would they secure a greater extension of life and diminution of morbidity for more people? When planning for the rational use of communal funds, it is sensible to seek to maximize access and contribution to the greatest number of people as a reasonable test of what it means to use communal resources for the common good. However, not everything done out of the common purse need be cost effective. It is unclear how one could determine the cost effectiveness of symphony orchestras or art museums. Societies have a proclivity to save the lives of identifiable individuals while failing to come to the aid of unidentified, statistical lives that could have been saved with the same or fewer resources. Any decision to provide expensive life-saving treatment out of communal funds must at least frankly acknowledge when it is not a cost-effective choice but instead a choice made because of special sympathies for those who are suffering or because of special fears that are engendered by particular diseases.

The moral framework of secular, pluralist societies in which rights to health care are more created than discovered will allow such choices as morally acceptable, even if they are less than prudent uses of resources. It will also be morally acceptable for a society, if it pursues expensive life-saving treatment, to exclude persons who through their own choices increase the cost of care. One might think here of the question whether active alcoholics should be provided with liver transplants. There is no invidious discrimination against persons in setting a limit to coverage or in precluding coverage if the costs are increased through free choice. However, societies may decide to provide care even when the costs are incurred by free decision.

Though none of the foregoing is unique to transplantation, the issue of transplantation has the peculiarity of involving the problem not only of the allocation of monetary resources and of services but of that of organs as well. In a criticism of John Rawls' *Theory of Justice*, which theory attempts to provide a justification for a patterned distribution of resources that would redound to the benefit of the least-well-off class, Robert Nozick tests his readers' intuitions by asking whether societal rights to distribute resources would include the right to distribute organs as well.[41] He probably chose this as a test case because our bodies offer primordial examples of private property. The example is also forceful, given the traditional Western reluctance, often expressed in religious regulations, to use corpses for dissection. There is a cultural reluctance to consider parts of the body as objects for the use of persons. No less a figure than Immanuel Kant argued for a position that would appear to preclude the sale or gift of a body part to another.[42] This view of Kant's, one should note, is very close to the traditional Roman Catholic notion that one has a duty to God regarding one's self not to alter one's body except to preserve health.[43]

The concern to have a sufficient supply of organs for transplantation has expressed itself in recent political proposals and counter-proposals regarding the rights of individuals to sell their organs, the provision of federal funds for the support of organ procurement, the study of the medical and legal issues that procurement may raise, and even the taking of organs from cadavers by society with the presumption of consent unless individuals have indicated the contrary.[44–49] It will be easier to show that persons have a right to determine what ought to be done with their bodies, even to the point of making donor consent decisive independently of the wishes of the family, than to show that society may presume consent. A clarification of policy, to make donor decisions definitive, would be in accord with the original intentions of the Uniform Act of Donation of Organs and would ease access to needed organs. It would not impose on people the burden of having to announce to others that they do not want their organs used for transplantation. The more one presumes that organs are not societal property, the more difficult it is to justify shifting the burden to individuals to show that they do not want their organs used. If sufficient numbers of organs are not available, it will be unfortunate, but from the point of view of general secular morality, not unfair. Free individuals will have valued other goals (e.g., having an intact body for burial) more highly than the support of transplantation. One will have encountered again one of the recurring limitations on establishing and effecting a general consensus regarding the ways in which society ought to respond to the unfortunate deliverances of nature.

LIVING WITH THE UNFORTUNATE, WHICH IS NOT UNFAIR

Proposals for the general support of transplantation are thus restricted by various elements of the human condition. There is not simply a limitation due to finite resources, making it impossible to do all that is conceivably possible for all who might marginally benefit. There are restrictions as well that are due to the free decisions of both individuals and societies. Individuals will often decide in ways unsympathetic to transplantation programs that would involve the use of their private resources, including their organs. Insofar as one takes seriously respect for persons, one must live with the restrictions that result from numerous free choices. One may endeavor to educate, entice, and persuade people to participate. However, free societies are characterized by the commitment to live with the tragedies that result from the decisions of free individuals not to participate in the beneficent endeavors of others. There are then also the restrictions due to the inability to give a plausible account of state authority that would allow the imposition of a concrete view of the good life. Secular, pluralist societies are more neutral moral frameworks for negotiation and creation of ways to use their common resources than modes for discovering the proper purpose for those resources. If societies freely decide to give a low priority to transplantation and invest instead in generally improving health care for the indigent in the hope of doing greater good, there will be an important sense in which they have acted within their right, even from particular moral perspectives that may seem wrongheaded.

These reflections on the human condition suggest that we will need in the future to learn to live with the fact that some may receive expensive life-saving treatment while others do not, because some have the luck of access to the media, the attention of a political leader, or sufficient funds to purchase care in their own right. The differences in need, both medical and financial, must be recognized as unfortunate. They are properly the objects of charitable response. However, it must be understood that though unfortunate circumstances are always grounds for praiseworthy charity, they do not always provide grounds, by that fact, for redrawing the line between the circumstances we will count as unfortunate but not unfair and those we will count as unfortunate and unfair. To live with circumstances we must acknowledge as unfortunate but not unfair is the destiny of finite men and women who have neither the financial nor moral resources of gods and goddesses. We must also recognize the role of these important conceptual and moral issues in the fashioning of what will count as reasonable and necessary care, safe and efficacious procedures, nonexperimental treatment, or standard medical care. Though we are not gods and goddesses, we do participate in creating the fabric of these "facts."

ENDNOTES

[1] T. H. Engelhardt Jr. and A. L. Caplan, Eds., *Scientific Controversies* (London: Cambridge University Press, 1987).

[2] H. Newman, "Medicare Program: Solicitation of Hospitals and Medical Centers to Participate in a Study of Heart Transplants," *Federal Register*, 46 (January 22, 1981), pp. 7072–75.

[3] J. G. Copeland, et. al., "Heart Transplantation: Four Years' Experience with Conventional Immunosuppression," *Journal of the American Medical Association* 251 (1984), pp. 1563–66.

[4] W. C. DeVries, et. al., "Clinical Use of the Total Artificial Heart," *New England Journal of Medicine* 310 (1984), pp. 273–78.

[5] J. S. Dummer, et. al., "Early Infections in Kidney, Heart, and Liver Transplant Recipients on Cyclosporine," *Transplantation* 36 (1983), pp. 259–67.

[6] I Shunzaburo, et. al., "Current Status of Hepatic Transplantation," *Seminar in Liver Disorders* 3 (1983), pp. 173–80.

[7] T. E. Starzl, et. al., "Evolution of Liver Transplantation," *Hepatology* 2 (1982), 614–36.

[8] D. H. Van Thiel, et. al., "Liver Transplantation in Adults," *Hepatology* 2 (1982), 637–40.

[9] D. Wessell, "Transplants Increase, and So Do Disputes Over Who Pays Bills," *Wall Street Journal* 73 (April 12, 1984), pp. 1, 12.

[10] T. H. Spirito, "Letter of October 29, 1982," in *Organ Transplants: Hearings Before The Subcommittee on Investigating and Oversight,* 98th Congress, 1st Session (Washington, D. C.: Government Printing Office 1983), p. 236.

[11] P. A. Litos, "Letter of October 1, 1982," in ibid., p. 227.

[12] C. Fiske and M. Fiske, "Statements of Charles and Marilyn Fiske, and daughter Jamie, Liver Transplant Patient," in ibid., pp. 212–18.

[13] P. Gunby, "Organ Transplant Improvements, Demands Draw Increasing Attention," *Journal of the American Medical Association* 251 (1984), pp. 1521–23, 1527.

[14] _____, "Media-Abetted Liver Transplants Raise Questions of 'Equity and Decency.'" *Journal of the American Medical Association* 249 (1983), pp. 1973–74, 1980–82.

[15] J. K. Iglehart, "Transplantation: The Problem of Limited Resources," *New England Journal of Medicine* 309 (1983), pp. 123–28.

[16] _____, "The Politics of Transplantation," *New England Journal of Medicine* 310 (1984), pp. 864–68.

[17] M. J. Strauss, "The Political History of the Artificial Heart," in ibid., pp. 332–36.

[18] Ad Hoc Task Force on Cardiac Replacement, "Cardiac Replacement: Medical, Ethical, Psychological, and Economic Implication" (Washington, D. C.: Government Printing Office, 1969).

[19] Artificial Heart Assessment Panel, "The Totally Implantable Artificial Heart" (Bethesda, Md.: National Institute of Health, 1973), Department of Health, Education and Welfare, pul. no. NIH, pp. 74–191.

[20] A. Leaf, "The MGH Trustees Say No to Heart Transplants," *New England Journal of Medicine* 302 (1980), pp. 1087–88.

[21] B. A. Barnes, et. al., "Final Report of the Task Force on Liver Transplantation in Massachusetts" (Boston: Blue Cross and Blue Shield, 1983).

[22] H. T. Engelhardt, Jr., "Bioethics in Pluralist Societies," *Perspectives in Biology and Medicine* 26 (1982), pp. 64–78.

[23] _____, "The Physician-Patient Relationship in a Secular, Pluralist Society," in *The Clinical Encounter* (Dordrecht, Holland: D. Reidel, 1983), pp. 253–66.

[24] Aristotle, *Nicomachean Ethics*, ix 10.1170b.

[25] _____, *Politics*, vii 4a.1326b.

[26] H. T. Engelhardt Jr., *The Foundations of Bioethics* (New York: Oxford University Press, 1986).

[27] J. Rawls, *A Theory of Justice* (Cambridge, Mass.: Belknap Press, 1971).

[28] R. Nozick, *Anarchy, State and Utopia* (New York: Basic Books, 1974).

[29] H. Newman, "Exclusion of Heart Transplantation Procedures from Medicare Coverage," *Federal Register* 45 (1980), pp. 52296.

[30] R. A. Know, "Heart Transplants: To Pay or Not To Pay," *Science* 209 (1980), pp. 570–72, 574–75.

[31] R. W. Evans, et. al., "The National Heart Transplant Study: An Overview," *Heart Transplant* 2 (1982) pp. 85–87.

[32] Consensus Conference, "Liver Transplantation," *Journal of the American Medical Association* 250 (1983), pp. 2861–64.

[33] "Who Shall Be Dialyzed?" *The Lancet* 1 (1984), p. 717.

[34] H. J. Aaron, and W. B. Schwartz, "The Painful Prescription: Rationing Hospital Care" (Washington, D. C.: Brookings Institute, 1984).

[35] President's Commission for the Study of Ethical Problems in Medicine and Biomedical and Behavioral Research, "Securing Access to Health Care," vol. 1 (Washington, D. C.: Government Printing Office, 1983), p. 20.

[36] Ibid., p. 37.

[37] Ibid.

[38] Ibid., pp. 42–43.

[39] Ibid., pp. 43–46.

[40] Ibid., pp. 37–47.

[41] Nozick, *Anarchy*, pp. 206–7.

[42] I. Kant, *Kant's Werke: Akademie Textausgabe*, vol. 6 (Berlin: Walter de Gruyter, 1968), p. 423.

[43] G. Kelly, *Medico-moral Problems*, (St. Louis: Catholic Hospital Association, 1958), pp. 245–52.

[44] A. L. Caplan, "Organ Transplants: The Costs of Success," *Hastings Center Report* 13 (1983), pp. 23–32.

[45] G. Kolata, "Organ Shortage Clouds New Transplant Era," *Science* 221 (1983) pp. 32–33.

[46] T. D. Overcase, et al., "Problems in the Identification of Potential Organ Donors: Misconceptions and Fallacies Associated with Donor Cards," *Journal of the American Medical Association* 251 (1984), pp. 1559–62.

[47] J. M. Prottas, "Encouraging Altruism: Public Attitudes and the Marketing of Organ Donation," *Milbank Memorial Fund Quarterly* 61 (1983), pp. 278–306.

[48] U. S. Congress. House. "To Amend the Public Health Service Act to Authorize Financial Assistance for Organ Procurement Organizations, and for Other Purposes," by A. Gore, 98th Congress, 1st Session, House Report 4080: 1983.

[49] Ibid., Senate. by O. Hatch, Senate Report 2048: 1983.9

THE FAMINE RELIEF ARGUMENT
Peter Singer

Introduction, H. Gene Blocker

SOME CRITICS OF Utilitarianism have argued that this moral theory demands too little of us morally. For example, these critics claim that Utilitarianism would allow, and even sanction, the mistreatment of a minority by a majority if such behavior would result in a net increase in the overall happiness in the society. But other critics have argued just the opposite, that Utilitarianism demands too much of us. As these critics explain, Utilitarianism would require each of us to do our best to feed and house the poor around the world, leaving us with only the bare minimum that we need to survive. Indeed, we might even end up poor ourselves if we were to follow the strict dictates of Utilitarianism.

This principle of Utilitarianism profoundly challenges the early "liberal" tradition, which was first expressed by the English philosopher John Locke (1632–1704). According to this tradition, we each have the right to be free from government interference in the pursuit of our private goals in life, including the accumulation of property, so long as the exercise of those rights and freedoms does not interfere with the equal rights and freedoms of other individuals. This doctrine is enshrined in the United States Bill of Rights, the first amendments to the U.S. Constitution, which secure the basic rights of speech, press, assembly, and so on.

Yet later "liberals" grew concerned about the extremes of poverty and the enormous disparities of rich and poor spawned by the nineteenth-century Industrial Revolution. These thinkers worried that the wealthy would use their property to accumulate more and more wealth. Because they were free to bequeath their riches to their children when they died, "the rich would only continue to get richer and the poor, poorer." Such "liberals" wondered whether human rights should also include the right of everyone to be free from hunger, and to obtain a decent education, a job, an adequate income, housing, health care, and so on. As these thinkers saw it, without the fulfillment of such basic rights, people could hardly be expected to exercise and enjoy in any practical sense the other, loftier rights outlined in the Constitution.

Utilitarians, for their part, do not assume that every human being is born with a set of inalienable human rights. Indeed, the first Utilitarian, Jeremy Bentham, called this idea "nonsense on stilts." Bentham rejected the idea of inalienable rights because "rights" could not be scientifically measured. He used the expression "on stilts" to reflect what he saw as the pompous and self-righteous way supporters of the French and American revolutions expressed themselves.

From a Utilitarian point of view, our only obligation is to do whatever we can to increase the happiness of everyone. But if that is true, as Peter Singer argues in this selection, then doesn't it follow that everyone has a moral *obligation* to alleviate the pain and suffering that hunger and inadequate shelter inflict on people around the world? Aren't we obligated to help simply because doing so would obviously and significantly increase the happiness of people all over the world?

Cleary, following Singer's Utilitarian call would mean immense transfers of money from the rich to the poor. To be sure, a wealthy person also has an obligation not to so impoverish herself and her family—their suffering would only add to the world's unhappiness and thus violate the core principle of Utilitarianism. But Singer maintains that relatively wealthy people (including the majority of people living in the United States) should keep only what they need to meet life's basic needs – adequate food, housing, and so on. Whatever we normally spend on luxuries (such as a sports car, expensive vacations, lavish entertainment, and so on) should instead be used to relieve the suffering of the world's poor. Thus, according to Singer's interpretation of Utilitarian principles, an American who earns $40,000 a year but could meet the basic needs of life (in America) with $20,000 a year is morally obligated to give away the other $20,000 to feed the poor in America and abroad.

Of course, many people want lots of things besides what they need to live a bare-minimum existence. Especially in America, people tend to feel that they *need* an expensive home and car, and fine clothes, vacations, and entertainment. But as Singer points out, the unhappiness that would result from giving up such luxuries is far less than the happiness that $20,000 would bring to thousands of people who are literally starving to death. Moreover, he laments, we don't really "need" all the things that advertisers have brainwashed us to "want."

Singer realizes that most people are not going to rush out to follow his moral injunction. Nevertheless, he contends that there are no moral grounds for keeping money that we don't need for our basic survival. As he sees it, our refusal to do all we can to relieve suffering around the world stems from a simple, immoral sense of selfishness.

As you read Singer's article, consider how you would respond to his argument. If you agree with him, are you going to do as he prescribes? Why or why not? If you disagree with him, how would you challenge his argument—beyond simply admitting that you are indeed selfish and want to keep as much wealth for yourself as possible? Is there any morally sound reason for keeping more money than you need to meet the bare necessities of life? Do you think that Garrett Hardin, whom Singer cites in this selection, provides a sound counter-argument: that helping the poor would just make the problem of poverty worse by encouraging further overpopulation around the globe? And even if we *could* feed everyone in the world, would doing so deplete the capital reserves in the developed part of the world needed for continued scientific, technological, and economic progress? If so, is such a consequence worse, from a Utilitarian perspective, than allowing millions of people to starve to death? Finally, ask yourself who decides what we "need," as opposed to what we "want." In the United States today, for instance, do we "need" a university education, a car, a house in the suburbs? Where do we draw the line between "needs" and "wants"?

———

R obert McNamara . . . has suggested the term absolute poverty. The poverty we are familiar with in industrialized nations is relative poverty—meaning that some citizens are poor, relative to the wealth enjoyed by their neighbours. People living in relative poverty in Australia might be quite comfortably off by comparison with old-age pensioners in Britain, and British old-age pensioners are not poor in comparison with the poverty that exists in Mali or Ethiopia. Absolute poverty, on the other hand, is poverty by any standard.

•   •   •

Absolute poverty is . . . responsible for the loss of countless lives, especially among infants and young children. When absolute poverty does not cause death it still causes misery of a kind not often seen in the affluent nations.

———

"The Famine Relief Argument," by Peter Singer, reprinted from *Practical Ethics,* 1979, Cambridge University Press.

Malnutrition in young children stunts both physical and mental development. It has been estimated that the health, growth and learning capacity of nearly half the young children in developing countries are affected by malnutrition. Millions of people on poor diets suffer from deficiency diseases, like goitre, or blindness caused by a lack of vitamin A. The food value of what the poor eat is further reduced by parasites such as hookworm and ringworm, which are endemic in conditions of poor sanitation and health education.

Death and disease apart, absolute poverty remains a miserable condition of life, with inadequate food, shelter, clothing, sanitation, health services and education. . . . Absolute poverty is probably the principal cause of human misery today.

This is the background situation, the situation that prevails on our planet all the time. It does not make headlines. People died from malnutrition and related diseases yesterday, and more will die tomorrow. The occasional droughts, cyclones, earthquakes and floods that take the lives of tens of thousands in one place and at one time are more newsworthy. They add greatly to the total amount of human suffering; but it is wrong to assume that when there are no major calamities reported, all is well.

The problem is not that the world cannot produce enough to feed and shelter its people. People in the poor countries consume, on average, 400 lbs of grain a year, while North Americans average more than 2000 lbs. The difference is caused by the fact that in the rich countries we feed most of our grain to animals, converting it into meat, milk and eggs. Because this is an inefficient process, wasting up to 95% of the food value of the animal feed, people in rich countries are responsible for the consumption of far more food than those in poor countries who eat few animal products. If we stopped feeding animals on grains, soybeans and fishmeal the amount of food saved would—if distributed to those who need it—be more than enough to end hunger throughout the world.

These facts about animal food do not mean that we can easily solve the world food problem by cutting down on animal products, but they show that the problem is essentially one of distribution rather than production. The world does produce enough food. Moreover the poorer nations themselves could produce far more if they made more use of improved agricultural techniques.

So why are people hungry? Poor people cannot afford to buy grain grown by American farmers. Poor farmers cannot afford to buy improved seeds, or fertilizers, or the machinery needed for drilling wells and pumping water. Only by transferring some of the wealth of the developed nations to the poor of the underdeveloped nations can the situation be changed.

That this wealth exists is clear. Against the picture of absolute poverty that McNamara has painted, one might pose a picture of 'absolute affluence'. Those who are absolutely affluent are not necessarily affluent by comparison with their neighbours, but they are affluent by any reasonable definition of human needs. This means that they have more income than they need to provide themselves adequately with all the basic necessities of life. After buying food, shelter, clothing, necessary health services and education, the absolutely affluent are still able to spend money on luxuries. The absolutely affluent choose their food for the pleasures of the palate, not to stop hunger; they buy new clothes to look fashionable, not to keep warm, they move house to be in a better neighbourhood or have a play room for the children, not to keep out the rain; and after all this there is still money to spend on books and records, colour television, and overseas holidays.

At this stage I am making no ethical judgments about absolute affluence, merely pointing out that it exists. Its defining characteristic is a significant amount of income above the level necessary to provide for the basic human needs of oneself and one's dependents. By this standard Western Europe, North America, Japan, Australia, New Zealand and the oil-rich Middle Eastern states are all absolutely affluent, and so are many, if not all, of their citizens. . . .

These, therefore, are the countries—and individuals—who have wealth which they could, without threatening their own basic welfare, transfer to the absolutely poor.

At present, very little is being transferred. Members of the Organization of Petroleum Exporting Countries lead the way, giving an average of 2.1% of their Gross National Product. Apart from them, only Sweden, The Netherlands and Norway have reached the modest UN target of 0.7% of GNP. Britain gives 0.38% of its GNP in official development assistance and a small additional amount in unofficial aid from voluntary organizations. The total comes to less than £1 per month per person, and compares with 5.5% of GNP spent on alcohol, and 3% on tobacco. Other, even wealthier nations, give still less: Germany gives 0.27%, the United States 0.22% and Japan 0.21%.

If these are the facts, we cannot avoid concluding that by not giving more than we do, people in rich countries are allowing those in poor countries to suffer from absolute poverty, with consequent malnutrition, ill

172

health and death. This is not a conclusion which applies only to governments. It applies to each absolutely affluent individual, for each of us has the opportunity to do something about the situation; for instance, to give our time or money to voluntary organizations like Oxfam, War on Want, Freedom From Hunger, and so on. If, then, allowing someone to die is not intrinsically different from killing someone, it would seem that we are all murderers.

Is this verdict too harsh? Many will reject it as self-evidently absurd. They would sooner take it as showing that allowing to die cannot be equivalent to killing than as showing that living in an affluent style without contributing to Oxfam is ethically equivalent to going over to India and shooting a few peasants. And no doubt, put as bluntly as that, the verdict *is* too harsh.

These are several significant differences between spending money on luxuries instead of using it to save lives, and deliberately shooting people.

First, the motivation will normally be different. Those who deliberately shoot others go out of their way to kill; they presumably want their victims dead, from malice, sadism, or some equally unpleasant motive. A person who buys a colour television set presumably wants to watch television in colour—not in itself a terrible thing. At worst, spending money on luxuries instead of giving it away indicates selfishness and indifference to the sufferings of others, characteristics which may be understandable but are not comparable with actual malice or similar motives.

Second, it is not difficult for most of us to act in accordance with a rule against killing people: it is, on the other hand, very difficult to obey a rule which commands us to save all the lives we can. To live a comfortable, or even luxurious life it is not necessary to kill anyone; but it is necessary to allow some to die whom we might have saved, for the money that we need to live comfortably could have been given away. Thus the duty to avoid killing is much easier to discharge completely than the duty to save. Saving every life we could would mean cutting our standard of living down to the bare essentials needed to keep us alive. To discharge this duty completely would require a degree of moral heroism utterly different from what is required by mere avoidance of killing.

A third difference is the greater certainty of the outcome of shooting when compared with not giving aid. If I point a loaded gun at someone and pull the trigger, it is virtually certain that the person will be injured, if not killed; whereas the money that I could give might be spent on a project that turns out to be unsuccessful and helps no one.

Fourth, when people are shot there are identifiable individuals who have been harmed. We can point to them and to their grieving families. When I buy my colour television, I cannot know who my money would have saved if I had given it away. In a time of famine I may see dead bodies and grieving families on my new television, and I might not doubt that my money would have saved some of them; even then it is impossible to point to a body and say that had I not bought the set, that person would have survived.

Fifth, it might be said that the plight of the hungry is not my doing, and so I cannot be held responsible for it. The starving would have been starving if I had never existed. If I kill, however, I am responsible for my victims' deaths, for those people would not have died if I had not killed them. . . .

Do the five differences not only explain, but also justify, our attitudes? Let us consider them one by one:

1. Take the lack of an identifiable victim first. Suppose that I am a travelling salesman, selling tinned food, and I learn that a batch of tins contains a contaminant, the known effect of which when consumed is to double the risk that the consumer will die from stomach cancer. Suppose I continue to sell the tins. My decision may have no identifiable victims. Some of those who eat the food will die from cancer. The proportion of consumers dying in this way will be twice that of the community at large, but which among the consumers died because they ate what I sold, and which would have contracted the disease anyway? It is impossible to tell; but surely this impossibility makes my decision no less reprehensible than it would have been had the contaminant had more readily detectable, though equally fatal, effects.

2. The lack of certainty that by giving money I could save a life does reduce the wrongness of not giving, by comparison with deliberate killing; but it is insufficient to show that not giving is acceptable conduct. The motorist who speeds through pedestrian crossings, heedless of anyone who might be on them, is not a murderer. She may never actually hit a pedestrian; yet what she does is very wrong indeed.

3. The notion of responsibility for acts rather than omissions is more puzzling. On the one hand we feel ourselves to be under a greater obligation to help those whose misfortunes we have caused. (It is for this reason that advocates of overseas aid often argue that Western nations have created the poverty of Third World nations, through

forms of economic exploitation which go back to the colonial system.) On the other hand any consequentialist would insist that we are responsible for all the consequences of our actions, and if a consequence of my spending money on a luxury item is that someone dies, I am responsible for that death. It is true that the person would have died even if I had never existed, but what is the relevance of that? The fact is that I do exist, and the consequentialist will say that our responsibilities derive from the world as it is, not as it might have been.

One way of making sense of the non-consequentialist view of responsibility is by basing it on a theory of rights of the kind proposed by John Locke or, more recently, Robert Nozick. If everyone has a right to life, and this right is a right *against* others who might threaten my life, but not a right *to* assistance from others when my life is in danger, then we can understand the feeling that we are responsible for acting to kill but not for omitting to save. The former violates the rights of others, the latter does not.

Should we accept such a theory of rights? If we build up our theory of rights by imagining, as Locke and Nozick do, individuals living independently from each other in a 'state of nature', it may seem natural to adopt a conception of rights in which as long as each leaves the other alone, no rights are violated. I might, on this view, quite properly have maintained my independent existence if I had wished to do so. So if I do not make you any worse off than you would have been if I had had nothing at all to do with you, how can I have violated your rights? But why start from such an unhistorical, abstract and ultimately inexplicable idea as an independent individual? We now know that our ancestors were social beings long before they were human beings, and could not have developed the abilities and capacities of human beings if they had not been social beings first. In any case we are not, now, isolated individuals. If we consider people living together in a community, it is less easy to assume that rights must be restricted to rights against interference. We might, instead, adopt the view that taking rights to life seriously is incompatible with standing by and watching people die when one could easily save them.

4. What of the difference in motivation? That a person does not positively wish for the death of another lessens the severity of the blame she deserves; but not by as much as our present attitudes to giving aid suggest. The behaviour of the speeding motorist is again comparable, for such motorists usually have no desire at all to kill anyone. They merely enjoy speeding and are indifferent to the consequences.

Despite their lack of malice, those who kill with cars deserve not only blame but also severe punishment.

5. Finally, the fact that to avoid killing people is normally not difficult, whereas to save all one possibly could save is heroic, must make an important difference to our attitude to failure to do what the respective principles demand. Not to kill is a minimum standard of acceptable conduct we can require of everyone; to save all one possibly could is not something that can realistically be required, especially not in societies accustomed to giving as little as ours do. Given the generally accepted standards, people who give, say, £100 a year to Oxfam are more aptly praised for above average generosity than blamed for giving less than they might. The appropriateness of praise and blame is, however, a separate issue from the rightness or wrongness of actions. The former evaluates the agent: the latter evaluates the action. Perhaps people who give £100 really ought to give at least £1,000, but to blame them for not giving more could be counterproductive. It might make them feel that what is required is too demanding, and if one is going to be blamed anyway, one might as well not give anything at all.

(That an ethic which put saving all one possibly can on the same footing as not killing would be an ethic for saints or heroes should not lead us to assume that the alternative must be an ethic which makes it obligatory not to kill, but puts us under no obligation to save anyone. There are positions in between these extremes, as we shall soon see.)

To summarize our discussion of the five differences which normally exist between killing and allowing to die, in the context of absolute poverty and overseas aid. The lack of an identifiable victim is of no moral significance, though it may play an important role in explaining our attitudes. The idea that we are directly responsible for those we kill, but not for those we do not help, depends on a questionable notion of responsibility, and may need to be based on a controversial theory of rights. Differences in certainty and motivation are ethically significant, and show that not aiding the poor is not to be condemned as murdering them; it could, however, be on a par with killing someone as a result of reckless driving, which is serious enough. Finally the difficulty of completely discharging the duty of saving all one possibly can makes it inappropriate to blame those who fall short of this target as we blame those who kill; but this does not show that the act itself is less serious. Nor does it indicate anything about those who, far from saving all they possibly can, make no effort to save anyone.

These conclusions suggest a new approach. Instead of attempting to deal with the contrast between affluence and poverty by comparing not saving with deliberate killing, let us consider afresh whether we have an obligation to assist those whose lives are in danger, and if so, how this obligation applies to the present world situation.

The argument for an obligation to assist. The path from the library at my university to the Humanities lecture theatre passes a shallow ornamental pond. Suppose that on my way to give a lecture I notice that a small child has fallen in and is in danger of drowning. Would anyone deny that I ought to wade in and pull the child out? This will mean getting my clothes muddy, and either cancelling my lecture or delaying it until I can find something dry to change into; but compared with the avoidable death of a child this is insignificant.

A plausible principle that would support the judgment that I ought to pull the child out is this: if it is in our power to prevent something very bad happening, without thereby sacrificing anything of comparable moral significance, we ought to do it. This principle seems uncontroversial. It will obviously win the assent of consequentialists; but non-consequentialists should accept it too, because the injunction to prevent what is bad applies only when nothing comparably significant is at stake. Thus the principle cannot lead to the kinds of actions of which non-consequentialists strongly disapprove— serious violations of individual rights, injustice, broken promises, and so on. If a non-consequentialist regards any of these as comparable in moral significance to the bad thing that is to be prevented, he will automatically regard the principle as not applying in those cases in which the bad thing can only be prevented by violating rights, doing injustice, breaking promises, or whatever else is at stake. Most non-consequentialists hold that we ought to prevent what is bad and promote what is good. Their dispute with consequentialists lies in their insistence that this is not the sole ultimate ethical principle: that it is *an* ethical principle is not denied by any plausible ethical theory.

Nevertheless the uncontroversial appearance of the principle that we ought to prevent what is bad when we can do so without sacrificing anything of comparable moral significance is deceptive. If it were taken seriously and acted upon, our lives and our world would be fundamentally changed. For the principle applies, not just to rare situations in which one can save a child from a pond, but to the everyday situation in which we can assist those living in absolute poverty. In saying this I assume that absolute poverty, with its hunger and malnutrition, lack of shelter, illiteracy, disease, high infant mortality and low life expectancy, is a bad thing. And I assume that it is within the power of the affluent to reduce absolute poverty, without sacrificing anything of comparable moral significance. If these two assumptions and the principle we have been discussing are correct, we have an obligation to help those in absolute poverty which is no less strong than our obligation to rescue a drowning child from a pond. Not to help would be wrong, whether or not it is intrinsically equivalent to killing. Helping is not, as conventionally thought, a charitable act which it is praiseworthy to do, but not wrong to omit; it is something that everyone ought to do.

This is the argument for an obligation to assist. Set out more formally, it would look like this.

FIRST PREMISE: If we can prevent something bad without sacrificing anything of comparable significance, we ought to do it.

SECOND PREMISE: Absolute poverty is bad.

THIRD PREMISE: There is some absolute poverty we can prevent without sacrificing anything of comparable moral significance.

CONCLUSION: We ought to prevent some absolute poverty.

The first premise is the substantive moral premise on which the argument rests, and I have tried to show that it can be accepted by people who hold a variety of ethical positions.

The second premise is unlikely to be challenged. Absolute poverty is, as McNamara put it, 'beneath any reasonable definition of human decency' and it would be hard to find a plausible ethical view which did not regard it as a bad thing.

The third premise is more controversial, even though it is cautiously framed. It claims only that some absolute poverty can be prevented without the sacrifice of anything of comparable moral significance. It thus avoids the objection that any aid I can give is just 'drops in the ocean' for the point is not whether my personal contribution will make any noticeable impression on world poverty as a whole (of course it won't) but whether it will prevent some poverty. This is all the argument needs to sustain its conclusion, since the second premise says that any absolute poverty is bad, and not merely the total amount of absolute poverty. If without sacrificing anything of comparable moral significance we can provide just one family with the means to raise itself out of absolute poverty, the third premise is vindicated.

I have left the notion of moral significance unexamined in order to show that the argument does not depend on any specific values or ethical principles. I think the third premise is true for most people living in industrialized nations, on any defensible view of what is morally significant. Our affluence means that we have income we can dispose of without giving up the basic necessities of life, and we can use this income to reduce absolute poverty. Just how much we will think ourselves obliged to give up will depend on what we consider to be of comparable moral significance to the poverty we could prevent: colour television, stylish clothes, expensive dinners, a sophisticated stereo system, overseas holidays, a (second?) car, a larger house, private schools for our children. . . . For a utilitarian, none of these is likely to be of comparable significance to the reduction of absolute poverty: and those who are not utilitarians surely must, if they subscribe to the principle of universalizability, accept that at least *some* of these things are of far less moral significance than the absolute poverty that could be prevented by the money they cost. So the third premise seems to be true on any plausible ethical view—although the precise amount of absolute poverty that can be prevented before anything of moral significance is sacrificed will vary according to the ethical view one accepts. . . .

Property rights. Do people have a right to private property, a right which contradicts the view that they are under an obligation to give some of their wealth away to those in absolute poverty? According to some theories of rights (for instance, Robert Nozick's) provided one has acquired one's property without the use of unjust means like force and fraud, one may be entitled to enormous wealth while others starve. This individualistic conception of rights is in contrast to other views, like the early Christian doctrine to be found in the works of Thomas Aquinas, which holds that since property exists for the satisfaction of human needs, 'whatever a man has in superabundance is owed, of natural right, to the poor for their sustenance'. A socialist would also, of course, see wealth as belonging to the community rather than the individual, while utilitarians, whether socialist or not, would be prepared to override property rights to prevent great evils.

Does the argument for an obligation to assist others therefore presuppose one of these other theories of property rights, and not an individualistic theory like Nozick's? Not necessarily. A theory of property rights can insist on our *right* to retain wealth without pronouncing on whether the rich *ought* to give to the poor. Nozick, for example, rejects the use of compulsory means like taxation to redistribute income, but suggests that we can achieve the ends we deem morally desirable by voluntary means. So Nozick would reject the claim that rich people have an 'obligation' to give to the poor, in so far as this implies that the poor have a right to our aid, but might accept that giving is something we ought to do and failing to give, though within one's rights, is wrong—for rights is not all there is to ethics.

The argument for an obligation to assist can survive, with only minor modifications, even if we accept an individualistic theory of property rights. In any case, however, I do not think we should accept such a theory. It leaves too much to chance to be an acceptable ethical view. For instance, those whose forefathers happened to inhabit some sandy wastes around the Persian Gulf are now fabulously wealthy, because oil lay under those sands; while those whose forefathers settled on better land south of the Sahara live in absolute poverty, because of drought and bad harvests. Can this distribution be acceptable from an impartial point of view? If we imagine ourselves about to begin life as a citizen of either Kuwait or Chad—but we do not know which—would we accept the principle that citizens of Kuwait are under no obligation to assist people living in Chad?

Population and the ethics of triage. Perhaps the most serious objection to the argument that we have an obligation to assist is that since the major cause of absolute poverty is overpopulation, helping those now in poverty will only ensure that yet more people are born to live in poverty in the future.

In its most extreme form, this objection is taken to show that we should adopt a policy of 'triage'. The term comes from medical policies adopted in wartime. With too few doctors to cope with all the casualties, the wounded were divided into three categories: those who would probably survive without medical assistance, those who might survive if they received assistance, but otherwise probably would not, and those who even with medical assistance probably would not survive. Only those in the middle category were given medical assistance. The idea, of course, was to use limited medical resources as effectively as possible. For those in the first category, medical treatment was not strictly necessary; for those in the third category, it was likely to be useless. It has been suggested that we should apply the same policies to countries, according to their prospects of becoming self-sustaining. We would not aid countries which even without our help will soon be able to feed their populations. We would not aid countries which, even with our help, will not be able to limit their population to a level they can feed. We would aid those countries where our help might make the difference between success and failure in bringing food and population into balance.

Advocates of this theory are understandably reluctant to give a complete list of the countries they would place into the 'hopeless' category; but Bangladesh is often cited as an example. Adopting the policy of triage would, then, mean cutting off assistance to Bangladesh and allowing famine, disease and natural disasters to reduce the population of that country . . . to the level at which it can provide adequately for all.

In support of this view Garrett Hardin has offered a metaphor: we in the rich nations are like the occupants of a crowded lifeboat adrift in a sea full of drowning people. If we try to save the drowning by bringing them aboard our boat will be overloaded and we shall all drown. Since it is better that some survive than none, we should leave the others to drown. In the world to-day, according to Hardin, 'lifeboat ethics' apply. The rich should leave the poor to starve, for otherwise the poor will drag the rich down with them.

Against this view, some writers have argued that over-population is a myth. The world produces ample food to feed its population, and could, according to some estimates, feed ten times as many. People are hungry not because there are too many but because of inequitable land distribution, the manipulation of Third World economies by the developed nations, wastage of food in the West, and so on.

Putting aside the controversial issue of the extent to which food production might one day be increased, it is true, as we have already seen, that the world now produces enough to feed its inhabitants—the amount lost by being fed to animals itself being enough to meet existing grain shortages. Nevertheless population growth cannot be ignored. Bangladesh could, with land reform and using better techniques, feed its present population of 80 million: but by the year 2000, according to World Bank estimates, its population will be 146 million. The enormous effort that will have to go into feeding an extra 66 million people, all added to the population within a quarter of a century, means that Bangladesh must develop at full speed to stay where she is. . . .

What will happen then? Population cannot grow indefinitely. It will be checked by a decline in birth rates or a rise in death rates. Those who advocate triage are proposing that we allow the population growth of some countries to be checked by a rise in death rates—that is, by increased malnutrition, and related diseases; by widespread famines; by increased infant mortality; and by epidemics of infectious diseases.

The consequences of triage on this scale are so horrible that we are inclined to reject it without further argument. How could we sit by our television sets, watching millions starve while we do nothing? Would not that be the end of all notions of human equality and respect for human life? Don't people have a right to our assistance, irrespective of the consequences?

Anyone whose initial reaction to triage was not one of repugnance would be an unpleasant sort of person. Yet initial reactions based on strong feelings are not always reliable guides. Advocates of triage are rightly concerned with the long-term consequences of our actions. They say that helping the poor and starving now merely ensures more poor and starving in the future. When our capacity to help is finally unable to cope—as one day it must be—the suffering will be greater than it would be if we stopped helping now. If this is correct, there is nothing we can do to prevent absolute starvation and poverty, in the long run, and so we have no obligation to assist. Nor does it seem reasonable to hold that under these circumstances people have a right to our assistance. If we do accept such a right, irrespective of the consequences, we are saying that, in Hardin's metaphor, we would continue to haul the drowning into our lifeboat until the boat sank and we all drowned.

If triage is to be rejected it must be tackled on its own ground, within the framework of consequentialist ethics. Here it is vulnerable. Any consequentialist ethics must take probability of outcome into account. A course of action that will certainly produce some benefit is to be preferred to an alternative course that may lead to a slightly larger benefit, but is equally likely to result in no benefit at all. Only if the greater magnitude of the uncertain benefit outweighs its uncertainty should we choose it. Better one certain unit of benefit than a 10% chance of 5 units, but better a 50% chance of 3 units than a single certain unit. The same principle applies when we are trying to avoid evils.

The policy of triage involves a certain, very great evil: population control by famine and disease. Tens of millions would die slowly. Hundreds of millions would continue to live in absolute poverty, at the very margin of existence. Against this prospect, advocates of the policy place a possible evil which is greater still: the same process of famine and disease, taking place in, say, fifty years time, when the world's population may be three times its present level, and the number who will die from famine, or struggle on in absolute poverty, will be that much greater. The question is: how probable is this forecast that continued assistance now will lead to greater disasters in the future?

Forecasts of population growth are notoriously fallible, and theories about the factors which affect it remain speculative. One theory, at least as plausible as any other, is that countries pass through a 'demographic transition' as their standard of living rises. When people are very poor and have no access to modern medicine their fertility is high, but population is kept in check by high death rates. The introduction of sanitation, modern medical techniques and other improvements reduces the death rate, but initially has little effect on the birth rate. Then population grows rapidly. Most poor countries are now in this phase. If standards of living continue to rise, however, couples begin to realize that to have the same number of children surviving to maturity as in the past, they do not need to give birth to as many children as their parents did. The need for children to provide economic support in old age diminishes. Improved education and the emancipation and employment of women also reduce the birthrate, and so population growth begins to level off. Most rich nations have reached this stage, and their populations are growing only very slowly.

If this theory is right, there is an alternative to the disasters accepted as inevitable by supporters of triage. We can assist poor countries to raise the living standards of the poorest members of their population. We can encourage the governments of these countries to enact land reform measures, improve education, and liberate women from a purely childbearing role. We can also help other countries to make contraception and sterilization widely available. There is a fair chance that these measures will hasten the onset of the demographic transition and bring population growth down to a manageable level. Success cannot be guaranteed; but the evidence that improved economic security and education reduce population growth is strong enough to make triage ethically unacceptable. We cannot allow millions to die from starvation and disease when there is a reasonable probability that population can be brought under control without such horrors.

Population growth is therefore not a reason against giving overseas aid, although it should make us think about the kind of aid to give. Instead of food handouts, it may be better to give aid that hastens the demographic transition. This may mean agricultural assistance for the rural poor, or assistance with education, or the provision of contraceptive services. Whatever kind of aid proves most effective in specific circumstances, the obligation to assist is not reduced.

One awkward question remains. What should we do about a poor and already overpopulated country which for religious or nationalistic reasons, restricts the use of contraceptives and refuses to slow its population growth? Should we nevertheless offer development assistance? Or should we make our offer conditional on effective steps being taken to reduce the birthrate? To the latter course, some would object that putting conditions on aid is an attempt to impose our own ideas on independent sovereign nations. So it is—but is this imposition unjustifiable? If the argument for an obligation to assist is sound, we have an obligation to reduce absolute poverty: but we have no obligation to make sacrifices that, to the best of our knowledge, have no prospect of reducing poverty in the long run. Hence we have no obligation to assist countries whose governments have policies which will make our aid ineffective. This could be very harsh on poor citizens of these countries—for they may have no say in the government's policies—but we will help more people in the long run by using our resources where they are most effective. (The same principles may apply, incidentally, to countries that refuse to take other steps that could make assistance effective—like refusing to reform systems of land holding that impose intolerable burdens on poor tenant farmers.) . . .

Too high a standard? The final objection to the argument for an obligation to assist is that it sets a standard so high that none but a saint could attain it. How many people can we really expect to give away everything not comparable in moral significance to the poverty their donation could relieve? For most of us, with commonsense views about what is of moral significance, this would mean a life of real austerity. Might it not be counter-productive to demand so much? Might not people say: 'As I can't do what is morally required anyway, I won't bother to give at all.' If, however, we were to set a more realistic standard, people might make a genuine effort to reach it. Thus setting a lower standard might actually result in more aid being given.

It is important to get the status of this objection clear. Its accuracy as a prediction of human behaviour is quite compatible with the argument that we are obliged to give to the point at which by giving more we sacrifice something of comparable moral significance. What would follow from the objection is that public advocacy of this standard of giving is undesirable. It would mean that in order to do the maximum to reduce absolute poverty, we should advocate a standard lower than the amount we think people really ought to give. Of course we ourselves—those of us who accept the original argument, with its higher standard—would know that we ought to do more than we publicly propose people ought to do, and we might actually give more than we urge others to give. There is no inconsistency here, since in both our private and our public behaviour we are trying to do what will most reduce absolute poverty.

For a consequentialist, this apparent conflict between public and private morality is always a possibility, and not in itself an indication that the underlying principle is wrong. The consequences of a principle are one thing, the consequences of publicly advocating it another.

Is it true that the standard set by our argument is so high as to be counterproductive? There is not much evidence to go by, but discussions of the argument, with students and others have led me to think it might be. On the other hand the conventionally accepted standard—a few coins in a collection tin when one is waved under your nose—is obviously far too low. What level should we advocate? Any figure will be arbitrary, but there may be something to be said for a round percentage of one's income like, say, 10%—more than a token donation, yet not so high as to be beyond all but saints. (This figure has the additional advantage of being reminiscent of the ancient tithe, or tenth, which was traditionally given to the church, whose responsibilities included care of the poor in one's local community. Perhaps the idea can be revived and applied to the global community.) Some families, of course, will find 10% a considerable strain on their finances. Others may be able to give more without difficulty. No figure should be advocated as a rigid minimum or maximum; but it seems safe to advocate that those earning average or above average incomes in affluent societies, unless they have an unusually large number of dependents or other special needs, ought to give a tenth of their income to reducing absolute poverty. By any reasonable ethical standards this is the minimum we ought to do, and we do wrong if we do less.